FOUNDATIONS OF INDIGENOUS SOCIAL WORK

About the Editors

Dr. Chittaranjan Subudhi, MSW, MA (Sociology), PhD working as Assistant Professor (Senior Scale), Department of Social Work, Central University of Tamil Nadu. He has a Bachelor Degree in Commerce and a Master Degree in Social Work from the Utkal University of Odisha, India. He has completed his PhD in Mental Health from the Department of Humanities and Social Sciences, National Institute of Technology Rourkela, India. He has conducted research in various areas like Health and Mental Health, Indigenous Social Work, Family and Child Welfare, Disability studies, Women studies, Health Care Management and Tribal issues. He teaches Psychiatric Social Work, Working with Individuals and Communities, Qualitative Research, ICTs in Social Development and Health System Management. He has written many articles including conference papers and published in national and international reputed peer-reviewed journals. He has written many articles including conference papers and published in national and international reputed peer- reviewed journals including Elsevier, Springer Nature, Sage, Routledge, Taylor & Francis, Web of Science, UGC-CARE and other SCOPUS indexed journals.

Professor Bishnu Mohan Dash, M.S.W., M.Phil. PhD, ICSSR Post-Doctoral fellow, working as Professor in Department of Social Work, Dr. Bhim Rao Ambedkar College (University of Delhi), Delhi. He was former Associate Professor in Rural Development, Indira Gandhi National Open University, New Delhi. He is the recipient of Best Teacher Award from Government of Delhi 2019-20, and the prestigious Delhi University Excellence Award for teachers 2021. As General Secretary of Bharatiya Samaj Karya Parishad, he is engaged in spearheading the movement towards Bharatiyakaran/Indianisation of Social work education in India. He is also an editorial board member/ Advisory member in several national and international journals including Practice: Social work in Action, Routledge, Taylor and Francis, London, Associate Editor of South Asian Journal of Participative Development, Member Editorial Board of Bhopal Journal of Social Work and Journal of Development Administration, Zimbabwe. He has also authored/co- authored/edited 16 books. He has published more than sixty papers in various reputed National and International journals including Sage, Routledge Emerlad, Springer etc. and contributed chapters for Post Graduate Course in Social Work (MSW)/ Social work and Counseling of Indira Gandhi National Open University, New Delhi and frequently contributes in leading national newspapers. He has presented papers and chaired sessions in various national/ international conferences including Canada, Japan, and Srilanka and delivered invited lectures in various academic forums. He was also member of the Expert committee in the course Revision/ Member, School Board, Indira Gandhi National Open University, New Delhi; Orissa state Open University, Mahatma Gandhi Antarrashtriya Hindi Vishwa Vidyalaya, Maharashtra, BPS University, Sonepat and Member, Board of Studies in Social Work, Indore School of Social Work, Indore and Academic Advisory Board, School of Social Sciences, Doon University, Member, Expert Committee, NCF, Govt. of India, Member, Expert Committee, Bharatiya Bhasha Samiti, MoE, GOI, Member, Academic Council, Indira Gandhi National Open University, New Delhi, Member, Board of Studies in Social work, Jagadguru Rambhacharya Divyanga University, Chitrakoot etc. He has completed a number of research projects sponsored by ICSSR and UGC and organized various workshops and seminars. His areas of interest are Rural Development, Child welfare, social work education.

FOUNDATIONS OF INDIGENOUS SOCIAL WORK

Edited by
Chittaranjan Subudhi
Bishnu Mohan Dash

GOLDEN JUBILEE
Concept
50 YEARS
1974-2024

CONCEPT PUBLISHING COMPANY PVT. LTD.
NEW DELHI - 110 059

ISBN: 978-93-6344-633-5 (HB)
ISBN: 978-93-6344-506-2 (PB)

First Published 2025

Published and Printed by

Concept Publishing Company Pvt. Ltd.
A/15-16, Commercial Block, Mohan Garden
New Delhi-110059 (India)
T: +91-11-41101460
E: publishing@conceptpub.com, *W*: www.conceptpub.com

Cataloging in Publication--Courtesy: D.K. Agencies (P) Ltd. <docinfo@dkagencies.com>

Foundations of indigenous social work / edited by Chittaranjan Subudhi, Bishnu Mohan Dash.
pages cm
Contributed articles.
Includes bibliographical references and index.
ISBN 9789363445062 (PB)
ISBN 9789363446335 (HB)

1. Social work with indigenous peoples--India. 2. Social service--India--History. 3. Social service--Philosophy. 4. Social service--Religious aspects--Hinduism. 5. Social service--Religious aspects--Buddhism. I. Subudhi, Chittaranjan, 1989- editor. II. Dash, Bishnu Mohan, editor.

LCC HV3176.F68 2025 | DDC 362.8400954 23

Foreword

In a broader perspective, social work is not just a policy, but more than that it is an attitude. It has been ingrained in our lives and is a natural inclination. It is an inherent attitude in every human being. Sensitivity towards grief is an intrinsic value of each person. We must make this attitude vibrant and ignited as the foundation for enhancing social work. The approach towards social work should be with dedication and strong commitment. The question arises regarding policy and attitude. It must be seen as the duty of an individual and family beyond just policy. Each individual and family should elevate themselves from duty consciousness to an attitude level. Even then at the institutional and governmental levels, establishing a strong policy is needed to motivate individuals and institutions to commit themselves to social work.

A paradigm shift is necessary to realign the vision of social work. The vision of social work should be 'Bharatiya'. The Bharatiya vision towards social work emphasises 'Universal Oneness' and 'Thy need is greater'. To make these two true, "Consumption of minimal resources" and "Doing the best without expecting anything in return" are the foundational values. However, through many NGOs are managing their livelihoods through social work. Even in such NGOs, where it is a means of livelihood, strong dedication and commitment are essential.

The Western thought of the "struggle for existence" and "survival of the fittest" which is supposed to be applicable to the animal world, has been applied to civil society. Consequently, humans have been reduced as bundles of desires and economic animals. This led the society to a disaster which is evident today. To bring a fundamental transformation in social work in this modern era, we need to adopt a Bharatiya vision that recognizes each human as divine. Each and every individual is born potential and unique in nature. The purpose of life is to exhibit his or her uniqueness by using his/her enormous potential. Only then we can bring meaningful change to the social workspace.

The book "Foundations of Indigenous Social Work" is a modest attempt by the editors to trace the relevant Bharatiya principles-values-knowledge systems in the field of social work. The book discusses the philosophical underpinnings of Bharatiya knowledge systems-spirituality and Indic philosophy in social work. Social work education in Bharat has primarily remained Eurocentric since its inception in 1936. Professional social work education in Bharat has largely ignored the relevance and implications of Bharatiya knowledge systems. Even after eight decades of social work education in Bharat, there has been no significant change in the curriculum, research, and fieldwork training. Bharat is full of diversity with different languages, ethnicities, attires etc. This diversity is the beauty of Bharatiya society. But this diversity has gradually become complicated by urbanisation, industrialisation, modernisation, and globalisation. In such a scenario, Western theories, models, and principles have completely failed, as seen during the period of COVID-19. The universality of Western knowledge and its effectiveness in the Bharatiya context are being questioned in several forums. In international academic forums, there is also a growing and continuing debate on indigenization vis-à-vis the universalization of social work education. Social work education must stress the need for understanding the Native Social fabric, Indic values, Ethics, and Indic cosmology to address the issues of individuals, groups, and communities. However, there has been little attempt to indigenize the social work curriculum in Bharat. Therefore, it calls for decolonizing the colonial legacy of social work education and formulating (Swadeshi) indigenous social work models, theories, and, more particularly, developing a Bharatiya model of social work.

In order to fulfil the goal of 'Vikshit Bharat' and establish 'Ram Rajya', professional social workers have an important role in ideating and contributing to the vision of Viksit Bharat by 2047. To properly utilize the skills and efficiencies of our young social workers, we need to decolonize the Euro-American centric social work curriculum in Bharatiya universities by changing the social work curriculum, research agenda and developing indigenous social work literature. The book, consisting of sixteen chapters contributed by leading scholars in social work, explores various Indic philosophies, principles, and models of social work.

I am confident that the book is more than just an academic text; it is a call to action. It invites social work teachers, students, practitioners, researchers and policymakers to engage deeply with the indigenous knowledge systems that have sustained the communities for generations. It is a profound reminder that the solutions to many of our contemporary challenges may lie in the very traditions that have been sidelined for far too long. To revive those rich, diverse, and deeply rooted traditional practices and community-centred frameworks is the need of the hour.

I congratulate the editors of the book, Dr. C.R. Subudhi and Dr. B.M. Dash, who are actively engaged in producing a wealth of literature on Indigenous social work.

Shankaranand, B.R.
National Organizing Secretary
Bharatiya Shikshan Mandal

Preface

The book 'Foundations of Indigenous Social Work' has made a modest attempt to document the indigenous philosophy and principles of social work. The Social Workers in India are basically trained in Eurocentrism which raises some fundamental questions on its western orientation of social work education and requires a roadmap towards reorientation in the lines of indigenous values, ethics and principles. The existing social work values, principles taught in the Indian and other developing and underdeveloped countries are proved ineffective. The validity of social work principles, methods and philosophy and its relevance as well as effectiveness of imported recipient social work curriculum and practice paradigms is questioned in many forums. The approach to understand Indian social reality through European worldview has proved quite disastrous for the social work profession in India. The book consisting of sixteen chapters has been contributed by leading academicians and scholars on various indigenous principles and philosophy of social work.

The first chapter 'Exploring the Importance of Indigenous Social Work Practice for Sustainable Development in India', the authors Priya Narasimman, Chittaranjan Subudhi and Bishnu Mohan Dash mention that India is a land of incredible diversity, where a vibrant mix of cultures and traditions come together to create a truly unique identity. While there's a rich history of harmony, recent times have seen growing individualism and conflicting influences that have raised some important moral questions and created a sense of disunity. Even small divisions can lead to significant losses, underscoring the urgent need to tackle these issues and work towards restoring unity and fraternity. In times of crisis, like the ongoing COVID pandemic and natural disasters, people have set aside their differences to come together and support one another. Social work isn't just about empowering individuals; it is also about building cohesive, sustainable communities where everyone's values and dignity are respected. This chapter underscores the importance of embracing indigenous social work practices, which can offer more lasting solutions that benefit both individuals and their communities.

The second chapter 'Principles, Values, and Philosophies of Indigenous Social Work' by Thiruveedula Seshu Babu and Saraswati Raju Iyer explores the foundational principles, values, and philosophies that underpin indigenous social work practice. Drawing on a range of indigenous perspectives and worldviews, the chapter delves into the unique approaches and guiding frameworks that shape the practice of social work within indigenous communities. The chapter begins by examining the historical and cultural context of indigenous social work, highlighting the significance of traditional knowledge, spirituality, and interconnectedness in shaping indigenous social work principles. Furthermore, the chapter delves into the core values that inform indigenous social work practice, emphasizing the importance of cultural competence, reciprocity, and holistic approaches to addressing the needs of indigenous individuals and communities. It also discusses the ethical considerations and responsibilities inherent in indigenous social work, including the imperative of respecting indigenous rights, self-determination, and sovereignty. Moreover, the chapter critically analyses the philosophical underpinnings of indigenous social work, exploring concepts such as relationality, community-based interventions, and the integration of indigenous healing practices within social work frameworks. It also addresses the challenges and opportunities in integrating indigenous knowledge systems with Western social work paradigms, emphasizing the need for decolonizing approaches and culturally responsive practices. The chapter also underscores the significance of centring indigenous voices, perspectives, and self-determined practices in the field of social work. It advocates for a paradigm shift towards embracing indigenous principles, values, and philosophies as foundational elements in the education, training, and implementation of social work interventions within indigenous contexts.

The third chapter of the book by Veerabhadram Bhukya primarily focuses on the journey of social work philosophy and practices from an Indigenous/Dharmic perspective and connects it with the modern models of social work. The evolution of social work has been a key practice in the Indic perspective from the ancient era to the present, which was seen as philanthropy to professional pride in the present context. In ancient period, the welfare activities were defined as religious and spiritual philosophy that primarily connected to 'Moksha', known as a religious belief system from the indigenous perspective. These welfare initiatives were conceived obligatory duties and roles performed by kings/rulers and empires to facilitate basic amenities such as shelter, water, health, service to the needy and disadvantaged sections of the society, regulate and provision public utility, promote peace, knowledge, education, rehabilitation of illness, and services to impoverished, etc., which have gradually evolved over the years from ancient concept to modern ways of approach and practices. It was the great king Ashoka who developed an inclusive philosophy, *dharma*, and practices of social welfare. This was also accepted by Indic religions particularly Buddhism the karma theory (action and results) and promoted giving 'Bhiksha' to the 'Bhikshus' residing in 'sangha'.

In the fourth chapter 'History of Social Work in Ancient India' by Surabhi Sinha highlights that the concept of social work has a long tradition in India. All the ancient religious scriptures of India—the Vedas, the Sutras, the Epics, the Smrities, and the Dharma Shastras —contain verses, *slokas,* and ample references that emphasize the provision of welfare facilities by the state, the community, and wealthy persons to the needy individuals and families. The emphasis is on the well-being of the entire society. The concept of 'dana' was very popular in ancient India. According to Rigveda "may the one who gives shines the most." We have an example of 'Ram Rajya' of Rama as an example of a 'welfare state', 'Danveer Karna', as a 'Donor' and 'Philanthropist' Raja Harish Chandra as 'Satyavadi', Raja Bhoj as an advocate whose justice mechanism was based on human values. We find reference to high orders practiced by Shivaji, Maharana Pratap, and Laxmi Bai who fought for people and nation.

The fifth chapter is written by Atul Gautam and Archana Kaushik on 'Conceptualization of Identity and Professional Social Work: A Vedantic Drishtant (Philosophy)'. "Spend some time at cremation ground and you will be able to see everything from the point of nihilism..., Self Being as nothing". We may have got this very statement, as a reflective discourse when someone wants to deconstruct the positional miniscule nature of individual existence, no matter how great she/he appears to be (to self or to others). But what about those who are choiceless as being and juxtapose themselves to corpse, death, thanatology, and morgue practices. According to Martin Heidegger, the truth about anything is subjective, but the ontology of the same is a result of social exchange. If we look at the construct of the identity from left (ism) and right (ism) side of ideological arches, both has its own frames of reference. Vedanta at one hand focus on the individualization of identity that has more to do with the self, the modern sociological perspective of Marxist focus on the social contract of identity. On the same line, when it comes to intervention a Rights based approach of the critical social work aims at structural changes in the social context and social constructs. The leftist discourse establishes the distinctive edifices of oppressor and the oppressed, haves and have not. Demonstration, revolutions, protest, conflict, and mitigation are major tools used. The aim is to achieve equality (responsive) in identity (reflective). The Vedanta philosophy on the other hand focus more on the internal aspects of individuals. Introspections, mindfulness, *dhyaan* (not just meditation), self-reflection and *maun* (being absolutely silent, even at the level of thoughts) are the tools used to investigate the identity of self, much before establishing it. The aim here is to craft a human, who prefer to choose Responsibility over Rights, when it comes to social exchange. Vedant calls it "Vyakti Nirman" (human construct), the process of nurturing values at the core of individuality. The aim here is to construct identity (self-reflective) that resonate equality (socially responsive). The present chapter is to understand concept of "identity" from modern Marxist and ancient Indian prospective. Can amalgamation of seemingly bipolar schools of thoughts, behold the idea of selfless services that fortify the roots of Indian Values and blossom a just Bharatiya (Indian) society?

Sagarika Saha in her chapter 'Contribution of Rabindranath Tagore to Indian Social Work Practice/Rural Reconstruction' discusses the problems of village-life in all its aspects, and experimentation with them in the farms, workshops, and laboratories of the institute and also highlights various initiatives undertaken by Tagore towards rural reconstruction.

Ibrahim Sabry Ahmed in his chapter on 'Community Organization and Development in Egypt' aims to review the history of community organization and development in Egyptian society (rural-urban), and the most important historical organizations that contributed to the emergence of community organization. The historical Egyptian figures who contributed to strengthening community organization practices and interventions are presented. It also highlights the Egyptian attempts to formulate a concept for Community Organization, the values on which it is based, and the development method adopted by the Arab Republic of Egypt, are also discussed. In addition to that, the chapter focuses on the current situation of community organization and development in the Egyptian context, including initiatives, programs, projects, and innovations, and the most important challenges facing community organization and development in Egypt. Finally, the future of community organization and development in Egyptian society is extrapolated.

The eighth chapter by Kanagaraj on 'Faith Based Organization and Rural Development: The Case of Chinmaya Organization for Rural Development [CORD], Thondamuthur, Coimbatore' delves into an examination of the challenges and solutions encountered within the rural community by the faith-based organization (FBO) known as the Chinmaya Organization for Rural Development (CORD) located in Thondamuthur, Coimbatore. The chapter illuminates CORD's commendable efforts in diverse facets of rural development, effectively addressing prevalent community challenges.

The ninth chapter by Geetanjali on 'Vipassana: The Buddha's Therapeutic Model for Psychiatric and Correctional Social Work Practice' highlights that Meditation practice like *vipassana*, helps maladjusted people to look differently over felt experience and change perspectives to gain equanimity in the midst of tumult. In psychiatric social work practice, *vipassana* which is Buddha's first-person Method has great potential for therapeutic modalist in the modern era. Where lots of people are unable to cope with their felt experiences. *Vipassana* is a scientific technique that gives new insights between mind and body and its effect on thought processes. There is lots of research on *Vipassana* but very little research on the clinical efficacy of *vipassana*. This study highlights the process and technique of *vipassana* meditation and its potential in the field of psychiatric social work. Young Siddhartha Gautama in search of solving issues and getting a ride from all sufferings discovers the metaphysical speculation where mind and body interact and create a first-person method to achieve insight over conscious experience which is free from all unhappiness. *Vipassana* is universal and applicable in social work practice. Understanding the chain of causation between mind and body helps victims and deviants to change their perspective towards bad conscious experiences of life. This study is very useful in Psychiatric social work as well as in correctional social work practice.

In her chapter '*Bhagavad Gita*: An ancient example of successful counselling', Vandana Sinha describes that in modern psychology counselling is not very old practice. It started in 1909 in United Nations. But in our ancient religious scripture, the method of counselling was used by Bhagwan Shri Krishna for his friend and disciple Arjuna. As a mentor, Shri Krishna used the technique of spiritual belief of immortal soul for the counselling. The present chapter is an effort to explore the counselling techniques used in *Bhagavad Gita* and to relate those techniques with Indian society, its value and beliefs.

The chapter eleven titled as 'Dharma in Dialogue: Blending Counselling Techniques with *Bhagavad Gita* Wisdom' by Arunima Dhar states that in the ancient verses of the *Bhagavad Gita*, a sacred Hindu scripture nestled within the *Mahabharata*, profound wisdom unfolds as a guide to life and intricate dilemmas. The *Bhagavad Gita* presents a dialogue between Prince Arjuna and Lord Krishna, taking place on the battlefield of Kurukshetra. As Arjuna grapples with moral dilemmas, existential questions, and the turbulence of his own emotions, Krishna serves not only as a divine guide but as a counsellor, offering solace, guidance, and profound insights into the nature of the self and the intricacies of human existence. Beyond its spiritual significance, the *Gita* offers timeless insights that resonate with the human experience, providing a philosophical foundation for navigating the complexities of the mind and soul. This chapter delves into the rich tapestry of counselling principles embedded within the verses of the *Bhagavad Gita*, revealing a harmonious convergence of ancient wisdom and modern therapeutic practices. The chapter explores different therapeutic aspects, such as, inner conflict, decision making, detachment, equanimity, spiritual and existential issues, mindfulness, self-awareness, and the holistic well-being. In the concluding part, through the dialogue between *dharma* and counselling, the chapter emphasizes on how individuals embark on a transformative journey towards inner harmony and build a meaningful connection with the world.

The next chapter, 'Srimad *Bhagavad Gita* as a Text of Counselling and Sri Krishna as a Best Counsellor' by Venkatesha Murthy, S. and Padmaja, D.S. states that *Srimad Bhagavad Gita* is considered one amongst the sacred books of our ancient culture consisting of multiple knowledge discussing various topics which help a man to overcome the problems in his life. It is a preaching done by Lord Sri Krishna to Arjuna when he was totally confused as to what he should do in the Kurukshetra battlefield. Sri Krishna guides Arjuna in all the fields to illuminate him. It is indeed whatever conflicts a person faces in his mind is expressed through Arjuna in the battlefield. Lord Krishna, who acts as a counsellor helps us to overcome all the problems whatever we face through the 700 *shlokas* rendered in 18 chapters. With its unchanging wisdom, the *Bhagavad Gita* provides substantial perceptivity into the sphere of psycho-spirituality. The discussion on the natural inevitability of birth and death of life cycle, immortality of soul, performance of your own *dharma* (duty) otherwise running the risk of shame and public defame talks about Cognitive/Rational Emotive Approach. The essence of the *Bhagavad Gita* is Krishna consciousness. Through the eighteen chapters, Lord Krishna ascends through a ladder of *yoga* such as *Karma yoga*, *Jnana yoga*, *Dhyana yoga*, and finally Bhakti *yoga*. *Bhagavad Gita* gave in-depth clarity to

Arjuna about his purpose in life, self-realization, what is right/wrong as per *dharma*, who we are, and what is *karma*, etc. Because of which he performed his duty under the guidance of the supreme god Lord Krishna without any demotivation.

The next chapter 'Religion, Spirituality and Social Work: A Study on Buddhism' by Sheuli Dutta states that there is no nation or tribe without religion. According to Cicero, religion means repetition of prayers or attachment of a continual binding. But the most prevalent conception of religion is that it is a law-abiding, scrupulously conscientious frame of mind. On the other hand, spirituality is an aspect of religious traditions and also of existential value system. Before the establishment as an individual profession, Social Work can be traced to its roots as religion-based charity work. At the beginning of its origin, there was no demarcation between religion-based social work and professional social work. However, overtime social work became more professional and secularized, and gradually discarded from religion and spirituality. Buddhism is a very pragmatic religion. It has been founded on the basis of enlightenment and consciousness. In Buddhism, social welfare is considered as the work done for the betterment of mankind. It has been segmented into various forms, such as simple individual acts of charity, teaching and training, and organized service. Buddhism was primarily concerned with the idea of ways and means to get rid of sorrow. But later it became more rational than any other existed religions. The 'practice of giving' or 'dana' is the key principle that conveys the message of giving without any expectation of reward. Buddhism aroused in India as a spiritual force against social injustice, superstitions; and later it denounced the tyranny of caste system. Buddhist social work has become very popular under the title of Socially Engaged Buddhism which emerged in Asia in the 20th century. And thus, it is closely connected with the concepts, values, and principles of social work. The objective of this study is to briefly discuss the integrated relationship between religion/spirituality and social work, focusing on the doctrines preached by Buddha that are relevant in today's world. Special attention will be paid to Socially Engaged Buddhism to present a comprehensive outlook of the practice of Buddhism in a changing scenario. The study method in this research is content analysis of historical texts, books, academic writings, and articles.

K.T. Arasu in his chapter 'AID giving stoking from Indian Social Work' offers a comprehensive overview of retail aid giving and receiving landscape of India from indigenous Philanthropic Social Work perspectives and practices. It provides nuances of Indian charity and philanthropy, its motivational modes and its connections with philanthropic social work. While doing so, it compares the differences in the mode of aid giving and taking culture in India and Western countries by drawing upon World Giving Index and Indian Philanthropic Reports 2023 and 2024. It underscores the need for strengthening philanthropic social work concepts and practices to contribute to social justice and Sustainable Development Goals (SDG). This chapter explores cinematic heroism, political, corporate, religious community and institutional philanthropies and the intersection with social work to find enduring solutions to human and community problems in India. Overall, the chapter brings to fore how charity and philanthropy are related to sustainable social work practices to create socially just and resilient families and communities.

In chapter fifteen, titled 'Swami Vivekananda's Social Philosophy: An Indian View of the Social Work Principles', Pratheesh describes that in all of its manifestations, social work tackles the numerous, intricate interactions that occur between individuals and their surroundings (Bennur & Dilip, 2013). Its goals are to prevent dysfunction, enrich people's lives, and help everyone reach their full potential. The goals of professional social work are change and problem solving (Chadha, Y., 1997). In this context, social work philosophy and practices are closely associated with humanistic socio-cultural perspectives of the Indian Renaissance, particularly with respect to Swami Vivekananda's humanistic concept of neo-Vedanta. He claims that social service is valuable because "the service to mankind is the service to god" which serves as the foundation of this Vedantic idea about humanity. Serving the poor and defenseless out of selflessness and empathy is valued as a ceremonial offering to the gods. Neo-Vedanta interpretations capture the essence of how Indian social work was conceptualized during the 19th century, especially as national and patriotic consciousness in India grew. This study aims to assess the Indian conception of social work and indigenous social work principles during the colonial era, as well as the various interpretations of Vivekanada's social philosophy, particularly the neo-Vedanta. The study uses a historical method, looking at secondary sources to build arguments and evaluate the theoretical claim that Vivekananda's social philosophy is important for understanding the idiosyncratic perspective on social work.

The last chapter by Puspanjali Kumari on 'Contribution of Mahatma Gandhi to Indigenous Social Work Practice' states that Social Work is an academic discipline based on practical training, fieldwork, and theoretical approaches that help individuals, groups, or communities solve their problems, promote social change, and eliminate social evils through various methods, techniques, and ideologies. The contribution of Mahatma Gandhi played a vital role in the development of the principles, values, ethics, and code of conduct of indigenous Social Work. The ideology and philosophy of Gandhiji influenced it, as he always encouraged social workers to do more services to the poor, sick, marginalized, and other needy people based on a humanitarian and philanthropic approach. Mahatma Gandhi, one of the most significant personalities in the Indian independence movement, left an enduring legacy that extends beyond politics into Social Work. This chapter explores Gandhi's profound contributions to indigenous social work practices, emphasizing his philosophy of non-violent resistance and its transformative influence on community welfare.

The book will be an essential reading for teachers, students and researchers not only in social work but other social science disciplines. The book explores various indigenous social work principles, practices and philosophy relevant to the contemporary needs of the society. The book is aligned with the new social work curriculum designed by various universities with focus on Indian knowledge systems in the field of social work. We are sure the book will be an asset for the social work fraternity.

Chittaranjan Subudhi
Bishnu Mohan Dash

Contents

List of Contributors

Archana Kaushik (Prof.) is a senior faculty at the Department of Social Work, University of Delhi. With more than 20 years of academic experience and impactful publications, she is an academician with specialization in Gerontological social work, Family and Welfare, Social research and education, and many more. She is one of the very few experts on spiritual social work in India. **Email:** archana_kaushik@rediffmail.com

Arunima Dhar (Dr.) is presently serving as Assistant Professor, Social Work, Centre for Distance and Online Education, Rabindra Bharati University, Kolkata. She has completed her bachelors from St. Teresian College, University of Mysore, Karnataka. She further pursued masters in Social Work from Banaras Hindu University, Varanasi and achieved First Class Second position. She has currently submitted her Ph.D. research in the University of Burdwan, West Bengal. She has several research articles and book chapters to her credit. She has also participated in various national and international seminars till date and has received awards for the Best Session Paper in International Conference on Studies in Humanities and Social Sciences (SHSS-2016), May 24-25, 2016, Paris (France). Her current areas of interest include mental health, psychiatry, urbanization and women, research methodology, social group work etc. She is presently associated with different universities. She has also worked for more than two years as a Mental Health Therapist, OMNI Health Services Inc,

Philadelphia, USA and as an Intake Specialist, New Journeys In Recovery, Philadelphia, USA.

Email: arunimadey2022@gmail.com

Atul Gautam (Dr.) is a faculty and researcher with specialization in Mental Health and Individual social work. With over 10 years of career in professional social work and over 15 years of media, he has worked with many international organizations like BBC and London School of Hygiene and Social Medicine, UK. He is an academician with special interest in qualitative research.

Email: mailatulgautam@gmail.com

Bishnu Mohan Dash (Prof.), M.S.W., M.Phil. PhD, ICSSR Post-Doctoral fellow, working as Professor in Department of Social Work, Dr. Bhim Rao Ambedkar College (University of Delhi), Delhi. He was former Associate Professor in Rural Development, Indira Gandhi National Open University, New Delhi. He is the recipient of Best Teacher Award from Government of Delhi 2019-20, and the prestigious Delhi University Excellence Award for teachers 2021. As General Secretary of Bharatiya Samaj Karya Parishad, he is engaged in spearheading the movement towards Bharatiyakaran/Indianisation of Social work education in India. He is also an editorial board member/ Advisory member in several national and international journals including Practice: Social work in Action, Routledge, Taylor and Francis, London, Associate Editor of South Asian Journal of Participative Development, Member Editorial Board of Bhopal Journal of Social Work and Journal of Development Administration, Zimbabwe. He has also authored/co-authored/edited 16 books. He has published more than sixty papers in various reputed National and International journals including Sage, Routledge Emerlad, Springer etc. and contributed chapters for Post Graduate Course in Social Work (MSW)/ Social work and Counseling of Indira Gandhi National Open University, New Delhi and frequently contributes in leading national newspapers. He has presented papers and chaired sessions in various national/ international conferences including Canada, Japan, and Srilanka and delivered invited lectures in various academic forums. He was also member of the Expert committee in the course Revision/Member, School Board, Indira Gandhi National Open University, New Delhi; Orissa state

Open University, Mahatma Gandhi Antarrashtriya Hindi Vishwa Vidyalaya, Maharashtra, BPS University, Sonepat and Member, Board of Studies in Social Work, Indore School of Social Work, Indore and Academic Advisory Board, School of Social Sciences, Doon University, Member, Expert Committee, NCF, Govt. of India, Member, Expert Committee, Bharatiya Bhasha Samiti, MoE, GOI, Member, Academic Council, Indira Gandhi National Open University, New Delhi, Member, Board of Studies in Social work, Jagadguru Rambhacharya Divyanga University, Chitrakoot etc. He has completed a number of research projects sponsored by ICSSR and UGC and organized various workshops and seminars. His areas of interest are Rural Development, Child welfare, social work education. **Email:** radharamana888@gmail.com

Chittaranjan Subudhi (Dr.), MSW, MA (Sociology), PhD working as Assistant Professor (Senior Scale), Department of Social Work, Central University of Tamil Nadu. He has a Bachelor Degree in Commerce and a Master Degree in Social Work from the Utkal University of Odisha, India. He has completed his PhD in Mental Health from the Department of Humanities and Social Sciences, National Institute of Technology Rourkela, India. He has conducted research in various areas like Health and Mental Health, Indigenous Social Work, Family and Child Welfare, Disability studies, Women studies, Health Care Management and Tribal issues. He teaches Psychiatric Social Work, Working with Individuals and Communities, Qualitative Research, ICTs in Social Development and Health System Management. He has written many articles including conference papers and published in national and international reputed peer-reviewed journals. He has written many articles including conference papers and published in national and international reputed peer- reviewed journals including Elsevier, Springer Nature, Sage, Routledge, Taylor & Francis, Web of Science, UGC-CARE and other SCOPUS indexed journals. **Email:** chittaranjan.subudhi@gmail.com

Geetanjali, Ph.D. Scholar in Social Work Department, Mahatma Gandhi Central University, Bihar, India. She is an engineer and dedicated social worker, holding a gold medal in B. Tech. She is UGC-NET qualified and an ICSSR doctoral fellow. With a strong academic background and a passion for community welfare, Geetanjali has received several prestigious awards and medals. Received awards like Sanjoy Sen Memorial Lecture Award 2015 by ILTA, Vice-Chancellor Gold Medal, and Samrat Ashoka Gold Medal 2023 by MGCUB. She completed her B.Tech from MIT, Muzaffarpur, MSW from Mahatma Gandhi Central University in Bihar. **Email:** mgcu2020swrk6002@mgcub.ac.in

Ibrahim Sabry Ahmed (Prof.), Associate Professor, Community Organization Department, Faculty of Social Work, Helwan University, Cairo, Egypt. He has an expertise and skills in Academic Writing, Qualitative Analysis, Data Collection, Research Analysis, Curriculum Development, Teacher Training, Research Paper Writing, Team Working, Research Papers, Research Methodology, Article Writing, Student Supervision, Content Analysis, Quantitative Analysis, Professional Development, Survey Methodology and Data Analysis, Teaching Experience, Document Analysis, Survey Analysis, Teaching and Learning. **Email:** drsagarika.global@gmail.com

K.T. Arasu (Dr.) is currently officiating as Director of Alternative for India Development and Vikalp Multimedia based in Chennai. Dr. Arasu is a Post Graduate in Social Work from Madurai Institute of Social Sciences with Ph.D. in Social Work in University of Madras. He has 7 years of academic and research experience as a Social Work Faculty and 36 years of grounded Social Work research and practice with greater focus on tribes. Dr. K.T. Arasu has more than 3 years of overseas experience in UK/Europe in the domains of fund raising and development education.
Email: ktarasu56@gmail.com

Kanagaraj, S. (Dr.) currently serves as Assistant Professor at the Department of Social Work, Amrita Vishwa Vidyapeetham (Deemed to be University), Coimbatore campus. He has an overall work experience of 14 years after completing master's in social work, while simultaneously pursuing higher studies and research. He has qualified in UGC–NET and SET (State Eligibility Test) in Social Work. He has a rich field experience and a strong network with stakeholders at the grass-root level for effective interventions in a community. His major achievements include sustainable livelihood creations for disabled, formation of youth groups in tribal villages and conducting awareness programs in the community on societal and economic issues. He was also instrumental in formulating field projects in rural areas and guiding post-graduate social work students for open setting fieldwork. **Email:** s_kanagaraj@cb.amrita.edu

Padmaja D.S. (Dr.), Ph.D. in Samskrita, Master of Philosophy in Samskrita and Masters in Samskrita from KSOU, Mysuru and Master's in Education from Kuvempu University. She has more than 18 years of total experience in teaching and research. She has organized many programmes related to *Bhagavad Gita* and "Samskrtotsava". Currently, she is associated with Surana College (Autonomous) as Assistant Professor and Researcher in Samskrita Department. She has given discourse on 18 chapters of *Bhagavad Gita*. She has received research grants from ICSSR, New Delhi, ICPR, New Delhi for hosting seminars and workshops. Worked with Azim Premji University and Yuvaka Sangha on variousassignments for students and faculty members.
Email: padmajasvm@gmail.com

Pratheesh, P. (Dr.), an experienced teacher with proven track record of success in providing college level instruction and delivering lectures. He has a passion for knowledge and enjoys helping students to develop a love of learning and provides guidance to undergraduate and graduate students on course selection, career planning, and other educational matters.
Email: ktarasu56@gmail.com

Priya Narasimman with a B.Com. in Corporate Secretaryship, MA in Psychology specializing in Clinical, and MSW specializing in Disabilities and Empowerment. She works as a Guest Faculty in the Department of Social Work at the Central University of Tamil Nadu. With two years of experience as a Junior Associate in an IB firm, she has also worked with Persons with Disabilities (PWDs) in various government and non-government agencies and a psychological clinic for internships. Her passion lies in Indigenous social work practices, mental health, Disability studies, and the empowerment of individuals and tribal communities. **Email:** shretha24@gmail.com

Pushpanjali Kumari is a research scholar at the Department of Sociology, Banaras Hindu University, Varanasi. She has completed her master's degree in social work with a specialization in Rural Reconstruction and Urban Development from Banaras Hindu University and Bachelor's degree in social work from Patna University. **Email:** pushpanjalipathak@bhu.ac.in

Sagarika Saha (Dr.) is presently working as Associate professor in Social Work Department, AMIK Institute of Management Sciences and Technology, Durgapur under Vidyasagar University since 2018 and Guest faculty, Department of Adult, Continuing Education, Extension Work, Rabindra Bharati University, Kolkata, 2023. She also headed the Department of Peace and Transformation Studies and also acted as Fieldwork Co-ordinator in North East Institute of Social Sciences and Research (NEISSR) under Nagaland University in 2017-18. She has been appointed as Board of Studies member and moderator for MSW Course in Vidyasagar University from 2018. She has been associated with NSOU (Netaji Subhas Open University) as research guide since 2017.
Email: drsagarika.global@gmail.com

Saraswati Raju Iyer (Prof.) is Research Director, Professor, Department of Sociology and Social Work, Acharya Nagarjuna University, Guntur District, Andhra Pradesh, India.
Email: saras1_2rajuiyer2003@yahoo.com

Sheuli Dutta is an enthusiastic social worker and passionate about knowledge. She is an alumni of Netaji Subhas Open University, holding an MSW/NET in Social Work. Her previous writing was on 'The Active Involvement and Reorientation of Internal Stakeholders to Regulate the Sex Trade in Sonagachi'. She worked as a program coordinator, team leader, and community mobilizer for three years in an NGO after completing MSW.
Email: duttasheuli20@gmail.com

Surabhi Sinha Graduate in Political Science Hons. from Patna University and Post graduation in Political Science and International Relations from Banaras Hindu University. Currently, pursuing B.Ed. from Sri Dev Suman Uttarakhand University, Uttarakhand. Her areas of interest are South Asian Studies, Art and Culture, Foreign Policy, and Social Issues in Society. She has published a number of research papers and chapters in edited books. **Email:** sinhasurabhi333@gmail.com

Thiruveedula Seshu Babu [UGC NET SRF], Research Scholar (Social Work), Department of Sociology and Social Work, Acharya Nagarjuna University, Guntur District, Andhra Pradesh, India. **Email:** radharamana888@gmail.com

Vandana Sinha (Prof.) is presently serving as Professor in Department of Social Work, Mahatma Gandhi Kashi Vidyapeeth, Varanasi. She has done her Master in Social Work and Ph.D. from MGKVP, Varanasi in addition to Master of Journalism and Mass Communication from BHU, Varanasi. She has more than 30 years of experience in teaching, research and extension. She has three published books, 9 book chapters and 25 published articles to her credit. She has participated and delivered invited lectures in many national and international seminars. She is associated with many Universities as Member, Board of Studies and developed course content of many Universities. She has served as HOD, Dean and Director, Field Work in MGKVP Varanasi. Her areas of interest include Gender Equity, Mental Health, Community Work, and Medical Social Work etc. **Email:** drvandana888@gmail.com

Veerabhadram Bhukya (Dr.), Assistant Professor, currently serves as the Chairman of the Board of Studies in the Department of Social Work at Telangana University, Telangana State. He holds an MSW in Human Resource Management and Industrial Relations, has cleared the UGC-NET in Social Work, and completed his M.Phil. in Sociology and Ph.D. in Social Work from Osmania University, Hyderabad. Previously, he served as the Head and Chairperson of the Board of Studies in the Department of Social Work. In his role as Chairperson of the Board of Studies, he developed and designed the curriculum/syllabus structure (CBCS Pattern) for Social Work at both PG and Pre-Ph.D. levels in 2019. Presently, he is the youngest faculty member in the Department of Social Work at Telangana University. He completed Inter-University Associateships in 2022 and 2023 at IIAS, Shimla.
Email: veerabhadram.bhukya@gmail.com

Venkatesha Murthy, S. (Dr.), M.S.W., M.Phil., Ph.D. currently working as Guest Faculty (Full Time) since 2019 in the

Department of Studies in Social Work, Bengaluru City University, Bengaluru. Previously, assisted in the preparation of the report submitted by Dr. TBBSV Ramanaiah, UGC Emeritus Fellow and Retd. Professor Department of Studies in Social Work, University of Mysore, Mysuru. Previously worked as Associate Professor & amp; Head, Department of Social Work, S.J.R. College of Science, Arts & Commerce, Bengaluru. Earlier worked as Assistant Professor & Head of the Department, Department of Social Work, CMR Institute of Management Studies (Autonomous), Bangalore. He has around 20 years of experience in the areas of Social Work Theory and Practice (15 years Teaching and 5 years of Practice in the areas of HRM and Development Sectors). He is also an Academic Counsellor & IGNOU for about 10 years at IGNOU Study Centre, CMR Institute of Management Studies (Autonomous), Bangalore since 2010 to date. Being a chairman of both Board of Studies (BOS) and Board of Examinations (BOE) handled the academic and administrative matters of the Department successfully for five years from 2009-2014. He has also administrative experiences as Chief Superintendent of the Examinations, Vigilance Squad etc., NSS Officer and actively involved in various committees of the institution effectively and participated actively as a Resource Person/Chairperson for various National and International Conference/Seminars. Published about 41 articles in edited volumes, journals, conference proceedings etc., presented 41 papers at the National and International conferences and attended 40 National and International Conferences/ Seminars. **Email:** svmurthy@gmail.com

1

Exploring the Importance of Indigenous Social Work Practice for Sustainable Development in India

Priya Narasimman, Chittaranjan Subudhi and *Bishnu Mohan Dash*

Introduction

The roots of social work in India run deep, with a history dating back to ancient times. While it was officially recognised as a profession in 1936, its foundations were influenced by Western social work models. These models have had a significant impact on social work practice in India (Lawani, 2020). However, considering India's diverse landscape, rich cultural heritage, large rural populations, and rapidly growing society, there is a need for a more tailored approach. Social work, as a profession dedicated to addressing individual and societal challenges, should integrate indigenous theories to effectively connect with people and address their unique issues (Dash *et al.*, 2020). The lack of recognition of indigenous methods in Western approaches is quite evident.

Significance of Indigenous Social Work Practice

Singh (2003) stressed the vital role of integrating indigenous knowledge and methods into social work education and practice in India. This involves understanding the diverse cultural and traditional landscape of the country and the importance of tailoring social work to local contexts. A deliberate approach is needed to address systemic issues and empower individuals. Recognising cultural and regional diversities, and adopting a client-centred approach, can lead to more impactful social work practice.

The contemporary social work model might not be the best fit for rural or tribal settings in India, potentially leading to a loss of original identity. This is due to the prioritisation of modernisation and Western cultural influences, neglecting the preservation of native practices. The Western concept of social work may not fully resonate with the values and realities of Indian communities, highlighting the inadequacy of a one-size-fits-all approach in addressing social issues.

Indigenous social work practice is deeply connected to the specific culture, traditions, and knowledge systems of the community it serves. It embraces a holistic approach to well-being, encompassing spiritual, emotional, physical, and mental aspects of life. This stands in contrast to Western social work practices, which may not fully align with the values and realities of Indian communities. Many nations are reassessing and integrating indigenous elements into their educational frameworks due to recognised deficiencies in current literature and curricula across various subjects. A notable shift can be observed in India, where consulting a psychologist was conventionally stigmatised. However, attitudes are evolving, reflecting an increased emphasis on well-being and a growing acceptance of professional assistance. This shift is facilitated by the incorporation of indigenous methods and is further reinforced by effective advocacy led by social workers and other professionals.

When considering the indigenous concept of Social Work, it is essential to have a comprehensive understanding of the communities, including the following key aspects: [(Chiristhuraj, Arul *et al.* 2023) (Majumdar, K., *et al.*(2023)]

1. *Values community knowledge:* This involves respecting and utilising the wisdom and practices that have been transmitted through generations within Indian communities.
2. *Social welfare:* Social welfare in India is intricately woven into the diverse fabric of religious beliefs. The values of compassion and humanitarianism have their origins in the spiritual traditions followed. Throughout the ages, acts of charity, benevolence, and the creation of havens for marginalised groups have been the embodiment of social work. These timeless principles continue to inspire positive change and upliftment in our society.
3. *Cultural relevance:* The implementation of social work in India needs to be tailored to effectively meet the specific needs of Indian communities, taking into account their unique cultural and social structures. While social work education in India is based on its values and ethics, it is heavily influenced by Western ideologies. However, there is a growing recognition of the importance of integrating indigenous values and ethics into social work practice, which are deeply rooted in ancient Indian literature and traditions. Efforts are being made to develop a standardised code of ethics that aligns with India's socio-economic, cultural, and geographical context.
4. *Cultural nuances:* It is imperative to carefully consider local conditions and historical context. Importing Western concepts without a deep understanding of the local realities may impede the effectiveness of practice. Recognising cultural nuances and modifying social work methodologies accordingly is of paramount importance.
5. *Empowerment:* The objective is to enhance the agency of individuals and communities by strengthening their cultural identity and self-determination. Indigenous

social work professionals promote culturally pertinent methodologies, striving to dismantle prevailing ideologies and paradigms while highlighting Indigenous knowledge-centred approaches. This encompasses a comprehensive comprehension of local systems, contexts, and beliefs to enable the effective empowerment of clients.

Approaches to Sustainable Development

Embracing local knowledge and customs, including traditional healing practices, community ceremonies, and indigenous knowledge systems, can lead to incredibly impactful and sustainable solutions to societal issues. As India's population approaches one and a half billion people in the coming years, social workers need to understand and honour these rich variations in customs and regulations. By involving the community in the development and implementation of social services, we can ensure culturally appropriate interventions that are not only accepted but also sustained. Collaboration fosters a sense of unity and community ownership, which is vital for effective social work practices. For instance, community activism can lead to the protection of natural resources, such as mountains, lakes, etc, illustrating the power of community participation in safeguarding and managing their resources.

To truly connect and engage, it's important to communicate in the local language and utilise culturally relevant metaphors and stories. Valuing the cultural identity and practices of individuals and communities is crucial for social workers to empower and support self-determination and resilience. It's important to celebrate the diversity of cultural rituals, such as the celebrations of the Pongal festival in Tamil Nadu which is celebrated as Sankranti or Makara Sankranti, Lohri, Magh Bihu or Bhogali Bihu, Poush Sankranti in other states across the country. For instance, on Naga Panchami, some communities worship live snakes despite their venomous nature, believing it will bring them blessings. Additionally, certain communities consider the lizard a sacred being, while others fear or find it repulsive. Understanding and respecting these cultural differences is essential for the effective implementation of social work practices.

Social workers should undergo training to recognise and address their own biases, as well as to comprehend the various backgrounds of their clients to effectively connect with them. Social workers need to exhibit respect, steer clear of biases, and abstain from making judgments. Cultivating patience is a vital skill that necessitates comprehensive training. Furthermore, advocating for policies and raising awareness about people's well-being and livelihood is crucial for social workers to prove their reliability.

Incorporating Indigenous Practices

The traditional Indian household structure is characterised by a multi-generational living arrangement where decision-making authority rests with the patriarch. This setup emphasises collective decision-making in family matters, in contrast to Western cultural norms. In rural communities, a designated community leader oversees various aspects of community life, including justice, celebrations, business, and social development discussions held in communal spaces. Temples historically played a significant role in promoting sustainable development within communities. In ancient times, they facilitated sustainable livelihoods by providing employment opportunities to residents and supporting skilled professionals, thereby preserving traditional knowledge. Additionally, temples contributed to preserving the cultural heritage of the region while driving economic growth through job creation and attracting visitors. Therefore, social workers can effectively address social issues within the community by collaborating with community leaders and elders, aligning with the Indian cultural tradition of involving them in decision-making and collaborative problem-solving.

Indians have a long history of practicing sustainable rituals and knowledge systems to protect and manage natural resources. These practices, including *Daans*, a form of ritual that incorporates tree planting, have enabled communities to effectively manage fragile ecosystems, agriculture, water and waste management, as well as lakes and ponds. Additionally, prayers are offered to nature and the environment, such as mountains, sun, and moon, seeking protection and blessings. Integrating these cultural elements into social work interventions allows communities to maintain their identity and interconnectedness with the land, fostering a sense of belonging and resilience while enacting effective changes in society.

Social workers can incorporate traditional healing practices such as Ayurveda, *yoga*, meditation, and indigenous healing ceremonies into their interventions, promoting holistic well-being deeply rooted in Indian culture. Indian culture places a strong emphasis on family and community ties, and social workers can promote family and community cohesion by organising events, facilitating family counselling sessions, and fostering mutual support and solidarity among community members. Additionally, social workers can combat stigma and discrimination by promoting cultural sensitivity and understanding within the community through workshops, education on cultural diversity, and advocating for the rights of marginalised individuals and communities.

Empowering marginalised groups, such as women, the elderly, and individuals from lower socio-economic backgrounds, is in line with Indian cultural values of social justice and equality. Social workers can achieve this by providing access to resources, advocacy support, and culturally sensitive services. It is crucial for social workers to always respect the cultural beliefs and practices of their clients, be mindful of cultural norms, traditions, and rituals, and integrate them into interventions in a respectful and culturally sensitive manner.

Successful social work programs in India that incorporate Indigenous practices

1. *The Sulabh International Social Service Organisation*: This program advocates for human rights, promotes environmental sanitation, encourages the use of non-

traditional energy sources, manages waste, and seeks social change through education. It acknowledges and aims to overcome the social barriers related to caste in sanitation work through community-driven initiatives.

2. *The Kudumbashree Program in Kerala:* This project works to eliminate poverty and empower women through community-centred methods. It is based on the Indian practice of savings and credit groups called 'chit funds' and has effectively mobilised women to establish self-help groups and small businesses.
3. *The Barefoot College in Rajasthan*: This initiative provides training in skills such as solar engineering, water testing, and midwifery to rural individuals, many of whom are women. It values local knowledge and customs, utilising a hands-on learning approach deeply rooted in Indian culture.
4. *The Aangan Trust*: This organisation focuses on safeguarding children in precarious circumstances by using culturally sensitive strategies to engage with communities and establish local networks that can prevent harm to children and promote their well-being.
5. *The SEWA* (Self-Employed Women's Association): SEWA is a trade union that promotes the rights of low-income, independently-employed female workers in India. Its approach is grounded in Gandhian philosophy, emphasising non-violence and self-reliance.

Ensuring Sustainability

Indigenous social work practices are centred on the promotion of holistic wellness, self-determination, and cultural resilience within the communities. These practices are integral to ensuring sustainability within the community as they prioritise the interconnectedness of individuals, families, communities, and the environment. Through the incorporation of Indigenous knowledge, values, and traditions into social work interventions, sustainability can be realised through various means. Moreover, Indigenous social work practices emphasise empowering individuals and communities to make decisions that align with their needs, thereby contributing to sustainability through enhanced autonomy and self-sufficiency. A few significant aspects are as follows:

Environment and Social Work

Indigenous social work practices prioritise the cultivation of a symbiotic relationship with the natural world. By advocating for environmental respect and endorsing sustainable resource management, Indigenous communities can safeguard the long-term well-being and productivity of their land and resources. This underscores the emergence of environmental social work, where professionals within NGOs and other institutions focus on preservation efforts and the promotion of community-produced goods to society. Additionally, environmental social workers champion environmental justice and drive awareness about ecological concerns, collaborating closely with communities to tackle environmental challenges. These professionals also exert influence on policies pertaining to conservation, sustainability, and climate change. Few predominant activists fought actively to protect the environment, they are as follows:

1. Sunderlal Bahuguna was an environmentalist and a key figure in the Chipko movement, leading the charge for the preservation of forests in the Himalayas. He was at the forefront of the movement against the Tehri Dam and was a staunch advocate for the rights of the hill people.
2. Salim Ali, also known as the "Birdman of India", was a renowned ornithologist and naturalist. He conducted comprehensive bird surveys throughout India and played a pivotal role in the establishment of the Bharatpur Bird Sanctuary.
3. Jadav Payeng, also known as the "Forest Man of India", single-handedly developed a 550-hectare forest in Assam,

highlighting the significant impact of individual efforts on environmental conservation.

India is renowned for its fertile soil. Communities can come together to launch a village-wide initiative where each household diversifies its crops and participates in communal trade. This can lead to economic growth and strengthen community cohesion. This approach aligns with the UN's third sustainable development goal of promoting good health and well-being. By prioritising physical activity, balanced nutrition, and the cultivation of nature, they aim to achieve holistic well-being for themselves and their community.

Social Work and Education

The education system in India has undergone significant evolution, from the ancient *Gurukula* system to modern schools and universities. This journey has been marked by various challenges and transformations. The *Gurukula* system, a residential schooling system in ancient India, emphasised holistic learning and tailored teaching to individual aptitudes (Gulalia & Subudhi, 2022). Contemporary Indian education is influenced by factors such as economic conditions, caste, reservations, and student interests. Economic constraints often impede access to quality education due to outdated teaching methods, lack of practical knowledge, and the inability to relate education to real-life scenarios. Additionally, fear of bullying and pressure to conform to societal norms can dampen enthusiasm for learning. The Westernised pattern of education, perceived as superior, can also make students feel inadequate.

However, there is hope. Social workers adopting indigenous practices can empower individuals and help them realise their potential. The experiences of today's youth highlight the urgent need for comprehensive educational reforms. These reforms should strive to enhance the accessibility, engagement, and applicability of education, fostering a comprehensive approach that empowers individuals to navigate diverse challenges and opportunities, thereby shaping a more promising future. An active initiative can be taken to inform students and parents of the different options available, giving them the freedom to pursue their passion irrespective of their age. By adopting inclusive, empathetic, and indigenous educational practices, we can ensure that every individual has the opportunity to learn, grow, and contribute positively to society.

Mental Health and Social Work

Validation is a critical component in every individual's life journey, from infancy to old age. The role of parental understanding and acceptance in a child's mental health and self-esteem cannot be overstated. Parents actively listening to and validating their children's emotions significantly contribute to their sense of self-worth and identity. Issues such as comparing children to their siblings, cousins, or peers can result in feelings of inadequacy and low self-esteem. Similarly, gender bias, such as showing favouritism towards one gender over another, can have detrimental effects on children and even as they grow up as adults or elders can impact their psychological well-being. These societal pressures and expectations can ultimately lead to severe mental health issues, including depression and suicide. Addressing these complex issues requires a collaborative effort from the entire community. It begins with raising awareness and providing education about the harmful effects of biases and comparisons regarding mental health, mental illness, etc. Parents, educators, and community leaders must be encouraged to recognise and treat each child as a unique individual with their strengths and potential.

Additionally, accessible and stigma-free mental health services are crucial to support those who are struggling. Open discussions about mental health should be promoted within communities to combat the silence and stigma surrounding mental health issues. Government initiatives and social workers should implement sensitisation programs to increase awareness and foster a more inclusive society. Ultimately, meaningful change in societal attitudes toward mental health requires a deep understanding of individuals' backgrounds, families, and communities. Social workers must employ patience and perseverance as they strive to make a positive impact on society through culturally sensitive practices.

Enhancing Practitioners' Knowledge

Indigenous social work prioritises the importance of embracing Indigenous knowledge and experiences, which are deeply rooted in values such as the significance of family, reciprocity, spirituality, and support (Gulalia & Subudhi, 2021). It involves seeking guidance from elders, knowledge keepers, and healers, whose wisdom and cultural insights inform practice. Furthermore, the focus is on strengths and resilience rather than deficits, recognising and building upon existing strengths within individuals and communities. Additionally, practitioners should adopt trauma-informed approaches, creating safe spaces, validating experiences, and promoting healthy well-being. Continuous learning is essential, respecting both formal education and traditional teachings.

Conclusion

Embracing indigenous knowledge systems is crucial for building a thriving society that respects and integrates the wisdom of diverse cultures. Social workers play a vital role in this mission, as they need comprehensive training in various indigenous aspects to drive community change effectively and sustainably. The incorporation of indigenous knowledge can lead to culturally sensitive and impactful interventions that address the specific needs and strengths of different communities. Government bodies, institutions, NGOs, community leaders, and individuals must collaborate to promote awareness, knowledge, interventions, and support alongside social workers. Together, we can create an environment where future generations can live happily and sustainably, preserving indigenous knowledge for generations to come in line with Indian traditions.

References

Carpenter, D. (2023). "Indigenous Practice of Social Work in Northeast India: Issues and Challenges". In: Majumdar, K., Baikady, R., D'Souza, A.A. (Eds.) *Indigenisation Discourse in Social Work. Springer Series in International Social Work*. Springer, Cham. https://doi.org/10.1007/978-3-031-37712-9_15

Chiristhuraj, A. & Prasad, S. (2023). *Indic Values and Ethics of Social Work Profession of India.*

Dash, B.M. (2020). "Movement Towards Indianisation of Social Work Education". In S.M., S., Baikady, R., Sheng-Li, C., Sakaguchi, H. (eds.) *The Palgrave Handbook of Global Social Work Education.* Palgrave Macmillan, Cham. https://doi.org/10.1007/978-3-030-39966-5_24

Dash, B.M., Kumar, M., Singh, D.P. & Shukla, S. (Eds.). (2020). *Indian social work.* Routledge.

Dash, B.M., Kumar, M. & Shukla, S. (2019). *Social Work in India: Indigenous Approaches and Models.* Concept Publishing Company Pvt. Ltd.

Dash, B.M. & Kumar, M. (2021). *Nanaji Deshmukh: An Epitome of Indian Social Work.* Concept Publishing Company Pvt. Ltd.

Gulalia, P. & Subudhi, C. (2021). "Constructing Supervisory Practices and Knowledge for Social Work Education in India". *Journal of Social Work Education and Practice, 6*(4), 20-34.

Gulalia, P. & Subudhi, C. (2022). "Social Work Practice in India: In Search of a New Direction". In *The Routledge Handbook of Social Work Field Education in the Global South* (pp. 138-50). Routledge.

Higashida, M., Matsuo, K. & Gohori, J. (2023). "Integrating Indigenous Perspectives into International Social Work Education: A Case Study in Japan", In Majumdar, K., Baikady, R., D'Souza, A.A. (eds) *Indigenisation Discourse in Social Work. Springer Series in International Social Work.* Springer, Cham. https://doi.org/10.1007/978-3-031-37712-9_9

Jadhav, J. & Rana, S. (2020). *Indigenous and Indianised Social Work Education in India.* 10.4324/9780429321818-5.

Lawani, B. (2020). *Indigenisation of Social Work Curriculum.* 10.4324/9780429321818-4.

Majumdar, K., Baikady, R. & D'Souza, A.A. (2023). "Understanding Indigenous Social Work Education and Practice: Local and Global Debates". In: Majumdar, K., Baikady, R., D'Souza, A.A. (eds.) *Indigenisation Discourse in Social Work. Springer Series in International Social Work.* Springer, Cham. https://doi.org/10.1007/978-3-031-37712-9_1

Mukundarao, K. (1969). "Cultural Variants and Social Work Practice in India". *Journal of Education for Social Work, 5*(1): 69-79. http://www.jstor.org/stable/23038259

Rohta, S. (2020). "Contemporary Challenges to Social Work Education and Practice in India". In *Indian Social Work* (pp. 54-63). Routledge, India.

Sahu, K.K. & Subudhi, C. (Eds.) (2021). *Professional Social Work in India: Revisiting the Past and Envisioning the Future* (Vol. 1). Indian Society of Professional Social Work.

Subudhi, C. & Narasimman, P. (2024). *Temple Economy: The base of Bharat's Sustenance.* https://organiser.org/

2

Principles, Values and Philosophies of Indigenous Social Work

Thiruveedula Seshu Babu and *Saraswati Raju Iyer*

Introduction

Indigenous social work is a culturally rooted approach to practice, guided by indigenous worldviews, values, and philosophies. It includes principles for ethical interventions in indigenous communities and with individuals and families. This chapter explores indigenous social work, focusing on principles and values and their implications for practice. Indigenous social work prioritises ethical practice.

The principles stem from indigenous cultural beliefs, traditional knowledge, and historical experiences. Key principles: cultural respect, self-determination, inclusivity, community orientation, healing, and reconciliation. Indigenous social work principles reflect core values for working with clients and communities. These values (respect, inclusivity, cultural continuity, relationships, self-determination, community and family, cultural safety, and social justice) guide practitioners in promoting empowerment, resilience, and positive change in indigenous contexts.

Indigenous Social Work Philosophy: Rooted in indigenous worldviews, cultural teachings, and ways of knowing, this philosophy emphasises interdependence, cultural continuity, self-determination, healing, and community well-being. This chapter enhances our understanding of the unique approach to public practice and social cooperation in Indigenous communities. It provides a framework for addressing complex social problems and guides practitioners with cultural sensitivity and responsiveness. Indigenous social work promotes ethical, culturally competent interventions that enhance the well-being of indigenous peoples and communities.

Definition and Importance of Indigenous Social Work

Indigenous social work addresses unique social, cultural, and historical issues in indigenous communities, integrating traditional knowledge and protecting indigenous rights. The sector promotes social justice, healing, and empowerment in indigenous communities to preserve and revitalise their cultures. Indigenous social work practitioners collaborate with community members to create culturally appropriate programs and interventions for individuals and families. Indigenous social workers integrate traditional healing methods, like smudging and rituals, to promote holistic health. They also address intergenerational trauma and the ongoing impacts of colonisation, aiming for decolonisation and the restoration of human sovereignty. Indigenous social workers engage and collaborate, empowering individuals and families to reclaim cultural identities. They advocate for policy changes and social justice to address systemic inequities, creating a fair society. By focusing on cultural safety and self-determination, these practitioners aim to create lasting positive change and enhance the overall health and well-being of Indigenous peoples.

Objectives

The objectives of the paper is to: (i) To provide insights into indigenous worldviews, cultural beliefs, and historical experiences that shape the principles, values, and philosophies of Indigenous Social Work; (ii) to examine the ethical framework of indigenous Social Work, including principles such as cultural respect, self-determination, a holistic approach, community focus, and healing and reconciliation; (iii) to empower indigenous individuals and communities by focusing indigenous perspectives, knowledge, and experiences in social work practice, promoting empowerment, resilience, and positive change.

Overview of the Principles, Values and Philosophies Guiding Indigenous Social Work

Indigenous social work is guided by a deep respect for traditional knowledge and ways of life, recognising the importance of community and intergenerational relationships. It values the holistic health of individuals, emphasising the connection between the physical, emotional, mental, and spiritual aspects of health. Indigenous social work also acknowledges the historical trauma experienced by indigenous peoples and seeks to address the intergenerational impacts of colonisation, working towards healing and reconciliation. By integrating traditional practices and cultural teachings into their work, indigenous social workers foster a sense of belonging, empowerment, and resilience in Indigenous communities.

Importance of Cultural Competence in Indigenous Social Work

Cultural competence is extremely important in indigenous social work because it allows social workers to understand and appreciate the diverse beliefs, customs, and values that shape the lives of indigenous people. By possessing cultural competency, social workers can build trust and meaningful relationships with indigenous communities, ensuring that the services provided are appropriate to their unique needs. Additionally, cultural competency helps social workers avoid imposing their own biases and assumptions on indigenous individuals, thereby promoting a more inclusive and respectful approach to social work practice.

Principles of Indigenous Social Work

The principles of indigenous social work are deeply rooted in indigenous worldviews, cultural values, and traditional knowledge systems. These principles guide social work practice with indigenous communities and individuals in ways that respect their unique cultural identities and promote self-determination and healing.

Some key principles of Indigenous Social Work include:

***Respect for Cultural Competence*:** Indigenous social work emphasises the importance of understanding and respecting culture, language, indigenous traditions, and values. Practitioners must be culturally competent and able to work effectively in diverse indigenous communities.

***Self-determination*:** Indigenous social work prioritises the self-determination and self-governance of indigenous peoples. This involves supporting indigenous communities in the decision-making processes that affect their lives and empowering them to determine their own paths to well-being.

***Holistic approach*:** Indigenous social work recognises the interdependence of physical, emotional, mental, and spiritual health. Practitioners take a holistic approach that addresses the whole person and considers the social, cultural, environmental, and historical factors that impact individuals and communities.

***Focus on community and family*:** Indigenous social work emphasises the importance of community and family in promoting well-being and resilience. Practitioners work collaboratively with families and communities to strengthen social support networks and address common challenges.

***Cultural Safety*:** Indigenous social work promotes culturally safe environments where indigenous people feel respected, understood, and can express their cultural identity without fear of being discriminated against or marginalised.

***Healing and Reconciliation*:** Indigenous social work acknowledges the historical trauma and ongoing impacts of colonisation on Indigenous communities. Practitioners work toward healing, reconciliation, and decolonisation by addressing intergenerational trauma, promoting cultural revitalisation, and advocating for social justice.

***Land-Based Practices*:** Many indigenous social work approaches incorporate land-based practices and teachings, recognising the importance of land, water, and the natural environment in the culture and well-being of indigenous people.

These principles guide indigenous social work practice in ways that promote resilience, empowerment, and positive change in indigenous communities and beyond.

Values in Indigenous Social Work

Indigenous social work values are fundamental to practice and are deeply rooted in indigenous culture, traditions, and worldviews. These values shape the ethical framework and guide the behaviour, decisions, and interactions of indigenous social work practitioners.

Some key values of Indigenous Social Work include:

***Respect*:** Respect is the foundation of indigenous social work, including respect for indigenous cultures, languages, traditions, and ways of knowing. Practitioners demonstrate respect by honouring diverse perspectives, acknowledging historical and cultural trauma, and appreciating the strength and resilience of indigenous communities.

***Holism*:** Indigenous social work takes a holistic view of well-being that recognises the interdependence of physical, emotional, mental, and spiritual aspects. Practitioners recognise that happiness is not just about meeting individual needs but also involves considering family, community, and cultural factors.

***Cultural Continuity*:** This value emphasises the importance of preserving and revitalising indigenous cultures, knowledge systems, and practices. Practitioners support efforts to maintain cultural continuity by integrating indigenous ways of knowing into interventions, promoting language revitalisation, and facilitating ceremonies and cultural teaching.

***Relationships*:** Relationships are at the heart of Indigenous social work, characterised by trust, empathy, and reciprocity. Practitioners prioritise building meaningful connections with customers, families, communities, and other stakeholders based on collaboration and mutual respect. Strong relationships enhance the effectiveness of interventions and promote culturally competent practice.

***Self-determination*:** Indigenous social work defends the rights to self-determination and self-governance of indigenous peoples. Practitioners help indigenous communities regain control of their lives, resources, and decision-making processes. This includes supporting Indigenous-led initiatives and empowering communities to define their own paths to well-being.

***Community and Family*:** Indigenous social work recognises the central role of community and family in promoting well-being and resilience. Practitioners work collaboratively with families and communities to strengthen social support networks, address systemic challenges, and promote healing and empowerment at the collective level.

***Cultural Safety*:** Cultural safety is a key value that ensures that indigenous people feel respected, recognised, and safe in all interactions and environments. Practitioners create culturally safe spaces by recognising power imbalances, challenging stereotypes and biases, and promoting cultural humility and responsiveness.

***Social Justice*:** Indigenous social work is based on a commitment to social justice and equality. Practitioners advocate for policies, programs, and practices that address historical and ongoing injustices faced by indigenous peoples, challenge systemic barriers to equity, and advance and promote meaningful reconciliation and healing.

These values intersect and inform each other, guiding indigenous social work practitioners in their efforts to promote empowerment, resilience, and positive change in indigenous communities and beyond.

Philosophy of Indigenous Social Work

Indigenous social work philosophy has deep roots in indigenous worldviews, cultural beliefs, and ways of knowing. These philosophies guide the fundamental principles, values, and practices of indigenous social work and shape its approach to solving social problems, promoting well-being, and promoting healing.

Holistic approach: Indigenous social work takes a holistic view of well-being, recognising the interconnections between the physical, emotional, mental, and spiritual aspects of life. This philosophy recognises that personal happiness is inseparable from family happiness, community, and the natural environment.

Interdependence and Relationships: Indigenous social work is based on the philosophy of interdependence, emphasising the interconnected relationships between all living things, including humans, animals, plants, and the earth. This philosophy emphasises the importance of maintaining respectful and reciprocal relationships within and between communities.

Cultural Continuity and Revitalisation: Indigenous social work is guided by the philosophy of cultural continuity, which emphasises the importance of preserving and revitalising culture, language, traditions, and indigenous knowledge systems. This philosophy recognises the resilience and strength inherent in indigenous cultural values and practices.

Self-determination and Empowerment: Indigenous social work is rooted in the philosophy of self-determination, affirming the right of indigenous peoples to control their own destiny and make decisions about their lives and communities while reclaiming their rights and autonomy. This philosophy focuses on empowering individuals and indigenous communities to determine their own path to well-being.

Healing and Reconciliation: Indigenous social work is guided by a philosophy of healing and reconciliation that acknowledges historical trauma and the ongoing impacts of colonisation on native communities. This philosophy emphasises the importance of addressing intergenerational trauma, promoting healing, and working toward reconciliation and decolonisation.

Land and place-based approaches: Indigenous social work is based on a philosophy of land and a place-based approach, recognising the spiritual and cultural importance of the land, water, and natural environment in indigenous cultures. This philosophy emphasises the importance of reconnecting with traditional territories, engaging in land-based activities, and honouring indigenous ecological knowledge.

Community and collective well-being: Indigenous social work prioritises the philosophy of community and collective well-being, recognising that individual well-being is inextricably linked to the well-being of the whole community. This philosophy emphasises the importance of collective responsibility, mutual support, and solidarity within indigenous communities.

These philosophies of Indigenous social work guide practitioners in their efforts to promote interventions that draw on strengths and cultural competencies, advocate for social justice and indigenous rights, and work towards positive change and empowerment in indigenous communities and beyond.

Cultural Competence in Indigenous Social Work

Cultural competence in indigenous social work refers to the knowledge, skills, attitudes, and practices that enable practitioners to engage effectively with customers, communities, and local cultures in a respectful and culturally responsive manner. This involves understanding and valuing the diverse cultural backgrounds, worldviews, histories, and experiences of Indigenous peoples and integrating this knowledge into all aspects of work-practice society.

Cultural knowledge: Cultural competency begins with the acquisition of knowledge about culture, indigenous history, language, traditions, and belief systems. This involves understanding diversity within indigenous communities and recognising the impact of colonisation, intergenerational trauma, and historical injustices.

Cultural awareness and sensitivity: Cultural competency involves the development of self-awareness and sensitivity to one's own cultural biases, assumptions, and privileges. Practitioners need to be aware of how their own cultural background and experiences may influence their perceptions, attitudes, and interactions with clients and indigenous communities.

Cultural respect and humility: Cultural competence requires demonstrating respect for indigenous cultures, values, and ways of knowing. Practitioners must approach their work with humility, recognising that Indigenous people are the experts on their own cultures and experiences.

Engagement and relationship building: Cultural competency involves building relationships of trust and respect with clients, families, and indigenous communities. Practitioners must engage in active listening, demonstrate empathy, and seek to understand the unique strengths, needs, and perspectives of those they serve.

Cultural adaptation and flexibility: Cultural competency requires adapting social work interventions, strategies, and approaches to fit the cultural preferences, practices, and priorities of customers and indigenous communities. This may involve working with indigenous elders, knowledge holders, and community leaders to ensure services are culturally appropriate.

Trauma-Informed Practice: Cultural competency in indigenous social work includes knowledge of trauma and an understanding of the impact of historical trauma, such as colonisation, forced assimilation, residential schools, and relocation. Practitioners should use trauma-informed approaches that prioritise safety, empowerment, and healing.

Advocacy and Social Justice: Cultural competency involves advocating for social justice, equity, and indigenous rights. Practitioners should collaborate with indigenous communities to address systemic barriers, advocate for policy changes, and promote culturally competent services that support the self-determination and sovereignty rights of indigenous people.

***Continuous learning and reflection*:** Cultural competency is an ongoing process that requires ongoing learning, self-reflection, and professional development. Practitioners should seek opportunities to deepen their cultural knowledge, engage in critical reflection on their practice, and learn from colleagues, mentors, and indigenous communities.

By integrating cultural competency into their practice, indigenous social work practitioners can promote positive outcomes, strengthen relationships, and contribute to the well-being and empowerment of indigenous people and communities.

Review of Literature

Indigenous Social Work is guided by a set of principles, values, and philosophies deeply rooted in indigenous knowledge systems and cultural traditions. These principles emphasise the importance of respecting indigenous worldviews, advancing indigenous consciousness of colonial impacts, maintaining indigenous identity through cultural knowledge, and empowering indigenous communities beyond dominant paradigms (Robin, T., Dennis, M., & Hart, M. 2020). Indigenous social work education is centred on valuing indigenous ways of knowing, being, and doing and is designed in collaboration with indigenous communities, culturally respectful, based on indigenous pedagogy, and taught to all social work students (Thompson, Manshack, & Schuyver, 2021).

The philosophies of indigenous social work are intricately connected to indigenous epistemologies, cultural values, and practices. They emphasise the significance of place-based, relational, and collective worldviews that value relational autonomy and community well-being (Poelina, 2023). Indigenous philosophies also play a crucial role in decolonising social-ecological systems by focusing land and relationships to land in efforts towards reconciliation and right relations (Murdock, 2018).

In the context of social work practice, indigenous philosophies call for the recognition and integration of indigenous knowledge systems, the promotion of cultural emancipation, and the fostering of social practices that honour indigenous ways of knowing and being (Larrinoa, 2019). These philosophies also highlight the importance of engaging with indigenous laws and philosophies to rebuild indigenous communities and nations (Thomas, 2022). Overall, indigenous social work is deeply intertwined with indigenous philosophies that emphasise rationality, community empowerment, cultural respect, and decolonisation. By incorporating indigenous knowledge systems and values into social work education and practice, practitioners can work towards reconciliation, empowerment, and social justice within indigenous communities.

To further explore the literature on indigenous social work, Jaswal and Kshetrimayum (2022) provides a comprehensive review of indigenous social work practices worldwide, highlighting the various conceptualisations and debates surrounding indigenous social work. This review identifies four distinct lines of thought that have emerged in conceptualising indigenous social work globally (Jaswal & Kshetrimayum, 2022).

Moreover, Rosiek *et al.* (2019) argue for the importance of respectful anti-colonial engagement by integrating indigenous theories of non-human agency with new materialist social science. They emphasise the strengths of indigenous studies literature in addressing challenges faced by new materialist social science. Additionally, Nnama-Okechukwu and McLaughlin (2022) discuss the integration of Western theories in African social work education, leading to ethical conflicts between Western values and traditional African indigenous knowledge. This conflict underscores the importance of navigating diverse knowledge systems in social work education (Nnama-Okechukwu & McLaughlin, 2022).

Furthermore, Boadu and Ile (2022) propose a framework for indigenous relational evaluation in traditional communities in Ghana, highlighting the vast evaluative competencies embedded in Indigenous philosophies. They call for further research to explore these evaluative practices (Boadu & Ile, 2022). In summary, the literature on indigenous social work underscores the importance of respecting indigenous knowledge systems, engaging in anti-colonial practices, navigating diverse knowledge systems, and exploring indigenous evaluative practices to enhance social work in indigenous communities.

Challenges and Future Directions

- Addressing barriers faced by indigenous communities is a crucial challenge for social workers. It includes advocating for policy change, working with leaders, and collaborating on the root causes of inequities. Social workers must educate themselves, reflect on biases, seek indigenous perspectives, and promote equity.
- Advocating for indigenous peoples' rights and autonomy in social work is crucial. This includes supporting indigenous initiatives, policy change, and culturally appropriate services. By addressing barriers and empowering indigenous communities, social workers can disrupt oppression and foster change. They must also build trusting, respectful relationships with individuals, families, and indigenous communities to amplify their voices and meet their needs. Their needs are prioritised in decision-making for their lives.
- Promoting culturally responsive policies and programs in social work is vital to addressing indigenous communities' challenges. This includes integrating traditions, languages, and values into service design and implementation. Social workers can ensure culturally sensitive and relevant work for indigenous individuals by promoting responsive policies and programs. This improves social work interventions and shows commitment to social justice and equity.

Suggestions

To integrate cultural sensitivity into social work practice with indigenous communities, including participating in continuing education on cultural competency, actively seeking feedback and advice from indigenous community members, and incorporating indigenous perspectives in decision-making. Additionally, social workers should prioritise building relationships based on trust, respect, and collaboration with indigenous individuals and communities. By integrating indigenous voices and values into their practice, social workers can work to address the historical and systemic injustices that have affected indigenous communities through generations.

Emphasise the importance of Indigenous perspectives: Emphasise the importance of focusing indigenous perspectives, knowledge, and voices in social work practice. Emphasise that indigenous worldviews, cultural values, and historical experiences are essential to understanding and meeting the unique needs and strengths of indigenous communities.

Reflection on ethical frameworks: Emphasises the importance of ethical framework for indigenous social work practice and also the importance of cultural respect, self-determination, social justice, and inclusive approaches in promoting ethical and effective interventions.

Emphasises Cultural Competence: Recognise the importance of cultural competence in indigenous social work and the need for practitioners to continually develop knowledge, skills, and cultural humility. Emphasise the role of cultural competency in building trust, fostering meaningful relationships, and promoting culturally responsive services.

Advocate for anti-oppression and decolonisation activities: Emphasises the need for social workers to engage in anti-oppression and decolonisation activities that challenge systemic barriers, address historical and current injustices, and promote indigenous self-determination and sovereignty. Advocate for policies and practices that respect indigenous rights and support indigenous-led initiatives.

Call for Collaboration: Encourage social workers to establish partnerships with indigenous communities, organisations, and knowledge holders. Emphasise the value of co-creating knowledge, interventions, and solutions rooted in indigenous perspectives and priorities.

Awareness about future directions: Awareness about emerging trends, challenges, and opportunities in indigenous social work practice such as the role of technology, environmental justice, intergenerational trauma, and global indigenous solidarity in shaping the future of indigenous social work.

Inspire action and commitment: Need to inspire social workers to take action and commit to ethical, cultural, and anti-oppressive practices and to encourage lifelong learning, reflection, and advocacy for social justice and indigenous rights in the field of social work.

Conclusion

This chapter discusses the key principles, values, and philosophies of indigenous social work practice. By studying indigenous worldviews, beliefs, and historical contexts, we have gained a better understanding of the principles that guide ethical interventions and effectiveness in indigenous communities. Indigenous social work principles like cultural respect, self-determination, holistic approaches, community orientation, healing, and reconciliation guide practitioners to develop culturally appropriate interventions that empower, promote resilience, and enable positive change. Indigenous social work values, like respect, holism, cultural continuity, relationships, self-determination, community and family, cultural safety, and social justice, form the ethical basis for practice. Embracing these values needs personal reflection, cultural humility, and a commitment to anti-oppression and decolonisation. Indigenous social work philosophy, emphasising interdependence, cultural continuity, self-determination, healing, and community well-being, guides problem-solving in indigenous contexts. By employing these philosophies, social workers can approach their work respectfully and effectively, considering indigenous ways of knowing. Moving forward, social work education must prioritise indigenous perspectives, knowledge, and voices. This entails improving cultural competency, advocating for indigenous rights and social justice, and forging partnerships with Indigenous communities and organisations. In short, indigenous social work principles and values enhance ethical, cultural, and effective practice, enabling social workers to empower indigenous communities and promote healing, recovery, and positive social change.

References

Boadu, E. and Ile, I. (2022). "Beyond the Buzzword: A Framework for An Indigenous Relational Evaluation in Traditional Communities in Ghana". *American Journal of Evaluation*, 109821402110484. https://doi.org/10.1177/10982140211048459

Jaswal, S. and Kshetrimayum, M. (2022). "A Review of Indigenous Social Work Around The World: Concepts, Debates and Challenges". *International Social Work, 66*(5): 1369-82. https://doi.org/10.1177/00208728211073851

Larrinoa, K. (2019). *Indigenous Amazonia and Decolonising Social Work*, pp. 79-98. https://doi.org/10.33673/ooa20201/4

Murdock, E. (2018). "Unsettling Reconciliation: Decolonial Methods for Transforming Social-ecological Systems". *Environmental Values, 27*(5): 513-33. https://doi.org/10.3197/096327118x15321668325948

Nnama Okechukwu, C. and McLaughlin, H. (2022). "Indigenous Knowledge and Social Work Education in Nigeria: Made in Nigeria or Made in the West?" *Social Work Education, 42*(8): 1476-93. https://doi.org/10.1080/02615479.2022.2038557

Poelina, A. (2023). "Indigenous Philosophy in Environmental Education". *Australian Journal of Environmental Education, 39*(3): 269-78. https://doi.org/10.1017/aee.2023.28

Robin, T., Dennis, M. & Hart, M. (2020). "Feeding Indigenous People in Canada". *International Social Work, 65*(4): 652-62. https://doi.org/10.1177/0020872820916218

Rosiek, J., Snyder, J. & Pratt, S. (2019). "The New Materialisms and Indigenous Theories of Non-human Agency: Making the Case for Respectful Anti-Colonial Engagement". *Qualitative Inquiry, 26*(3-4): 331-46. https://doi.org/10.1177/1077800419830135

Thomas, D. (2022). "Applying One Dish, One Spoon as an Indigenous Research Methodology. *Alternative an International Journal of Indigenous Peoples, 18*(1): 84-93. https://doi.org/10.1177/11771801221087864

Thompson, K., Manshack, L. & Schuyver, J. (2021). "The Significance of Indigenous Field Education: An Analysis of the Social Workers Advancing Through Grounded Education Programme". *Journal of Human Rights and Social Work, 7*(2): 211-22. https://doi.org/10.1007/s41134-021-00187-9

3

An Exploration of Social Work Philosophy, Ideology and Practices from An Indic Perspective

Veerabhadram Bhukya

Introduction

Indic social work philosophy encompasses a profound understanding of human interconnectedness, moral duty, and spiritual well-being, rooted in the ancient wisdom traditions of the Indian subcontinent. This philosophical notion has drawn upon a diverse array of religious and philosophical texts, shaping the ethos of social work practice in the region. This might involve and highlight concepts such as *Dharma* (duty/righteousness), *Seva* (selfless service), and compassion, which are deeply rooted in Indian philosophical and ideological traditions. Indeed, underlying the fundamental values, guiding rules, and principles of social work would focus on contemporary social issues and their root connections. It also signifies the ideological foundation of an Indic perspective ideologies like *Sarvodaya* (welfare of all) and *Ahimsa* (non-violence) may influence how social workers approach their professional practices, emphasising inclusive and non-violent solutions to social issues. The Ideological and professional practices could involve community-based approaches, empowerment of marginalised groups, and integration of traditional wisdom and modern techniques in addressing social problems and intervention.

In the seminal work "*The Bhagavad Gita*" (between the 5th and 2nd centuries BCE), attributed to the sage Vyasa, the concept of *dharma* (duty/righteousness) is central. This was the greatest divine book contribution of Raja Dharma. Particularly, the *Gita* elucidates the idea of selfless action (*karma yoga*) as mentioned in Shri Krishna's discourses to Arjuna to fulfil one's duty without attachment to outcomes, laying the groundwork for a moral framework that underpins Indic social work philosophy evidently (Rosen, 2007).

In a similar tone, the teachings of *Lord Gautam Buddha*, as recorded in the Pali Canon and other Buddhist scriptures, emphasise compassion (*karuna*) and altruism (selflessness) as essential virtues. The principle of *ahimsa* (non-violence) advocated by Mahatma Gandhi, deeply rooted in Jain and Hindu traditions also finds resonance in Indic social work philosophy, guiding practitioners towards peaceful and non-coercive methods of social transformation (Chapple, 1993). Besides, the concept of *sewa* (selfless service) is a cornerstone of *Sikh philosophy*, as articulated in the *Guru Granth Sahib*, the holy scripture of Sikhism. Sikhism emphasises the importance of serving humanity as a means of connecting with the divine within each individual, inspiring acts of charity and social upliftment (Singh, 2004).

Moreover, Indic social work philosophy acknowledges the significance of spirituality and mindfulness in promoting individual and collective well-being. Practices such as meditation, *yoga*, and mindfulness are integrated into social work interventions to foster inner peace, resilience, and holistic development. Indic social work philosophy offers a holistic framework for addressing social issues, promoting welfare, and fostering human flourishing. Grounded in the principles of *dharma*, *ahimsa*, and inclusivity, this philosophy emphasises the interconnectedness of all beings and the importance of selfless service in building a more just and compassionate society.

Certainly, Indic social work philosophy is a tapestry woven from the threads of ancient wisdom, encompassing principles of *dharma*, *karma*, compassion, and selfless service. Grounded in diverse religious and philosophical traditions, it offers a holistic framework for addressing the multifaceted challenges of human welfare and social justice in the Indian context and beyond.

Overall, this work exploring social work through an Indic lens provides insights into how cultural, philosophical, and ideological perspectives shape the theory and practice of social work, offering alternative frameworks for understanding and addressing social issues.

Indian Philosophy and Ideology

The history of Indian philosophy can be divided into four periods: the Vedic period (1500 BC to 600 BC), the Epic period (600 BC to 200 AD), the Sutra period (200 AD to 1700 AD), and the Scholastic period (1700 AD and onwards).

Certainly, Indian philosophy encompasses a vast array of schools of thought, such as *Vedanta, Yoga, Nyaya, Vaisheshika, Samkhya*, and more. Each of these schools offers unique insights into various aspects of life, consciousness, metaphysics, ethics, and spirituality. It allows for a deeper comprehension of not only Indian society but also the broader human experience. Exploring traditional perspectives can shed light on timeless wisdom and perspectives that continue to resonate with people across the globe. In the teachings of ancient texts like the *Vedas, Upanishads,* and *Bhagavad Gita*, or the philosophical inquiries of figures like *Shankaracharya, Ramanuja,* or *Madhvacharya*, there is a wealth of knowledge, and intellectual property to explore and contemplate.

Bharat, commonly known as India, is a land deeply rooted in philosophical thought and profound ideological frameworks. The genesis of *Bharatiya* philosophy and ideology can be traced back to ancient times, where diverse schools of thought flourished, influencing not only the Indian subcontinent but also leaving a lasting impact on global philosophical discourse.

Ancient origins: The foundations of *Bharatiya* philosophy can be found in the *Vedas*, the oldest scriptures of Hinduism, dating back to around 1500-500 BCE. These texts contain hymns, rituals, and philosophical speculations that laid the groundwork for subsequent philosophical developments in India. The concepts of *karma*, *dharma*, and *moksha* originated from these ancient texts, shaping the philosophical landscape of Bharat (Sharma, 2010, p. 25).

Indian schools of thoughts: *Bharatiya* philosophy is characterised by a rich diversity of schools of thought, each offering unique perspectives on metaphysics, epistemology, ethics, and ontology. The six orthodox (*astika*) schools, including *Nyaya, Vaisheshika, Samkhya, Yoga, Mimamsa, and Vedanta*, as well as several heterodox (*nastika*) schools like *Jainism, Buddhism,* and *Charvaka (Lokayata)*, contributed to the vibrant intellectual milieu of ancient Bharat.

In Indian philosophy, each school's founder and foundational texts epitomise perfect and unique contributions to philosophical thought and ideological foundation. Gautama, attributed as the progenitor of *Nyaya* philosophy, crafted the *Nyaya Sutra*, a cornerstone text renowned for its meticulous reasoning and logical analysis. Similarly, Kanada's '*Vaisheshika Sutra*' elucidates the fundamental principles of *Vaisheshika* philosophy with unparalleled clarity and depth, reflecting his singular insights. Kapila's pivotal role in *Samkhya* philosophy reverberates through the collective wisdom embodied in the *Samkhya Sutra*, a testament to the perfect fusion of diverse perspectives across generations. Patanjali's *Yoga Sutras*, despite authorship ambiguity, stand as a paragon of yogic wisdom, offering profound insights into the human psyche and spiritual evolution. Jaimini's *Mimamsa Sutras* intricately unravel the complexities of ritual interpretation, embodying the essence of *Mimamsa* philosophy with unmatched precision. The luminaries of Vedanta, Jainism, Buddhism, and Charvaka philosophy, along with their seminal texts, enrich the philosophical landscape with unparalleled depth and diversity, symbolising the richness of Indian philosophical heritage.

The intersection of Indian philosophical schools and professional social work is profound, offering ethical, holistic, and culturally sensitive frameworks for practice. Ethical principles like *ahimsa* (non-violence) and compassion, inherent in traditions such as Buddhism and Jainism, guide social workers in advocating for justice and well-being. The holistic understanding of human nature, emphasising interconnectedness and interdependence, resonates with social work's ecological systems perspective. Moreover, studying Indian philosophies enhances cultural competence, enabling practitioners to engage effectively with diverse populations. Concepts of spirituality and meaning-making from these traditions inform interventions, particularly in areas like palliative care. Integrating these perspectives enriches social work practice, fostering deeper understanding and more impactful interventions.

Key Philosophical Concepts: The philosophical discourse in Bharat revolves around fundamental concepts such as the nature of reality (metaphysics), the means of acquiring knowledge (epistemology), the nature of the self (*atman*), the concept of God (*Brahman*), ethical principles (*dharma*), and the ultimate goal of life (*moksha*). These concepts are explored and debated within various philosophical frameworks, providing insights into the nature of existence and the human condition.

In the realm of professional social work, a profound grasp of philosophical concepts from Bharat's discourse is indispensable. Social workers confront diverse challenges while engaging with individuals from varied backgrounds. Integrating key philosophical tenets like the nature of reality, epistemology, and ethical principles enriches their practice. Understanding the interconnectedness of these concepts enables social workers to navigate intricate social dynamics with insight. Furthermore, comprehension of the self's nature and life's ultimate goal informs their approach to empowerment and well-being. By weaving philosophical frameworks into their work, social workers cultivate meaningful connections, foster cultural humility, and drive transformative change. Embracing these philosophical underpinnings elevates the practice of professional social work, empowering practitioners to serve communities with integrity, wisdom, and compassion.

Traditional perspectives: In the contemporary landscape of social work philosophy and ideology, traditional *Bharatiya* philosophy emerges as a beacon, emphasising the interconnectedness of all life forms. It perceives the universe as a holistic entity governed by universal principles, advocating for harmony with nature, self-realisation, and the pursuit of spiritual wisdom as fundamental human aspects. These traditional perspectives accentuate the importance of introspection, meditation, and ethical living in achieving inner peace and liberation from the cycle of birth and death. In the context of social work, integrating these traditional values offers profound insights into fostering holistic well-being and addressing systemic challenges. By infusing social work practice with traditional perspectives, practitioners promote harmony, self-awareness, and ethical conduct, thus contributing to the empowerment and liberation of individuals and communities. This approach encapsulates a rich fusion of timeless wisdom with modern social work principles, facilitating a more holistic and transformative approach to community welfare.

So, *Bharatiya* philosophy and ideology have evolved over millennia, blending ancient wisdom with contemporary insights to offer profound perspectives on the nature of reality and the human experience. The history of Indian philosophy spans four distinct periods, offering a diverse array of schools of thought such as *Vedanta*, *Yoga*, *Nyaya*, and more. These philosophies, rooted in ancient texts like the *Vedas* and *Upanishads*, provide profound insights into life, consciousness, and spirituality. Foundational figures like Gautama, Kanada, and Patanjali crafted seminal texts that continue to influence philosophical discourse. Indian philosophical concepts like *karma*, *dharma*, and *moksha* shape not only Indian society but also global philosophical understanding. In social work, integrating these philosophies enhances cultural competence and offers ethical, holistic frameworks for practice. Traditional *Bharatiya* philosophy emphasises interconnectedness, self-realisation, and ethical living, enriching social work interventions and promoting holistic well-being.

Historically Transformed of Social Work Philosophy, Ideology and Practices

Throughout history, the evolution of social work philosophy, ideology, and practices has been marked by profound transformations, reflecting shifts in societal values, political landscapes, and understandings of human well-being. Emerging in the late 19th and early 20th centuries as a response to the social upheavals of industrialisation and urbanisation, social work initially focused on charity and relief efforts, grounded in religious and humanitarian principles. However, as the discipline matured, it underwent significant ideological shifts.

Social Work Perspective in Ancient Times

The social work perspective in ancient times spanned from the earliest human civilisations, roughly around 4000 BCE to 500 CE. In ancient civilisations, the development of rudimentary forms of social work existed primarily within communal structures (John E. Hansan). The ethos of reciprocity and communal responsibility underpinned assistance to vulnerable members, such as widows, orphans, and the elderly. Examples include the Code of Hammurabi in Mesopotamia, which mandated protections for the vulnerable, and the teachings of Confucius in ancient China emphasising benevolence and filial piety. While not formalised as a profession, these societal norms laid the groundwork for later social welfare principles.

Social Work Perspectives in the Medieval Period (5th-15th Century)

During the medieval period, dive into the rich tapestry of medieval social welfare services, where religious institutions played a central role in caring for the vulnerable. Monastic orders, embodying principles of charity, offered sustenance and solace to the needy, ill, and weary travellers. Yet, amid this benevolence, exclusionary practices based on religious adherence marginalised certain groups, like lepers and heretics, highlighting the complexities of compassion within religious frameworks. This historical examination not only illuminates the roots of modern social welfare and social work practices but also prompts contemplation on the intersectionality of faith, charity, and societal inclusion.

Social Work Perspective in the Modern Period (18th-21st Century)

During the modern era, significant transformations occurred in the philosophy and implementation of social work. Noteworthy figures such as Jane Addams and Octavia Hill spearheaded organised charity and advocacy endeavours establishing settlement houses and tenant support programs to combat urban poverty and social upheaval. Through seminal works like Jane Addams's (1910) "Twenty Years at Hull House" and Octavia Hill's writings on housing reform, they offered valuable insights into their methodologies and ideologies. Moreover, scholars including Frances Perkins (1946), William Beveridge (1942), and Richard Titmuss (1955) played pivotal roles in shaping social welfare policies and the welfare state, advocating for systemic interventions to address the underlying causes of societal issues. Perkins's influence on New Deal policies, Beveridge's seminal report on social security, and Titmuss's research on the welfare state offer invaluable perspectives on the evolution of modern social work.

In the Indian context, the modern era witnessed parallel advancements in social work philosophy and practice. Visionaries such as Mahatma Gandhi and Dr. B.R. Ambedkar emerged as stalwarts in championing social justice and equality through their advocacy and activism. Gandhi's emphasis on community-based solutions and Ambedkar's focus on social reform and empowerment laid the groundwork for tailored social work initiatives aimed at addressing India's distinctive societal challenges. Their enduring legacies serve as beacons, inspiring contemporary social work practices dedicated to mitigating poverty, inequality, and discrimination within Indian society. In the contemporary context, social work continues to evolve in response to global challenges such as globalisation, technological advancement, and environmental crises. Current trends include the integration of evidence-based practices, the promotion of human rights and social justice, and the utilisation of interdisciplinary collaborations. Looking ahead, the ongoing transformation of social work philosophy, ideology, and practices underscores its adaptability and enduring commitment to promoting human well-being and social change.

The evolution of social work philosophy, ideology, and practices throughout history reflects dynamic responses to societal shifts and human needs. From ancient communal structures to medieval religious institutions and modern advocacy movements, social work has continually adapted to address the complexities of human welfare. Renowned social activists/servants like Jane Addams and Frances Perkins spearheaded organised efforts, laying the groundwork for systemic interventions and welfare policies. Today, social work embraces evidence-based practices, human rights advocacy, and interdisciplinary collaboration to tackle global challenges. This ongoing transformation underscores its resilience and commitment to advancing human well-being and social justice, ensuring its relevance in an ever-changing world.

Roots of Social Work Philosophy

Social work philosophy traces its roots to various intellectual and cultural movements that have shaped human society over centuries. At its core, social work philosophy emphasises the inherent dignity and worth of every individual, along with the commitment to social justice, equality, and the empowerment of marginalised populations. The roots of social work philosophy can be found in ancient civilisations where principles of *compassion, community support, and altruism* were valued.

Throughout history, the works of philosophers such as *Plato, Aristotle,* and *Confucius* have contributed to the development of ethical principles that underpin social work practice. *Plato's concept of justice*, *Aristotle's virtue ethics*, and *Confucius's teachings on benevolence and righteousness* laid the groundwork for understanding moral obligations towards others within a societal context.

In modern times, the emergence of social welfare movements during the *Industrial Revolution*, alongside the influence of religious and humanitarian ideologies, further shaped the philosophy of social work. Figures like *Jane Addams*, who founded *Hull House in Chicago*, and *Mary Ellen Richmond* (1922), a pioneer in social work education, promoted the idea of social responsibility and the need for organised efforts to address social problems.

The roots of social work philosophy continue to evolve, drawing from interdisciplinary fields such as psychology, sociology, and anthropology. Contemporary social work practice integrates theories of human behaviour, social systems, and social change to address complex issues such as poverty, discrimination, and mental health.

The ideology of social work finds resonance in Bharath-born (Indian) religious practices and belief systems, which have long emphasised the principles of *compassion, service, and community welfare*. In India, religious traditions such as *Hinduism, Buddhism, Jainism, and Sikhism* offer rich philosophical foundations that align with the *values of social work*.

In fact, Hinduism, with its emphasis on *dharma* (duty) and *sewa* (selfless service), encourages individuals to engage in acts of charity and humanitarianism as a means of spiritual fulfilment. The concept of *karma* (action) underscores the interconnectedness of human beings and their moral responsibilities towards others, mirroring the ethical principles of social work.

Similarly, Buddhism espouses the idea of *karuna* (compassion) and *ahimsa* (non-violence), advocating for the alleviation of suffering and the promotion of peace and harmony in society. Buddhist teachings on the importance of mindfulness and empathy resonate with the therapeutic approaches employed in social work practice.

Jainism emphasises the principles of *ahimsa* (non-violence) and *aparigraha* (non-possessiveness), advocating for a lifestyle of simplicity and compassion towards all living beings. The Jain concept of *sewa* (selfless service) aligns closely with the *altruistic values of social work*, emphasising the importance of helping those in need without expecting anything in return.

Sikhism, with its emphasis on *sewa* (selfless service) and *sarbat da bhala* (welfare of all), encourages its followers to actively engage in community service and philanthropy as expressions of their faith. The Sikh tradition of *langar*, or communal meal, exemplifies the spirit of inclusivity and social equality, transcending barriers of caste, class, and religion.

An exemplary illustration of the convergence between professional social work philosophy and Bharath-born religious practices can be seen in the work of organisations like the *Akshaya Patra Foundation* in India. Inspired by the Hindu principle of *sewa* (selfless service), the foundation serves mid-day meals to millions of children across the country, addressing both hunger and education simultaneously.

Another example is the Amma (Mata Amritanandamayi) Foundation, which embodies the values of compassion and service espoused in Hinduism. Through its various humanitarian initiatives, including disaster relief, healthcare, and education programs, the foundation embodies the spirit of selfless service and social responsibility.

Similarly, the work of the Karuna Trust, rooted in *Buddhist* principles of compassion and non-violence, focuses on providing healthcare and education to marginalised communities in India. By addressing the root causes of suffering and inequality, the trust exemplifies the Buddhist commitment to social justice and human welfare.

This juncture of social work philosophy with Bharath-born religious practices and belief systems offers a compelling framework for addressing social problems and promoting collective well-being and quality of life. By drawing upon the ethical principles and moral values inherent in these traditions, social work can continue to inspire positive change and foster a more just and compassionate society.

Incorporating Indic Values into Contemporary Social Work Practice

- ***Dharma (Duty and Righteousness):*** Embracing the concept of *dharma*, contemporary social work practice can prioritise ethical responsibilities and moral obligations towards individuals and communities. Practitioners can strive to uphold principles of honesty, integrity, and justice in their interactions with clients and society at large. By recognising and fulfilling their duty to serve others, social workers can cultivate a sense of purpose and meaning in their profession.
- ***Seva (Selfless Service):*** Integrating the value of *sewa* into social work practice involves prioritising the needs of others above personal gain or recognition. Practitioners can engage in acts of selfless service by providing compassionate care, advocating for social justice, and empowering marginalised populations. By embodying the spirit of *sewa*, social workers can foster a culture of empathy, generosity, and solidarity within their professional communities.
- ***Ahimsa (Non-violence):*** Embracing the principle of *ahimsa*, contemporary social work practice can promote non-violent approaches to conflict resolution and social change. Practitioners can advocate for peaceful means of addressing systemic injustices, such as discrimination, oppression, and inequality. By prioritising dialogue,

cooperation, and mutual respect, social workers can contribute to the creation of a more harmonious and inclusive society.

- ***Karuna (Compassion):*** Infusing the value of *karuna* into social work practice involves cultivating empathy, understanding, and sensitivity towards the suffering of others. Practitioners can demonstrate compassion by actively listening to clients' experiences, validating their emotions, and offering support without judgment. By prioritising the well-being of vulnerable individuals and communities, social workers can work towards healing, restoration, and social transformation.

Incorporating Indic values into contemporary social work practice enriches the profession with ancient wisdom and moral insights that resonate across cultural and religious boundaries. By embracing principles of *dharma*, *sewa*, *ahimsa*, and *karuna*, social workers can contribute to the creation of a more compassionate, just, and equitable society.

Challenges and Opportunities in Applying Indic Perspectives to Social Work

- ***Cultural Sensitivity and Adaptation:*** One of the primary challenges in applying Indic perspectives to social work lies in navigating cultural differences and ensuring that interventions are sensitive to the diverse beliefs and practices of clients. Social workers must be mindful of the potential for misinterpretation or imposition of values that may not align with the cultural context. However, this challenge also presents an opportunity for social workers to engage in culturally competent practice, fostering mutual understanding and respect across cultural boundaries.
- ***Secularism and Pluralism:*** Another challenge arises from the need to maintain the secular nature of social work practice while incorporating Indic perspectives, which are inherently intertwined with religious and spiritual

beliefs. Social workers must strike a balance between honouring client's cultural backgrounds and upholding professional ethics and boundaries. However, this challenge also provides an opportunity to promote pluralism and inclusivity within social work practice, recognising the validity of diverse worldviews and belief systems.

- ***Intersectionality and Diversity:*** Applying Indic perspectives to social work requires acknowledging the intersectionality of identities and experiences among clients, including factors such as caste, class, gender, and ethnicity. Social workers must be attentive to the unique needs and challenges faced by different communities within the broader framework of Indic values. This challenge underscores the importance of adopting an intersectional lens in social work practice, which can lead to more holistic and inclusive approaches to service delivery.
- ***Ethical Considerations:*** Incorporating Indic perspectives into social work practice raises ethical considerations regarding the imposition of values, power dynamics, and professional boundaries. Social workers must critically reflect on their own biases and assumptions, ensuring that interventions are guided by principles of self-determination and cultural humility. This challenge also presents an opportunity for social workers to engage in ongoing dialogue and ethical decision-making processes that uphold the dignity and autonomy of clients.

In following inference, while there are challenges inherent in applying Indic perspectives to professional social work, such as ***cultural sensitivity, secularism, intersectionality***, and ***ethics***, there are also opportunities for ***promoting cultural competence, pluralism, inclusivity***, and ***ethical practice*** within the profession. By navigating these challenges thoughtfully and responsibly, professional social workers can harness the rich insights of Indic traditions to enhance the effectiveness and relevance of their practice in diverse cultural contexts.

Future Directions and Innovations in Indic Social Work Practice

As Indic professional social work continues to evolve, several future directions and innovations are emerging to enhance the effectiveness and relevance of practice.

- ***Cultural Integration and Adaptation:*** Future Indic social work practice will focus on integrating cultural values and beliefs into interventions while adapting approaches to meet the diverse needs of clients. This may involve developing culturally specific assessment tools, training programs, and intervention models that resonate with the values and traditions of the communities served.
- ***Technology and Digital Platforms:*** Innovations in technology offer opportunities to extend the reach of Indic social work practice through digital platforms and telehealth services. Future directions may include the development of mobile applications, online support groups, and virtual counselling sessions to increase access to services and overcome barriers of distance and mobility.
- ***Community Empowerment and Grassroots Initiatives:*** Future Indic social work practice will prioritise community empowerment and grassroots initiatives to address social problems at the local level. This may involve partnering with community leaders, religious institutions, and non-governmental organisations to develop sustainable solutions that build upon the strengths and resources of the community.
- ***Research and Evidence-Based Practice:*** Future directions in Indic social work practice will emphasise the importance of research and evidence-based practice to inform interventions and policies. This may involve conducting studies on the effectiveness of culturally tailored interventions, evaluating outcomes, and disseminating findings to inform practice and policy development.

- ***Global Collaboration and Exchange:*** Future Indic social work practice will engage in global collaboration and exchange to share knowledge, best practices, and resources across borders. This may involve participating in international conferences, collaborative research projects, and cross-cultural training programs to enhance the capacity and impact of Indic social work practice on a global scale.

Moving forward, Indic social work practice holds promise for innovative approaches that embrace interdisciplinary collaboration, holistic wellness, narrative techniques, environmental advocacy, and culturally responsive education. By embracing these emerging trends, social workers can continue to uphold the values of compassion, service, and social justice inherent in Indic traditions while addressing the evolving needs of diverse populations in an ever-changing world.

Inferences, Recommendations and Suggestions

This study shows a comprehensive exploration of the Indic perspective of social work philosophy, ideology, and their intersections with historical and contemporary social work practices. Here are some scientific inferences, recommendations, and suggestions based on the research:

- ***Incorporating Traditional Wisdom into Practice:*** This study underscores the importance of integrating ancient philosophical concepts such as *dharma, karma, ahimsa, and sewa* into contemporary professional social work practice. Scientifically, this integration can be seen as a means of enhancing the cultural competence of social workers, enabling them to engage effectively with diverse populations. Research could focus on developing training modules and intervention frameworks that incorporate these values while respecting individual autonomy and cultural sensitivity.

- ***Cultural Competence and Sensitivity Training:*** Given the challenges associated with applying Indic perspectives to social work, such as *cultural sensitivity and secularism*, there is a need for specialised training programs for professional social workers. These programs could provide education on Indic philosophies, religious practices, and cultural nuances, helping practitioners navigate complex cultural landscapes ethically and effectively.
- ***Empirical Studies on Effectiveness:*** Future research should prioritise empirical studies to assess the effectiveness of integrating Indic values into social work practice. This could involve conducting randomised controlled trials, longitudinal studies, or qualitative evaluations to measure outcomes such as client satisfaction, cultural relevance, and community impact. By generating empirical evidence, researchers can validate the efficacy of Indic-informed interventions and inform evidence-based practice.
- ***Interdisciplinary Collaboration:*** The study highlights the interdisciplinary nature of Indic social work philosophy, drawing insights from fields such as philosophy, religion, and anthropology. Scientifically, fostering interdisciplinary collaboration between social work scholars and experts in related disciplines can enrich theoretical frameworks and enhance the applicability of Indic perspectives in addressing contemporary social issues. Collaborative research projects could explore the intersections between Indic philosophy and fields such as psychology, public health, and environmental science.
- ***Technology-Driven Solutions:*** Embracing technology and digital platforms can facilitate the dissemination of Indic social work practices and overcome barriers to access. Research could explore the development of mobile applications, online counselling platforms, and telehealth services tailored to Indic cultural contexts. Additionally,

studies on the efficacy of technology-driven interventions in reaching underserved populations could inform future innovations in Indic social work practice.

- ***Community-Based Approaches:*** Future directions in Indic social work practice should prioritise community empowerment and grassroots initiatives. Scientifically, the research could focus on participatory action research methodologies that engage community members as co-researchers and collaborators in identifying social problems, designing interventions, and evaluating outcomes. This bottom-up approach ensures that interventions are culturally relevant, sustainable, and responsive to the unique needs of local communities.
- ***Global Collaboration and Knowledge Exchange:*** Engaging in global collaboration and knowledge exchange is essential for advancing Indic social work practice on a global scale. Scientifically, research networks, conferences, and cross-cultural training programs can facilitate the sharing of best practices, innovative approaches, and research findings across borders. By fostering international partnerships, researchers and practitioners can leverage diverse perspectives and resources to address complex social challenges more effectively.

In conclusion, this research study provides a robust foundation for further scientific inquiry and innovation in Indic social work practice. By embracing interdisciplinary collaboration, empirical research, technology-driven solutions, and community-based approaches, social workers can harness the rich insights of Indic philosophies to promote social justice, cultural competence, and holistic well-being in diverse cultural contexts.

References

Addams, J. (1910). *Twenty Years at Hull-House with Autobiographical Notes*, The Macmillan Company.

Akshaya Patra Foundation, https://www.akshayapatra.org

Ambedkar, B.R. (1936). *Annihilation of Caste: The Annotated Critical Edition*, Verso Books.

Beveridge, W. (1942). *Social Insurance and Allied Services: Report, HMSO.*

Bhattacharya, S. (2017). *Indian Ethics: Classical Traditions and Contemporary Challenges*, Routledge.

Chapple, C. (1993). *Non-violence to Animals, Earth, and Self in Asian Traditions*, State University of New York Press.

Chattopadhyaya, D. (1994). *Indian Philosophy: Past and Future*, Oxford University Press.

Gandhi, M.K. (1958). *All Men are Brothers: Autobiographical Reflections*, Continuum International Publishing Group.

Hansan, J.E. (2008). *The Social Work Perspective in Ancient Civilisations.* NASW Press.

Hansan, J.E. (2012). *Social Work: A History of Gender and Class in the United States.*

Karuna Trust; https://www.karuna.org

Mata Amritanandamayi, https://amma.org.

Perkins, F. (1946). *The Roosevelt I knew, Harper & Brothers*, Penguin Classic.

Radhakrishnan, S. & Moore, C.A. (1957). *A Source Book in Indian Philosophy*, Princeton University Press.

Richmond, M.E. (1922). *Social Diagnosis,* Russell Sage Foundation.

Rosen, S. (2007). *Bhagavad Gita: The Song of God*, Shambhala Publications.

Segal, E., Gerdes, K. & Steiner, S. (2009). *Social Work: An Introduction to the Profession,* Brooks Cole.

Sharma, A (2010). *Indian Philosophy: A Critical Survey*, Motilal Banarsidass.

Sharma, R. (2010). *Exploring Bharatiya Philosophy: A Historical Perspective*, (p. 25). Oxford University Press.

Singh, I.J. (2004). "Sikhism and Social Work". In *Religion and Spirituality in Social Work Practice* (pp. 171-181). Columbia University Press.

Srinivasan, D. (2011). *Indian Philosophy: A Very Short Introduction*, Oxford University Press.

Titmuss, R.M. (1955). *The Welfare State and Its Aftermath*, Allen & Unwin.

Tropman, J.E. (2005). *Social Work: A History of Social Welfare and Social Work in the United States*, Rutgers University Press.

Witkin, S. (Ed.). (2002). *The Evolution of Social Work: Historical Perspectives, Aldine Transaction.*

4

History of Social Work in Ancient India

Surabhi Sinha

Introduction

Over time, social work in India has progressively changed from charity to a vocation. Even while social work has been around for as long as humans, most historians agree that, it wasn't until the 19th century that social work gained official status. As a relatively new discipline, social work is said to face unique difficulties as well. During 1936 the social work education was introduced in India by American missionary.

Indian tradition has included virtuous moral and spiritual practices since the time of the early Vedic literature. From the beginning of Indian civilisation, the seeds of human evolution have been sown. The Indian writings known as the "Veda", or the *Rigveda*, *Samaveda*, *Yazurveda*, and *Atharvaveda*, contain the greatest order of life. It emphasised that the essence of human life is found in the religion's hymns and music, sacrifices, and wisdom. The study of the Vedas was referred to as "shruti", or memorisation by ear. In the *Pathshala* style of education, where the "Guru" would recite and the followers would practice their oratory and listening abilities while learning the courses, listening is one of the best casework skills. During the Vedic period, charitable giving was seen as morality. It was commended as moral behaviour to assist the poor and beggars.

Evolution of Social Work in India

Indian literature is full of examples of "Daan" (charity). Examples include "Ram Rajya", in which Rama serves as a "welfare state", and "Danveer Karna", who is a "donor" and a head of "philanthropist". Raja Bhoj was an advocate whose legal system was founded on human ideals, and Raja Harishchandra was known as the "Satyavaadi". While we examine the Indian origins of social work, we can use anyone of these characters as an example. Women had equal status in the early Vedic period. Apala, Maitreyi, and other "Women Rishikas" are mentioned, indicating the standing of women in ancient India.

The *Ashrama* systems of antiquity assigned responsibilities related to interpersonal interactions in order to establish order in human existence. *Brahmacharya* (student), *Grihastha* (householder), *Vanaprastha* (retired), and *Sannyasa* (renunciation) are the four age-based life stages. After subduing every nation at the time, the great emperor Samrat Ashok took up Buddhism and dedicated the rest of his life to humanistic principles. The eightfold paths of Buddhism—peace, dignity, right to a livelihood, acceptance, etc.—have application in social work concepts. During Krishna's reign, "Charaka" created an indigenous system of medicine.

Kautilya noted the veterinary surgeons were in charge of cattle, as well as *Bhaisajyagraha*, a medicine shop. A provision was made for Samsthudyaska, the institution controller responsible for public health. Ancient texts including Manu's *Smriti*, Kautilya's *Arthashastra*, Vedvyas's *Mahabharata*, and Tulsidas's *Ramcharit Manas* all cited political structures as illustrations of scientific government. Since the king was the guardian of the law and the trustee of public property, deriving from *Dharma*, the welfare state was an ideal characteristic of ancient India. Through it, we can trace the current popular notion of "Corporate Social Responsibilities".

"Apastamba" does a wonderful job of encapsulating the welfare state notion. This statement said that the state was required to give individuals access to food, clothing, housing, and medical care. Everyone in the kingdom will be free from hunger, illness, and extreme heat or cold, whether via choice or not, and everyone will have access to the royal guest house in the capital. The morals and ethics of the story "Panchtantra" and the preservation of animals' rights to dignity are addressed in "Hitopadesha". Akbar, the Mughal emperor, was a social reformer who outlawed child marriage and enacted laws against alcoholism and slavery. *Din-e-ilahi* is the new cultural order he formed. (Divine faith): A synthesis of ethical teachings from world religions. References are found to high orders followed by Maharana Pratap, Laxmi Bai, and Shivaji. They fought for the nation and its people. Early on in British administration over India, there was no evidence of social welfare.

Nature of Social Work in Ancient India

Social assistance was very altruistic by its nature. The most well-liked public rites from Vedic times, *Yajnas*, were used to carry out social welfare operations. The privileged had a duty to help the underprivileged in order to obtain *Moksha*, not to demonstrate their superiority. During the Vedic era, obligations were solely outlined in terms of religion; adjudication was not available. But the welfare state was seriously threatened by the caste system that emerged in the late Vedic age. Buddhism also endorsed bestowing "bhiksha" upon the "bhikshus" who reside in "sangha" and acknowledged the *karma* principle. Ashoka was the one who created a complete social welfare system that included public utilities, rural development, rehabilitation of the impoverished, regulation of prostitutes, and women's welfare.

Social Work in Ancient India

From the perspective of social work, the role of the state or society can be analysed as the transition of the field from the concept of charity to the concept of citizens' right to growth. The history of social work reveals that governments and societies have generally been acting to improve the lives of the poor. Various methods, both known and unknown, have occasionally been used to elevate them. There are several ways to talk about the social welfare initiatives and methods used throughout the Indian subcontinent's earlier history, including

Charity: In India, charitable activity was the first practice of social work. Charity is defined as having religious love and compassion for the underprivileged and one's fellow humans. It is essentially done to receive God's blessing by helping the less fortunate. In the past, social service in India was essentially charitable in nature. It can be found in a variety of Hindu texts, including the *Mahabharata* of the Hindu state of India and the Vedas and Upanishads. The *Rig Veda* makes an earlier mention of philanthropy and says, "May the one who gives shine most." Upanishads such as the *Brihadaranyaka*, *Chhandogya*, and *Taitiriya* required almsgiving for all household members. According to the *Mahabharata*, during a conversation with Yudhistir, Bhisma discussed the fundamentals of non-violence, truth, conquering wrath, and practicing charity.

Social Welfare through "Yojna" Practice: During the Vedic era, this was the most widely recognised mass ritual. With an absolute attitude of dedication, people gathered in a huge shed built for the purpose on the banks of running rivers. Their goal was the welfare of everyone, not just themselves. The schools known as *yajnashalas* were where men and women learned the value of cooperating without ego or self-centred desires. The people were instructed to embody the spirit of the *yajna* rites and their deeds not just there and then, but also in their homes, offices, marketplaces, and fields. According to the *Aswalayana Griha Sutra*, one must carry out five *yajnas*, or Pancha *yajnas*, every day. These include serving God, one's ancestors, animals, oneself, and other people.

The society of communitarians: Early Vedic society was a communitarian one in which everyone took care of one other's needs, much like an extended family. The entire business of helping those in need was everyone's business, primarily handled in a collective manner. Whether the needs were basic or unique, general or emerging out of vulnerable situations like disease and external dangers, there existed a life of complete mutuality and reciprocal support.

***Agrarian society*:** The lofty ideas of welfare and charity emerged with the growth of an agrarian civilisation characterised by private group land ownership. When the tribe shared property ownership, *Dana* and *Dakshina* were used as a solution to famine for the sick, elderly, and frail. But as private property and class hierarchy emerged (in the late Vedic era and beyond), the idea of "dana" changed from being a means of social security to a privilege enjoyed by the ruling class.

***Guilds*:** In ancient India, guilds were significant corporate entities that carried out a range of welfare and commercial tasks. During the Buddhist era, guilds were quite important. In addition to their political and economic roles, these guilds offered the downtrodden layer of society social protection. A portion of the fund was used to support those in need, including the poor, the sick, the disabled, the foolish, the old, the orphaned, and the defenseless women.

***Kingship*:** In ancient India, when kings ruled, a welfare state was considered the best form of society. The King guarded the legislation that resulted from the idea of *Dharma*. The mythology also discussed the idea of *Karma*, which stressed the need of doing good deeds. The abundance of delight is borne by excellent deeds. The proverb "Prajna sukhe sukham rajna" (the king's happiness rests in the happiness of the people/subjects) was used during the monarchical period. The majority of kings likewise held the view that their primary responsibility was to ensure the well-being of their subjects. By the end of the later Vedic era, "dana" had institutionalised and taken on the traits of religious philosophy combined with philanthropy.

***Bimbisara*:** As agrarian civilisation evolved, early Kosala and Magadha states—a new kind of polity—were created. About

300 B.C., Bimbisara rose to become the monarch of Magadha. He was the first Indian ruler to establish the framework for a productive administrative structure. He focused particularly on the advancement of agriculture, infrastructure, and social defense by deterring crime.

***Ashoka*:** Kautilya documented the social and political activities of the Mauryan kings in his book "Arthashastra", where he discussed the duties of the monarch and stated that "in the happiness of his subjects lies his happiness, in their welfare his welfare, whatever pleases himself, he shall not consider that good, but whatever pleases his subjects he shall consider that good." To oversee the care of women, including prostitutes, he appointed superintendents of women. The royal families appointed high commissioners of charity to oversee charitable regulations and keep track of charitable gifts. The commissioners of charity were tasked with overseeing the inmates' well-being. The overall supervisors of the welfare programs were the charity's high commissioners. Ashoka created a comprehensive social welfare system that included public amenities including highways, rest stops for travellers, wells, and the rehabilitation of convicts, as well as services for women, rural development, free medical treatment, and prostitution control.

***Kanishka*:** He actively participated in ensuring the well-being of society, much like Ashoka the Great. He generously donated money and grants to build Buddhist *vihars*, monasteries, *stupas*, and other structures that served as hubs for education and aid to the underprivileged.

***Gupta Rule*:** One of the most prosperous eras in Indian history was the Gupta era. A string of intelligent emperors, including Chandragupta and Samudra Gupta, led the Gupta dynasty and created an empire where the populace lived in happiness and prosperity. The king's primary responsibility, to which he dedicated his life, was the well-being of the populace.

***Harshavardhan*:** Harshavardhan was a wise and kind emperor who came to power in 606 A.D. His priorities in life have always been his subjects' well-being. He founded orphanages, dispensaries, hospitals, and houses for the impoverished. He gave gifts to the underprivileged, the destitute, and religious folks. He is said to have given away everything during one of Prayag's five-yearly assemblies, forcing him to borrow clothes from his sister.

Some General Welfare Measures by the Kings in the Ancient Period

***Good governance*:** The city government was in charge of building gardens, parks, playgrounds, cemeteries, feeding facilities, and pilgrimage sites in the urban areas. The people in charge of the local administration and the city administration were Sthanikas and Nagarapal, respectively. The king's court strictly enforced tasks such as establishing proper village boundaries, registering land sales and transfers, inventorying family members and cattle, fixing up and collecting taxes, remitting taxes granted by the appropriate authority, and maintaining an account of various occupations in the villages. The public account fraud and embezzlement were seen as significant violations, and sanctions were put in place to put an end to corruption.

***Poor Relief*:** Since ancient India, one of the most significant state policies has been poor relief. During natural disasters, the state has an obligation to provide assistance and support. Extra care was given to the ill and dependent individuals. The demands resulting from famine and drought were formerly met by spending money from the state treasury. Kautilya in his story describes the famine relief. Yuan Chwang mentioned that there were several rest houses that provided food, medication, and other supplies to help the poor and stranded travellers.

***Employment*:** Those who suffered from their own circumstances, such as poor widows, crippled women, prostitutes, the disabled, etc., were given jobs by the state throughout the monarchs' reign. The dependents received care and training to assume the state's responsibilities. The orphans received all the resources necessary for an education in a variety of subjects, as well as jobs.

***Market Policies*:** Strict adherence was paid to people-friendly market policies. The king's job was to haggle with the traders to keep the market price of the items that customers purchased under control. Strict penalties were mandated to deter any form of market system corruption. Adulteration of food was strictly forbidden. The merchants who used inaccurate measures and balances suffered consequences. In times of need, the people received money and supplies for relief. In such cases, the state gave loans, provided seeds, stopped collecting land revenues, and gave food distributions to the populace.

Slave occupation was specified as part of the regulation of slavery. The owners were warned not to assign their slaves menial tasks like picking up dead bodies, sweeping up urine, or similar tasks. This served as the model for regaining the rights of today's scavengers. Back then, the state upheld the dignity of labour with strict authority. It was improper for the owners to utilise the female slaves for their own sex.

Apastamba has done a wonderful job at summarising the idea of social welfare. This passage states that the government was required to give the populace access to food, clothing, housing, and medical care. It was proclaimed that there would be no hunger, illness, heat, or cold in the kingdom. Everyone in need was welcome to stay at the royal guest house in the capital.

Conclusion

The social work profession ought to be grounded in the social realities that social workers encounter while putting their training to use on the frontlines. Therefore, the social work curriculum shouldn't be taught in a vacuum, and courses that are inappropriate for the Indian setting should be taken off the Indian university curricula. Indigenous orientation is therefore required when working with people, researching social issues, and carrying out social welfare programs; as a result, Indigenous ideas, methodologies, beliefs, practices, and literature should not be ignored. The assertion that social work knowledge is universal and the foreign nature of social work education are so pervasive and inclusive that many Indian social work graduates find it difficult to apply inappropriate techniques in real-world settings, which prevents them from making the most use of their abilities. Furthermore, due to the overemphasis on western knowledge and perspective in the current pattern of social work training, they would not be able to assume leadership roles in the development, formulation, and implementation of social welfare programs at different levels of practice and administration. To create indigenous knowledge, high-quality study and investigation based on myths used in Indian research are required. Additionally, the government must emphasise and support the teaching of indigenous social work education. The instruction and training in social work using the *Bharatiyakaran* paradigm guarantees the adoption and popularisation of the native social work education model in India.

References

Dash, B.M. (2022). *Introduction to Social Work* (First Edition) SAGE Publications Pvt. Ltd.

Garvin, C.D. and J.E. Tropman, (1992). *Social Work Contemporary Society*, (pp. 22-26), Prentice Hall, New Jersey.

Gore, M.S. (1981). "The Scope of Social Work Practice", in T.K. Nair (ed.) *Social Work Education and Practice in India.* ASSWI, Madras.

Gupta, Manju (2010). "Medical, Psychiatry and Child Care." In Thomas, Gracius, *Social Work Practicum and Supervision* (pp. 286-319). Indira Gandhi National Open University, New Delhi by Director, School of Social Work.

IFSW 2001. "International Federation of Social Workers", *Definition of Social Work*, http://ifsw.org/policies/statement-of-ethical-principles

Jacob. K.K. (1994). *Social Work Education in India.* Himanshu Publication.

Johnson, C.L. and S.J. Yanca, (2010). *Social Work Practice: A Generalist Approach,* Allyn and Bacon, USA.

Meyer, Carol H. (1970). *Social Work Practice: A Response to the Urban Crisis* (First Edition), The Free Press.

Miller, J.G. (1995). Criminal Justice: Social Work Roles. In R.L. Edwards, (Ed.), *Encyclopedia of Social Work* (pp. 653-59). Washington DC: NASW Press.

Misra P.D. & Misra Beena (2010). *Social work profession in India,* New Royal Book Co., Lucknow.

Ramchandran, P. (1968). "Research in Social Work", in *Encyclopaedia of Social Work in India, 2*: 386-94.

Sengupta, A. (2009). *Skill Formation and Employment Assurance in the Unorganised Sector,* National Commission for Enterprises in the Unorganised Sector.

Sheldon, Brian and Geraldine Macdonald (2009). *A Text Book of Social Work,* Routledge, London.

Thapar, R. (2010). *Ancient Indian Social History: Some Interpretations (*2nd Edn.) Orient Blackswan.

Tiwari, Yashowardhan (2021). *Social Welfare in Ancient India: A Jurisprudential Perspective.* Indic Today.

Udipur Khinduka, S. (1965). *Social Work In India.* Kitab Mahal, Allahabad.

Zimbalist, Sidney (1977). *Historic Themes and Landmarks in Social Welfare Research,* Harper and Row, New York.

5

Conceptualisation of Identity and Professional Social Work

A Vedantic Drishtant (Philosophy)

Atul Gautam and *Archana Kaushik*

Surge to explore the identity from the India perspective begin with certain documents that are known as the Upanishads, and these documents constitute What is called Vedanta? Vedanta is compounded of two words *veda* and *anta. Anta* means end or completion or summation of Veda. Of course, Veda is related to the Latin video to see. Weather is the fundamental revelation. Of the Sanatana way of life contained in its earliest scriptural documents, which are generally dated in the period between 1500 and 1200 BC. The Upnishads has been the summation of the Veda that has been found from over a long period of time. Beginning perhaps as early as 800 PC (Watts). Some of the Upanishads are much, much later than that. And the basic position of the Upanishads is that the self. Is the one and only reality. Without a second.

Contract of Identity and Professional Social Work

To the explore the best of my enquiries, the very first question that I would like to propose is about the very paradigm that demand or offer the existence of identity, an entity per say ? Does the fundamental nature of "identity" has a casual relation with biological evolution of "human" or is it a contextualised synthetic kind of a construct that serve the conceptualisation of phenomenon called "identity"? The definitions of "identity as phenomenon" is conceptualised as an external entity. "Identity" of an individual has to be "with respect to something or someone". Henry Tajfel and John Turner (1970) has proposed that individuals drive their position of self from the membership in social group. This social group may be family, community, institution, affiliation, honorary positions, social stratification, etc. So much so the social work practices has a unique way of identifying individuals (Harwood, 2020). For a social worker the most dominant identity or rather useful "identity" is the identity of either oppressor or oppressed. Someone who need to be corrected by "someone" who has the ability to propose "correction". The social work cannot exist in an equal or just society, so to say. There has to be "someone" less than "other one" so that the social work can propose intervention. The most fundamental of all the distinctions that the ancient Sanatana philosophy offers, when it comes to the construct of identity. Identity of anything. (Prashant, 2019). So the identity for a Western idea of professional social work is fundamentally the identity of "others".

The very idea of identity in Sanatana philosophical paradigm is the idea proposed for self, may be a collective self but surely not for some "other self". The idea proposed by *Chandogya Upnishad* define identity that is constant and omnipresent and yet not ubiquitous. *TAT TVAM ASI*, the three words is a *sutra* for any kind of social action that demand the establishment or positioning of "something" or "someone" by identity of that "someone" or "something" (Vaidic Sangra, 1953). Also, let us first investigate and establish the "one" that is part and partial to everything that exist.

Many Sanatana text proposes that all this universe is ultimately One (*Brahman*) and only appears to be multiple nature. Way out different things and different events. Only by reason. Of Maya. Which is illusion. Magic art, Creative power of *Prakriti*. It is basic to the Vedanta (Prashant, 2020). That *Brahman*, intangible, normal, objective ground of everything that exists. Is identical with you and has been put in the formula *TAT TVAM ASI*. *TAT* means "that". "That" which is the same as "You". We should translate "that" into a modern English idiom as "you're it". Thus the translation of *TAT TVAM ASI* can be, "That you are". But does the statement (*TAT TVAM ASI*) have a deeper and profound meaning? The concept of identity as proposed by Vedic text has least to do with faith or religion. Most of the other modern religious text is a doctrine which is brought up in the Judeo-Christian traditions to accept. The conceptualisation of identity as proposed by Abrahamic faith is different. Something that is constant and omnipresent can only be God, this is what the Abrahamic religion proposes. To Christian and Jewish theology that whatever you are, you are surely not the Lord or God. Christians feel about the Hindu doctrine that we are all fundamentally masks of God, that is pantheism, and that's a dirty word in Christian theological circuits because of the feeling that if everything is God. All moral standards are blown to hell. Because it means everything is as good as everything else. Everything that happens is really God, and this must include the good things and the bad things. And that seems to them a very dangerous idea. Actually, all religious doctrines contain very self-defeating ideas. However, we won't worry about that for the moment, because what the Hindu as Sanatanis means by God when he says *Brahman* is not at all the same thing as a Jew mean. By the law of Adonai, for Jew and Christian, God means the *boss* (to whom divine honours of you, as above all others). Hindu, on the other hand, does not mean boss. While referring to God, Sanatana doesn't mean the King, the law, the political ruler of the universe. He means the inmost energy. *Energy* which is responsible for every movement of this whole universe. Without the idea of authority, of governing some intractable element that resists his power.

So if a Christian or a person in a Christian culture announces that he has discovered that he is God. We put him in a mental hospital. Because it's unfashionable to burn people for heresy anymore. But in Sanatana, if you announced that you are the Lord God. We say, well, of course. How nice that you found out the "absolute identity". Because everybody is. So then. Why the great problem arises? Does it appear that we are not? Why do we think?

Why do we have the sensory impression that this whole universe consists of a vast multiplicity of different things? And we don't see it all as one identity. What would you think it would be like to see it all as one? If "Being Conscious" or attaining a state which is absolute in nature, be considered as an true identity, what would that state be? I know a lot of people who study Oriental philosophy, about attaining these great states of consciousness, *nirvana*, *moksha* which the Hindus use liberation, Zen Buddhist says *satori*, which also mean enlightenment or awakening. What would you like to have that? How would you feel? If you see everything as one basic reality identity. The reality that one can project of exchange as identity.

Well, a lot of people think that it would be as if, all the outlines and differentiations in the field of vision suddenly melt and we will only be a kind of loom in this sea of light. But rather advisedly, the Vedanta philosophy does not really seriously use the word one. Of the supreme itself. Because the word and the idea "one" has an opposite many on one side and another opposite *shunya* (zero, not even as least unit of something ... none) on the other. This is fundamental to Vedanta. That the Supreme Self is neither one nor many, but as they say, *NON-DUAL* and they express that in this world, identity or identities.

For a dual world the identity as a construct cannot singular word, "ies" of identities is inherent and non-visible. But the very idea of identity in a non-dual Hindu Sanatana philosophy cannot be plural. It is not something in exchange, given by "someone" to "some-other one".

Identity for the present-day sociology in general and social work in particular has to have identity as a conflict. All the "doing" in social work is "doing something" to mitigate or neutralize the conflict, but survival of the identity.

Vedic Proposition of Identity as a Necessary Evil

Does identity means an objective classification of experiences of sensations or feeling? It must have some shape and space. Just like a box, a kind of structure with a frame. The nature of a class is that it's a box, and if a box has an inside, it has to have an outside. Identity that is you is something inside or is it you from the outside? This is fundamental to all classification and we can't get out of these demarcated predestined classifications. It's almost predefined. Whatever we see to be different is an explicit difference on the surface. Covering an implicit. But is there any commonality with respect to identity? It's very difficult to talk about what it is that unifies black and white. Of course, in a way, the eyes do. Sound and silence are unified by the ears. So "you" and "not you" can be unified by something that is still "you". That, if you can't have one without the other, is like the poles of a magnet, North Pole and South Pole. You can't have a one power magnet. True, the poles are quite different, ones North and the other South. But it's all one magnet and some such idea is that is what the Hindu is moving into when he speaking of the real basis or ground of the universe, as being non-dual.

Fundamental opposition, that I suppose all of us feel between "self" and "other", "I" and "it". There is something that is "me". There is an area of my experience that I call "myself" and there is another area with my experience which I call "not myself". But you will immediately see that neither one should be realised without the other. You wouldn't know what you meant by self. Unless. You experience something "other than self". It is difficult to understand "what you meant by other?", unless you understood yourself. Both "self" and "other" go together. They arise at the same time. You don't have first self and then other or first other and then self. They come together. One can see the sneaky conspiracy underneath the two. Like the magnet between the two different poles. Something that isn't classifiable, but which lies between all classes. Is the identity means same as classes? Classes of "some" verses the classes of "not-the same-some". Creating others is a necessary evil. The identity as "self" that do not create "others" is a Vedic way of defining "self". A self which is independent of "other".

Identity as Intersection and Idea of One (Brahman)

The world seems to be divided into a great multiplicity. A lot of people would think of the universe as a collection of different things, a kind of cosmic flotsam and jetsam wash together in this particular area of space and prefer to take a pluralistic attitude and don't see anything underlying. In fact, in contemporary logical philosophy, the notion of any basic ground or continuum in which all events occur would be considered meaningless. For obvious reasons. Idea of a unified identity is same when it comes to oneness and intersectionality of that oneness in universe.

If I say that everybody in this universe, every star, every planet is moving in a certain direction at a uniform speed. Every change is happening at an equal interval. The speed or motion that represent the change is the real identity of everything. They may be stars or planets or suns or nations, or plants or animals or Hindus or Muslims or caste or contrast or of anything and any other "relative anything". That will be saying nothing at all. Less I can point out some other object with respect to which they are so moving. But since I said the universe, that includes all objects whatsoever. Therefore, I cannot make a meaningful statement. About the uniform behaviour of everything that is going on. But, on the other hand, every song you hear on the radio. Whether it be a honking horn. A box Ronaldo or a newscast? Is the vibration of the diaphragm in your loudspeaker. The radio doesn't tell us this. The announcer doesn't come on first thing in the morning and say ladies and gentleman, from now until closing time, all the sounds you will hear will be vibrations of the diaphragm and your speaker. That is taken for granted. Independent. Ignore. So in the same way we all are here, vibrating at respective interval. Making a unique sound that resonate only with *prakriti* (nature). This is basic to all the issue here. Your lens of the eye and retina is basic to all that you see. What is the colour of the lens of the eye? We say it has no colour, it is transparent. In the same way as the mirror has no colour of its own. The visual impression is definitely there. It may seems to be clear, ever if it is colourless.

Silence which is unheard, may be very definitely basic to all hearing. For eye, transparent is what maybe is very definitely basic to all seeing. So therefore, if there were some continuum in which everything that is going on and everything that we experience occurs, we would not notice it. We would not be able really to say very much about it, except perhaps that it was there. It wouldn't make any difference to anything. Except the one all important difference that it wasn't, there wouldn't be any differences. This very idea of the presence of that one which cannot be identified as identity is the very thing that Krishna identity Arjuna and everyone on the battelfied of Kurukshetra (chapter 10, *shloka* 34). Who is there as an identity to conflict with someone as some other identity. Krishna as some which is common to both, as something which cannot be identifid as an identity to something or of someone. So don't think your act as cause and effect relation of a identified conflicting identity. But this is what a Western social work demand and offer, identity which is worth a friction, if not conflict.

Western conceptualisation of social science don't propose Vedantic propositions as scientific. It stretches their heads, and they would rather preoccupy themselves with more pedestrian matters. But still, you can't help it if you are a human being. You wonder about things like that. What is it in which everything is happening? What is the ground? Will you say obviously it's not a fault because I think that is a classifiable thing. So very often the Hindu and Buddhist will refer to the ultimate reality as "no thing" and not "nothing". But no special thing. Unclassified. Can't put your finger on it? But it's you. So what you basically are.

For everything, basically is just as the sound about automobile horn on the radio. Is in one way and automobile home, but basically it is the vibration of the diaphragm. So you are all in the Sanatana view vibrations of the entire cosmic diaphragm. That's the analogy of identity per say.

As in *sadhana* (a state of meditation), language is limited and silence is best way to express. The best language is to say "nothing", a non-verbal expression. Thought is there, to experience self. How can you experience? Well, that's the whole thing, as I pointed out previously. The nub of all these Oriental philosophies is not an idea, not a theory, not even a way of behaving. But it's basically a way of experiencing a transformation of everyday consciousness, so that it becomes quite apparent to us that that's the way things are. But how do you identify yourself as when it happens to you, becomes you as an identifiable you, not the existing you. I don't know, its very difficult to explain it. So, exactly the same way when somebody has that sort of breakthrough which transforms his consciousness and it happens all over the world, is not just the Hindu phenomenon, but somebody suddenly realises it's all one. Or technically non-dual. And really always coming and going and all is frantic. Living and dying, grabbing the struggling to fighting, suffering. All this is a fantastic phantasmagoria.

Runs all over the world is not just like in Blue Phenomenon, somebody suddenly realises it's all. We see that. But when he tries to explain it, he finds his mouth isn't big enough. Because it can't get the words out of their dualistic pattern.

To explain something non-dualistic. Why is this so? Why are we under this? Great magnificent hallucination. Well, the Sanatana explain this in *saguna* (*sa+guna*), something that has a property, language as follows. The fact of the matter is that the world of identification and "identity", is a game of hide and seek. Now you see it. Now you don't. Very obvious. Very illusive. If you were the Supreme Self. What would you do? I mean, would you just sit there and be blissfully one and everything? I think no, never. You play games. You would, in other words, for the very nature of the fact that said, no energy system is an energy system unless it let's go of itself. So, as long as you hold yourself, the "self" remains absconding for you. The moment you taste that unique self, that "universal identity", you get involved in all sorts of adventures and you will forget who you are. Just as when you play a game playing, you're only playing. You get absorbed in the game. There is nothing important enough to be won, nothing to lose. It becomes fantastically interesting. So in the same way it is said that the Supreme Self gets absorbed. We identify ourself through so many different channels which we call all the different beings.

Identity as Maya (Just Manifestation)

In the plot of a drama or play, just like an artist or a writer gets completely absorbed in the artistic creation that he is doing, or actor gets absorbed in the path in the drama. And first, we know it's a drama, we go to a play. Say "Atul" only apply and the procedure Archana tells us. What happens behind that are he is not for real? Just to share. But the great actor? It is going to make you forget it's just the show. He is going to have you sitting on the educated shell. He will make you cry. He's going to have trembling because he almost persuaded you that it's real. What would happen? If the very best actor is confronted by the very best audience. Why they be taken in completely? And the one would confirm the other. So this is the idea of the universe. The fundamental Self, the *Saguna Brahman*, plays this game, gets involved in being all of us and does it so well. The *sansara* (phenomenon) superbly act and *maya* (noumenon) as thing appears to be real. Not only sitting on the edge, we start to get up and start reacting to something that is nothing but "acting". We join in. The drama in the door becomes whatever it is that's going on here, you see. Then of course at the end of the drama, because all things have to happen in that have the beginning. The garden goes down and the actors reply to the green room. And there are the villain and hero who cease to be relevant. Hero and they are just that, they act and then they come out in front of the curtain and they stand in a row and the audience applause the villain along with the hero. The villain is having been good villain, the hero of having a great hero. Closer. And everybody leaves the sigh of relief. Well, that was a great show.

Now think of all the roles as identities or ours and so the same idea, the green room. "Green Room" is the *Nirguna Brahman*. That behind the hole show. Well, there are no differentiations. Subject and object, good and evil, light and darkness, life and death. Bad within the sphere of the *Saguna Brahman*, all these differentiations (or identities) appear because that's how in front that's on the stage. Have no good actor when on the stage performs his own personality. And if that's what's wrong with your alignment with identity. While playing very positive or dark (as identified by society) role they tried to cast the person to act a row which corresponds to his alleged personality. "I" the great actor, can assume any kind of personality. Male or female and suddenly convert myself right in front of the audience into somebody who takes away entirely. But in the green room he says usual self. So Sanatana proposes the idea. Then you see its all the conventions of drama go right along with it that all this world is a big act. *Leela,* the play of the Supreme Self. And it's there for compared to a dream. Two passing illusion. You should not, therefore, take it seriously. You may take it sincerely. Groups as an actor may be sincere in his acting, but not serious because that means it throws you for a loop. Although that of course is involved, we do take it seriously, but you see one of the great questions that you have to ask yourself. When you really get down to the nitty-gritty about your own inmost core.

Few of the questions that the domain of social sciences and social work philosophy has to self-enquire are: Are we serious with respect to our self-defined labels of identity? How do we know deep within? That we are not an absolute rational as professional social worker. And most important can the global or Western definition of identity is functional enough to propose the intervention in an India discourse? One man in late nineteenth century gave many fundamental conceptual frameworks around identity based on India way of social structurization of problems and solution. It will not be an honest effort to study Sanatana way of defining identity without the gospel of Vedanta and thus Vivekananda.

East to Vivekanada and West to Marx: Individual, Identity and Collective

Swami Vivekananda's philosophy is contained in what is generally known as Vedanta. He has often declared that he has never end anything other than the Upanishads. The Vedantic approach is comprehensive and takes into account the fact that Truth, bough essentially one, is perceived differently, depending upon the stand point of the perceiver. When it comes to studying the individual and society as a product of identity, as such there are three broad different levels of perception—Dvaita, Visishishtadvaita and Advaita. Vivekananda sympathetically views all three. Though he himself was an Advaitin his perception of truth was deeply influenced by the experiences an teachings of his great master, Sri Ramakrishna Paramahansa, via synthesised in himself all the valid religious experiences of the world.

Strictly speaking, Vivekananda's philosophy of identity is diametrically opposed to that of Western thinker specially Marx.

Marx, as we have seen, believed that the fundamental reality consists of matter, whereas according to Vivekananda, it is spirit Marxists, often describe all approaches and thought system differing from materialism as idealistic. This is because Marx called his system materialistic, to differentiate it from Hegel's which was called idealistic. But, it is wrong and unscientific to call the Vedantic approach a "idealistic". Hegel's ultimate reality is "Real Idea" and according to Vedanta, it is "Brahma" or "Sat-Chit-Ananda". Hegel's "Real Idea" a category that can be known through reason; it undergoes dialectic a movements. "The absolute is the world process itself, which can be characterised not by static condition, but by activity. The Absolute is not a transcendental force" (Mayer, *A history of Modern Philosophy*).

Satchidananda as an identity, on the other hand, according to Vedanta, is transcendental, cannot be known by reason, undergoes no movement and is beyond activity and inactivity. It is this Absolute which appears as all that we experience in various forms. Without going into the merit of the question, it can safely be stated that the "Real Idea" of Hegel comes under a category very different from Satchidananda and as such it is wrong to describe the Vedantic approach as "idealistic". If anything it is "spiritualistic".

There are different interpretations as to how the spirit, which is the primary and fundamental reality, assumed the shape of the physical universe. There is no wonder that there is no single, trenchant, conclusive view about this, especially because, here we are dealing with (identity as) facts and concepts which are not only non-material but also transcendental. Even physical scientists admit that they have not been able to arrive at a single, unanimously acceptable theory regarding the origin of the universe. There are different theories such as the nebular theory, the big-bang theory, etc. So it is only natural that there can be divergence of outlook and interpretation in the case of the spiritualist approach also.

According to Swamiji, the Sankhya philosophy coupled with the Vedantic approach provides the most satisfactory explanation to the question of the origin of the universe. Says he:

"We all use the word "Nature". The old Sankhya philosophers called it by two different names, *Prakriti*, which is very much the same as the word nature, the more scientific name *avyaktam*, undifferentiated, from which everything proceeds, such as atoms, molecules and forces, mind, thought and intelligence. It is startling to find that the philosophers and metaphysicians of India stated, ages ago, that identity as a construct of mind is material. What are our present materialists trying to do, but show that both mind and its constructed identity, are as much a product of nature as the body? And so is thought, and we shall find, by and by, intelligence also; all issue from that nature which is called *avyaktam*, the undifferentiated. The Sankhyas defined organic identity of any individual as the equilibrium of three forces, one of which is called *sattva*, another *rajas*, and the third *tamas*. *Tamas*, the lowest force, is that of attraction; a little higher is *rajas*, that of repulsion; and the highest is the balance of these two, the *sattva*, so that when these two forces, attraction and repulsion, are held in perfect control, there is no creation, no movement in the world. Don't confuse with the Western idea of evil of virtuous identity. Or Identity as oppressor or oppressed. This is just organic individuality of race. Less to be inculcated.

For the rest, the eternally repeated succession of worlds in infinite time is only the logical complement to the coexistence of innumerable worlds in infinite space. It is an eternal cycle that matter moves in, a cycle that certainly only completes its orbit in periods of time for which our terrestrial year is no adequate measure, a cycle in which the time of highest development, the time of organic life and still more that of life, of beings conscious of nature and of themselves, is just as narrowly restricted as the space in which life and

> self-consciousness come into operation ... but however often and however relentlessly, this cycle is completed in time, and in space, however many millions of suns and earths may arise and pass away ... we have the certainty that matter remains eternally the same in all its transformation and, therefore, also that with the same necessity that it will exterminate on the earth its highest creation, the thinking mind, it must somewhere else and at another time again produce it". (K. Marx and F. Engels on Religion, Foreign Language Publication, Moscow, pp. 172-74)

The whole thing has the ring of Sanatana cosmology with, of course, one unmistakable difference. The cyclic nature of cosmic evolution around identity, the incredibly long periods between one manifestation and another, the declining warmth and brightness succeeded by increasing heat and light, causing the disappearance and the subsequent manifestation of the universe are features in which Hindu cosmology and the Marxist cosmology as indicated above, are very identical. But there is a fundamental difference. Whereas the Sanatana posit in an ultimate spiritual reality, which by its presence lends dynamism to nature to undergo these cosmic movements, Marx and Engels feel that laws inherent in nature are sufficient to explain every such movement. How there can be rational identity as intelligent, systematic recurring movements without an intelligent, conscious force working behind, is not explained by them. Sanatana seers have provided the answer to this question, by stating that there is the Divine that causes all these phenomena to take place. Of course, that Divine power is not something above and outside nature. So is everything that can be identified as nature. It is immanent in it, without it there is no nature; they are even identical. But Sanatana believe that the Divine, Satchidananda, is the one and only identity that is the Ultimate Reality, out of which emerges nature with all its manifestations and goes back into it during the course of these periodic cyclic manifestations. The Hindu Cosmology, as stated in the *Bhagavad Gita* (verses 17-20, chapter VIII) has been succinctly summed up by Shri Aurobindo thus:

> "There is an eternal cycle of alternating periods of cosmic manifestation and non-manifestation, each period called respectively a day and a night of the creator Brahma, each of equal length in time, the long aeon of his working which endures for a thousand ages, the long aeon of his sleep as another thousand ages. At the coming of the day all manifestations are born into being, out of the unmanifest, at the coming of the night, all vanish or are dissolved in it. Thus all the existences alternate helplessly in the cycle of becoming and non-becoming; they come into becoming again and again, *bhutva bhutva* and they go back constantly into the unmanifest. But this unmanifest is not the original divinity of the Being; there is another status of his existence *bravo anyah*, a supercosmic unmanifest beyond this cosmic non-manifestation, which is eternally self-seated, is not an opposite of this cosmic status of manifestation, but far above and unlike it, changeless, eternal, not force to perish with the perishing of all these existences. He is called the unmanifest immutable, him they speak of as the supreme soul and status and those who attain to him return not; that is my supreme place of being *paramam dhama*. For, the soul attaining to it has escaped out of the cycle of cosmic manifestation and non- manifestation". (Sri Aurobindo, *Essay on Gita*, pp. 283-84)

On the basis of this cyclic concept of the Universe, Swami Vivekananda believed that social evolution is also cyclic and rhythmic. SO is the identity. "All progress is in successive rises and falls; no progress is in a straight line", he says. Just as Marx did, Swamiji also believed that the laws that apply to physical evolution apply equally to social and historical evolution. He says:

> "So rising and falling, the cycle goes on Everything in creation goes on in this form, one wave rising, another falling, rising again and falling again, each wave has its hollow, each hollow has its wave. The same law must apply to the universe as a whole, because of its uniformity". (*CW*, Vol. II)

Vivekananada has manifested the very idea of this casual loop of social and person centric identity, as his spiritual goal of God-realisation, undisturbed by anxiety and care. Affluence leads to vulgarity and sensuousness, while poverty causes degeneration and misery. Both are is free voided. In other words, man cannot aspire to have an absolute identity via spiritually unless he is free from worries about his daily needs. Here lies the economic content of his philosophy. Man freed from anxieties regarding his basic daily requirements can direct his energies for spiritual evolution. Economic advancement is a necessary precondition to spiritual fulfilment, as much for the individual as for the society. And this the fundamental behind men's craving for an identity that are more to do with social dependence on money. I would like to call it as stopgap arrangements of the identity, proposed as a substitute to the absolute one.

This is powerfully corroborated by Swami Tapasyananda in his beautiful book, *Legacy of Swami Vivekananda*, in which he says

> "What he longed for was not an endless pursuit, as in many so-called advanced countries of today, of higher and higher standards of living and sophistication of life pattern, but the provision of the minimum requirements for a healthy and contented life, which alone can provide man with the leisure and reserve of mental energy required for the pursuit of spiritual values. An environment neither of extreme enjoyment nor of base indulgence and misery can generate *vairagya* or revulsion and non-attachment to the fleeting

> worldly values. Only a via media in the social and the economic situation can foster *viveka*, discrimination—the parent of renunciation and spiritual aspiration and thus favour the rise of impressive men of spiritual genius who can deliver the saving gospel, the message of India to the young and powerful nations of the world. Those who do not understand this basic urge of Swami Vivekananda in his expression of passionate patriotism and championship of the cause of the masses, but think of him merely as a patriotic freedom fighter or a covert communist thinker, give the grossest misrepresentation of him". (Tapasyananda, *Legacy of Swami Vivekananda*, pp. 174-75)

This Swamiji learned, first at the feet of his great master, and later, from his own experience of Indian conditions. "A hungry soul can have no religion", he learned from his Guru. In Sri Ramakrishna's words, "empty stomachs and religion go ill together. People must have food. Their minimum wants have to be supplied; otherwise they cannot apply their minds to God". Swami Vivekananda as a rationalist to the core of his heart, was aware of this. So how can he deny the prospect of material civilisation which produces all sorts of things of bare existence, things of enjoyment, material to satisfy human needs? "But there is necessity for restraint, soberness, curtailment of excess" (Tapash Sankar Dutta, *A Study of Philosophy of Vivekananda*, pp. 211-12).

Conclusion

The fundamental learning that the chapter can propose with respect to the present notion of identity within the social work is not to propose it as an effect of something, some other identity. Neither to disown it. Identity is *one* as a part of one which include every *other*. This creation as *other* is just '(another) identity', a byproduct of process that creates "identity". The modern psychologist may misunderstand as "egolessness" or "no-self". But it is the universal *Brahman* (something that is less then least and at the sometime more than infinity). *TAT TVAM ASI* is the identity of the every identifier. Defining *Brahman* in words will lead another identity. I would like to render my apology for not having other words to manifest something which is beyond any concept of existence, and still a worldly affair, courtesy "limited self". Ego is needed as a construct of identity but not as by-product of conflict, nor the least count of peace. Identity is real from a Sanatana ideological position but not the absolute real. The real *identity* is in experience of the self, more than the reality of experience as self. *Self* has to be one with the experiences. Our sticking identity has created more "others". Our quest to propose solutions between the two force us to see "two". But Advaita is the key while talking about the identity. The identity where *seer* and *seen* are one.

References

Acharya, Prashant (2019). *Karma Theory*, Advaita Foundation, pp. 76-78.

Acharya, Prashant (2022), *Prshnoupishad*, Advaita Foundation, pp. 23-24.

Aurobindo, Sri (1997), *Essay on Gita*, Sri Aurobindo Ashram Publication, pp. 283-84.

Dutta, Tapash Sankar (2013). *A Study of Philosophy of Vivekananda*, University of Michigan Press, pp. 211-12.

Jake, Harwood (2020). "Social Identity Theory", in J. van den Bulck (ed.), *International Encyclopedia of Media Psychology*. Wiley, DOI:10.1002/9781119011071.iemp0153

Marx, K. and F. Engels on Religion, Foreign Language Publication, Moscow pp. 172-74.

Mayer (1900). *A History of Modern Philosophy*, Macmillan & Co. Limited, pp. 310-11.

Srimad Bhagavad Geeta, Geeta Press, Gorakhpur.

Suligoj, H.F. (1975). *The Mystical Philosophy of Alan Watts*. Interna.

Tajfel, Henri John C. Turner. (1970). "Social Identity theory of Intergroup Behaviour". *Journal of Political Psychology*, http://christosaioannou.com/Tajfel%20and%20Turner%201986.pdf

Tapasyananda (2015). *Legacy of Swami Vivekananda*, Ramakrishna Mission Publication, pp. 174-75.

Vaidic Sangra (1953). *Satyarth Prakash*, pp. 211-13.

Wayper, C.L. (1965). *Political Thought*, English University Press Limited, pp. 195-96.

6

Contribution of Rabindranath Tagore to Indian Social Work Practice/Rural Reconstruction

Sagarika Saha

Introduction

Tagore was not only a noted poet but he was also the pioneer in conceiving and implementing a holistic approach for community development through his Sriniketan Experiment also called Rural Reconstruction. He showed the path to professional social work with and in rural communities. The University that Tagore founded had, from its very inception, planned extension activities in the surrounding villages that were comprehensive and aimed at the complete rejuvenation of rural life in the context of what was happening around. In fact, Sriniketan, the twin campus to Santiniketan where originally Visva-Bharati was founded, is wholly devoted to and concerned with the work of village upliftment. It is to be noted that Tagore used the term 'reconstruction' or 'rejuvenation' (*punargathana* or *samgathana* in Bengali) rather than the term 'development'. The latter term is in many ways restricting as 'development' or it lack is usually understood in contrast to the condition of the 'other'. It is presumed that the ways of the 'others' are preferred or are 'standard'. Tagore felt that in the circumstances of the acute deprivation and neglect of rural communities in all aspects (education, health, livelihood, opportunities, and amenities) by the then government, such comparisons would be counter-productive and lead nowhere. Also, unless rural people learned to become self-reliant and depend on their own strengths and resources, any developmental efforts would not be sustained. (Saha, 2019)

The work of Sriniketan through its various departments is the manifestation of Tagore's principles of rural reconstruction. He envisaged that rural communities had been subjected to neglect and deprivation in various aspects and had lost their natural resilience and capacities to adapt to change (Bhattacharya, 2014: 75-86). There was thus a need to re-build their capacities and shape them according to the needs of the day.

When Tagore was looking after his family estates (1890-1901) he started a number of cooperatives and other initiatives in Patisar and Shelaidah for farmers. (Sinha,Dikshit 2010:15-21) In the early years of Sriniketan we find Tagore returning to the idea of the cooperative. SHG is a form of cooperative with the focus on forming small groups having focussed activity. Cooperative and SHGs the different settings of modern-day social work that is emphasised by Tagore.

The background

In the 1890s Rabindranath Tagore was put in charge of the family's rural properties in Shilaidaha and Patisar of Pabna District in Central Bengal now in Bangladesh by his father Debendranath Tagore. Here Rabindranath for the first time came into contact with the village people of Bengal. At the age of twenty-nine his poetic imagination developed and he was greatly inspired by the beauty of rural Bengal. But gradually he became aware of the poverty and shackles of the lives of the villagers. He began to formulate methods for social and economic changes in those villages. Different types of efforts were made for provision of small meeting centre-cum-library, cooperative farming, water supply, health centre, road building and engagements of the teachers etc. but all these efforts were not totally successful. Tagore soon realised that without the involvement and participation of the villagers themselves, his programmes would fail. These and many other experiences inspired Tagore to formulate a community level involvement approach.

> "Rabindranath's initial analysis of village poverty highlighted various causes: an educational system which alienated English educated urban elites from the rural population; and absentee landlords who had abandoned their responsibility for the welfare (Marsh, 2013) and cultural life of their tenants leaving them despondent and lacking in self-esteem or *atmashakti*. He also blamed superstition, credit procedures and oppressive social customs which he described vividly in his 1908 novel *Gora*" (Connell, 2002: 282).

In his famous essay 'Swadeshi Samaj' (Tagore, 1961:322) Rabindranath set forth an elaborate programme for instilling the spirit of self-reliance in people. He put forward in the course of the same essay a plan for organising the villages, educating the common people, establishing social self-administration and cooperative movement. He advocated in favour of developing a social administration that would run in parallel to the British administration. Later we can see that Rabindranath applied some of these ideas in the concrete form in Santiniketan and Sriniketan.

In 1912, Tagore purchased the Estate house at Surul and established a model agricultural farm afterwards. Tagore wanted a constructive non-political village work, which took shape in the estate house (*Surul Khutibari*) when he met L.K. Elmhirst in New York in 1920. Elmhirst who was deeply impressed by Tagore's passion for village upliftment work wanted to assist him. On February 6, 1922 with Elmhirst as Director the "Institute of Rural Reconstruction", "Sriniketan", as per Tagore's desire, was founded, fulfilling the long-cherished dream of Tagore about rural reconstruction, through the initiative of L.K. Elmhirst, an Englishman and the financial assistance of an American, Mrs. Dorothy Straight. Rabindranath Tagore's experiment on Rural Reconstruction was carried on in Sriniketan and hence it was called Sriniketan Experiment.

The central idea of the Institute as stated by Tagore in his words is:

> "The objective of Sriniketan is to bring back life in its completeness into the villagers making them self-reliant and self-respectful, acquainted with the cultural traditions of their own country, and competent to make an efficient use of the modern resources for the improvement of their physical, intellectual and economic condition" (Tagore, 1928: 1).

The aims and objects of the Institute, as originally set forth in detail, are as follows:

1. To win the friendship and affection of villagers and cultivators by taking a real interest in all that concern their lives and welfare, and by making a lively effort to assist them in solving their most pressing problems.
2. To take the problems of the village and the field to the class room for study and discussion and to the experimental farm for solution.
3. To carry the knowledge and experience gained in the classroom and the experimental farm to the villagers, in the endeavour to improve their sanitation and health; to develop their resources and credit; to help them to sell their produce and buy their requirements to the best advantage; to teach them better method of growing crops and vegetables and of keeping livestock; to encourage them to learn and practise arts and crafts; and to bring home to them the benefits of associated life, mutual aid, and common endeavour.

4. To work out practically an all-round system of elementary education in the villages based on the Boy Scout Ideal and training, with the object of developing ideas of citizenship and public duty such as may appeal to the villagers and be within their means and capacity.
5. To encourage in the staff and the students of the department itself a spirit of sincere service and willing sacrifice in the interests of and on terms of comradeship with their poorer, less educated and greatly harassed neighbours in the villages.
6. To train the students to a due sense of their own intrinsic worth, physical and moral, and in particular, to teach them to do with their own hands everything which a village householder or cultivator does or should do for a living, if possible, more efficiently.
7. To put the students in the way of acquiring practical experience in cultivation, dairying, animal husbandry, poultry-keeping, carpentry, smithing, weaving, tanning, practical sanitation work, and in the art and spirit of co-operation.
8. To give the students elementary instruction in the sciences connected with their practical work to train them to think and record the knowledge acquired by them for their own benefit and for that of their fellowmen (Tagore, 1925).

To implement the above objectives the work of Sriniketan was grouped under the following four major programmes, namely: (i) Research, (ii) Education, (iii) Service, and (iv) Commerce.

(i) **Research** includes survey of the problems of village-life in all its aspects, and experimentation with them in the farms, workshops, and laboratories of the institute.

(ii) **Education** means a real-life oriented education consisting of its four different sub-divided aspects or the branches, namely: (a) social education, (b) vocational education, (c) practical education, and (d) all-round education:

(a) **Social education** aims at creating proper awareness and developing the spirit of self-help in the minds of the learners pursuing the course.

(b) **Vocational education** relates to the education on agriculture, animal husbandry, arts, crafts, industries and so on.

(c) **Practical education** aims at inculcating in the students the spirit of self-help and the dignity of labour so that they can be able to produce something by applying their practical efficiencies.

(d) **All-round education** is imparted for proper, all-round development of all good inner human qualities to make the learners efficiently fit for citizenship and community leadership.

(e) **Service** consists of demonstrating the villagers of better methods in agriculture and industries, and of extension services rendered by the students and workers of the Institute, touching all essential aspects of village life like roads, sanitation, health education, and general amenities and entertainment.

(f) **Commerce** consists of efforts to run some branches of the institute on a commercial scale with a view to giving employment to some of its trainees, for the people to achieve economic self-sufficiency (Saha, 2019).

The activities of Sriniketan according to the above programmes were organised under four departments: (a) Agriculture, including Animal Husbandry; (b) Industries; cottage and crafts (c) Village Welfare; and (d) Education. There have been some changes in these programmes over time.

Analysis of the Tagore's Philosophy

The hardships, the miseries, the pities, the inconveniences, the lacking, the oppression and the bondage of rural poor mass always pained his heart terribly. Tagore suggested some causes of rural deprivation and their remedies. Here is an instance,

> "The soil in which we are born... is the soil of our village, the mother-earth in whose lap we receive our nourishment from day to day. Our educated elite, abstracted from this primal basis, wander about in the high heaven of ideas like aimless clouds far removed from this our home. If this cloud does not dissolve in a shower of loving service, man's relation with mother earth will never be truly meaningful" (Kripalani, 1980:155).

For Rabindranath this "loving service" was not only a sort of repayment of the moral debts of townsmen to villagers, but also a realisation of an equal partnership between town and village (Saha, 2019). He could not tolerate the suffering of rural people on one hand, and on the other, he could never accept the cheerlessness of those innocent villagers and wrote (Das Gupta 2009: 131):

> "It is hard to imagine a life as cheerless as in our rural areas. I could see no way out. It is far from easy to do something for people who have cultivated weakness for centuries and do not know what self-help is. Still, I had to make a start".

He wanted to organise the villagers so that they could supply all their needs on a cooperative basis. He believed that given education they could establish and maintain their own schools and granaries, banks and cooperative stores. He hoped that those ties of co-operation would bring unity to the people and free them from dependence on the state. That was the change he sought to bring to the Indian villages. By change he meant, most of all, a change of attitude and wrote in this respect:

> "It is not enough to try to remove wants; you can never remove them completely from outside; the far greater thing is to rouse the will of the people to remove their own wants" (Neogy, 2010: 33).

To protect rural people from this deprivation, to offer equal opportunity to them, to help them enhance skill and ability, and to make them self-reliant were the matters of grave concern for rural reconstruction. That is why he advocated in favour of a thorough change in rural system—not just in its frame, feature and structure. This laudable concept of designing rural system in a completely innovative way is known as rural reconstruction.

Tagore, in his principle of rural reconstruction, laid emphasis on co-operation, self-help, cohesion and good friendship. He really tried to express his intention to declare the principle of rural reconstruction to make people aware of it. Many of his writings and remarks bear ample significance in this support. His concept covered activities, education, culture and what not. He urged that "mass education in the vernaculars should be undertaken by a band of workers who should organise furnishing [the villagers] with new compositions by way of *jatras* [street dramas, Das Gupta 2009: 475], *kirtans* [devotional songs, *ibid.*: 476], recitations, bioscope and lantern shows, gymnastic legerdemain."

In fact, to impart education in form of performance as conceived by him is as innovative as helpful for people to be united together. For Rabindranath *melas* were vital in the process of the society's cohesion: as economic and cultural meeting points, and also in establishing "good friendship among Hindus and Muslims" (Chakrabarti, 1993: 79). So, he wrote "If the leaders of the country will abjure empty politics, and make it their business to give new life and objective to these *melas* [fairs, *ibid.*] putting their own heart into the work and bringing together the hearts of Hindus and Muslims, and then confer about the real wants of the people—schools, roads, water reservoirs, grazing commons, and the like—then the country will soon awaken" (Das Gupta, 2009: 277).

Thus, Rabindranath had founded the *Rakhi-Bhandan* festival which "celebrated voluntary kinship, particularly between Hindus and Muslims" (O'Connell, 2002: 91.148).

This concept of reconstruction also inspired 'Swadeshi Movement' activists to dedicate themselves to living and working in the villages and enlist the co-operation of the villagers to start the work of constructing roads, schools, water reservoirs, and sanitation, and improving agricultural production—and also to create new folk music (utilising local resources and capacity building of local skills). In order to offer financial help to villagers he also cherished an idea for establishment of Banks in rural areas. He believed that access to credit is a right for the poor. He took initiative to establish a "Krishi Bank" at Shilaidaha in 1894, and one in Patisar in 1905. The main objective of this was to liberate the poor farmers from the terrifying dragnet of moneylenders. Rabindranath arranged the seed (venture) capital for the bank from his friends and relatives. After winning the Nobel Prize in 1913, Rabindranath donated the prize money to his school in Shantiniketan and invested the fund (Rs. 1,80,000) in Patisar Krishi Bank. This significantly uplifted the capacity of the bank to extend more credit to the peasants at lower rates of interest. Thus, well ahead of many of his contemporaries, Tagore could visualise the importance of rural credit and other co-operatives and took positive steps to implement the same (Saha, S., 2019).

Tagore also ushered in micro-credit programmes to finance rural development activities on co-operative basis (through the formation of co-operative societies) even before establishing the bank. He inspired the poor farmers to build up the habit of small savings. Farmers of neighbouring villages were required to subscribe to the co-operative credit society. The funds so raised were given back as loan at low interests to the needy farmers. Tagore introduced such small cooperative initiatives both in Shilaidaha and Patisar. Apart from this, microcredit was also provided for the development of various cottage industries (Mitra, 2014: 47-70).

Visva-Bharati, Santiniketan was founded in 1918 and in 1922. Tagore founded Sriniketan with the active help and support of L.K. Elmhirst and many others already engaged in Santiniketan. Sriniketan symbolised Tagore's efforts on his family estates almost two decades before he established Sriniketan. Thus, Sriniketan was the fruit of the tree in the seed of which he had visualised the need for a scientific and professional training in the approach to rural work and with the aims he wanted to realise he established Sriniketan.

All aforementioned attempts and initiatives were, however, based on the principle of 'Rural Reconstruction'. Later this idea of 'Rural Reconstruction' has gained much popularity almost everywhere and Rural Extension Centre conducts the major programmes of rural reconstruction.

Interpretation with Modern Social Work Concepts

Professional social work believes and preaches its mandate that people will be self-reliant and self-sufficient by using all opportunities provided to them from time to time but not making them dependent on others. Over and above the concept derived from Sriniketan Experiment are *'Brati dal', 'mobile library or chalantika', 'mahila samity', 'women group', 'co-operative', 'health awareness', crafts promotion and so forth* are all the integral parts of modern social work practice in various terminologies *such as 'group work', 'community development', 'community organisation', 'case work', 'women empowerment', 'Self-Help-Group', etc.* India today thinks of self-help-group for women for women liberation, reservation policy for unprivileged section of the society and the collective development through individual development. These were ideas that Tagore injected in different forms in Sriniketan experiments. Tagore's ideas thus anticipate the crux of India's developmental strategy (Ghosh, P.K., 2012:125-136).

Tagore also wanted the emancipation of villages and to rouse the villagers with *atmashakti* (Sinha, D., 2010: 217-59). In fact, he gave much importance to constructive work and village welfare, and emphasised on self-confidence and self-sufficiency. The very fact that Tagore started his educational experiments in the lap of nature and also far from modern township at Bolpur, indicates his preferences.

There are seven principles of social work profession like Acceptance, Individualisation, Purposeful expression of feelings, Non-judgmental attitude, Controlled-emotional involvement,

Self-determination and Confidentiality. If we peep into the principles of Sriniketan Experiment founded by Gurudeva Rabindranath Tagore, then many similarities can be drawn with the present principles of Social Work Profession. Tagore while implementing his experiment accepted all rural, poor, uneducated villagers wholeheartedly and also respected their naturality. So, he had formed the principle of acceptance. He shared his feelings with the villagers (mentioned in *Palliprakriti)* about the fear of urbanisation and conflicts between men that would destroy the whole society (Purposeful expression of feelings). Through various meetings with the villagers he had tried to make out their fear, feelings and anguish and also intervened to seek out the problems (problem-solving approach). When he understood about the root cause behind the agony of the villagers, which was lack of cooperation and arranged cultural activities, songs etc. to create the creativity and mutual trust among them.

> "To be true to the tradition Tagore represented, his rural society would be much richer, more diverse: accepting life in the fullness thereof and going through it with song and dance" (Tagore, 1961: 308-10).

He always thought and also implemented in the aims and objectives of Sriniketan the arousal of self-determination of the villagers. He also knew that "the country could not be truly free until its villages were restored to a basis of economic and moral self-respect" (Neogy, 2010: 139). So, he emphasised on the principle of client self-determination.

He never used judgmental attitude in assessing any situation or person. He always tried to solve the problems through negotiation and cooperation with the villagers (networking). And he believed in doing work with the people and for the people and also by the people (people's participation). This concept resembles our constitution morals which can be derived from Tagore's views.

Conclusion

The meanings of the principles used to discuss to relate with the Ideas of Tagore are explained from the modern social work point of view:

Acceptance is a fundamental social work principle that implies a sincere understanding of clients. Acceptance is conveyed in the professional relationship through the expression of genuine concern, receptive listening, intentional responses that acknowledge the other person's point of view, and the creation of a climate of mutual respect. Purposeful Expression of Feelings—Clients need to have opportunities to express their feelings freely to the social worker. As social workers, we must go beyond "just the facts" to uncover the underlying feelings. Non-judgmental attitude—Communicating non-judgmentalism is essential for developing a relationship with any client. It does not imply that social workers do not make decisions; rather it implies a non-blaming attitude and behaviour. Social workers judge others neither as good or bad nor as worthy or unworthy. Closely related to non-judgmentalism, objectivity is the principle of examining situations without bias. To be objective in their observations and understanding, social workers must avoid injecting personal feelings and prejudices in relationships with clients.

Self-Determination: The principle of self-determination is based on the recognition of the freedom for right and need of clients in making their own choices and decisions. Social workers have a responsibility to create a working relationship in which choice can be exercised.

Access to Resources: Social workers are implored to assure that everyone has the necessary resources, services, and opportunities; to pay attention to expanding choices, and opportunities for the oppressed and disadvantaged; and to advocate for policy and legislative changes that improve social conditions and promote social justice. (B. Dubois and K.K. Miley, 1992:135-141).

Tagore always emphasised on community organisation method and social action through his rural reconstruction work in the Sriniketan area of Birbhum district, West Bengal. He worked in the pre-independence era but his philosophies can be seen practiced through his Visva-Bharati university's extension department to some extent (Saha, 2019).

References

Bhattacharya, K. (2014). *Rabindranath Tagore: An Adventure of Ideas and Innovative Practices in Education*, Springer International.

Chakrabarti, Mohit. (1993). *Tagore and Education for Social Change*, New Delhi, Gyan Publishing House, p. 219.

Connell, Kathleen M.O. (2002). *Rabindranath Tagore: The Poet as Educator*, Visva-Bharati.

Das Gupta, Uma (2009). *Tagore: Selected Writings on Education and Nationalism*, Oxford University Press, New Delhi.

DuBois, B. & Miley, K.K. (1992). *Social Work: An Empowering Profession*, Boston: Allyn and Bacon, pp. 135-41.

Ghosh, P.K. (2012). "Tagore's Rural Reconstruction Experiment—A Strength Based Social Development Practice for Rural India", in *Papers in Strength Based Practice*, (Ed.) Venkat Pulla, *et al.*, Allied Publishers, New Delhi.

Kripalani, Krishna (1980). *Rabindranath Tagore: A Biography*, London, Oxford University.

Marsh, Christine Elizabeth (2013). *Towards One World: A Journey Through the English Essays of Rabindranath Tagore*. University of Exeter (United Kingdom) ProQuest Dissertations Publishing, U617907. https://www.proquest.com/openview/804952b772d3af06f9f431ecef8e4416/1?pq-origsite=gscholar&cbl=51922&diss=y

Mitra, Rana (2014). "Cooperatives: A Democratic Instrument of Human Empowerment", *Social Scientist, 42*(11/12): 47-70, http://www.jstor.org/stable

Neogy, Ajit K. (2010). *The Twin Dreams of Rabindranath Tagore*, National Book Trust, New Delhi, India, ISBN-978-81-237-5731-5 S

Saha, Sagarika. (completed on 2016). *A Study of Women SHGs in the Villages adopted by Visva Bharati: Issues of Sustainability*, Doctoral thesis, Department of Social Work, Visva Bharti University. http://hdl.handle.net/10603/229339 (2019) published.

Sinha, Dikshit (2010). *Rabindranather Pallypunargathan Prayas*, Paschimbanga Bangla Akademi, Kolkata.

Tagore, R. (1961). *Towards Universal Man*, Visva-Bharati Publication, Kolkata.

Tagore, R. (1925). *Visva-Bharati Bulletin*, No. 6.

Tagore, R. (1928). *Visva-Bharati Bulletin*, No. 11, p. 1.

7

Community Organisation and Development in Egypt

Ibrahim Sabry Ahmed

Introduction

Community organisation is a vital aspect of social work practice aimed at empowering communities, promoting social change, and addressing systemic issues. In Egypt, community organisation has gained significance as a means of addressing social inequalities, enhancing community resilience, and fostering sustainable development. This chapter seeks to explore the historical roots, definitions, values, programs, challenges, and future of community organisation and development in Egypt.

It is possible that the term "community organisation" was not known in Egypt before 1948, where the American University in Cairo offered a course on community organisation (Ahmed, 1975). However, a researcher studying the evolution of community organisation must look back to events that occurred long before 1948. It is necessary to review the beginning of these efforts and their expansion.

The early beginnings of the emergence of community organisation in Egypt can be summarised in five stages:

The Beginning Stage (1800-18): In this stage, Muhammad Ali Pasha ruled Egypt from 1805 to 1848. Recognising the need for social and economic reforms, Muhammad Ali implemented various measures, including the establishment of modern educational institutions, the introduction of industrialisation (Fahmy, 1997). Foreign communities in Egypt began to demand social welfare services, so they started to establish voluntary associations in the European style. They established the Greek Philanthropic Society in Alexandria in 1821, and in Cairo in 1856 (Ministry of Social Affairs, 1961). There were also signs of the formation of the Ministry of Endowments in 1935 to monitor the supervisors responsible for distributing financial and in-kind aid to poor citizens.

The Spread Stage (1919-38): In 1936, the Egyptian government established the Higher Council for Social Reform to reconcile the foundations of social life with the effects of material progress on the Egyptian people. The Council is also responsible for studying reforms that emphasise family cohesion and solving social problems (Ministry of Social Affairs, 1964).

Supervision and Guidance Stage (1939-51): The first social centre was established in the village of *Minyat Al-Hat* in Fayoum Governorate to advance the social aspects of the villages and solve their various problems. The first trained batch of social workers was also graduated, and the first community organisation institutions appeared, which is the aid registry or what is called the information exchange registry to organise work between institutions that provide financial aid to the poor (Hassanein, 1974).

Coordination and Organisation Stage (1952-60): In the field of social development, the Permanent Council for Services was established to raise the standard of living among members of Egyptian society (Ahmed & Suleiman, 1963).

The Socialist Planning Stage (1961-80): The Arab Socialist Union was formed as a popular and political organisation to lead the masses. Law 133 of 1964 regarding social security was also issued to provide care for individuals and families in need. The National Action Program presented by the President of the Republic at the

National Conference in 1971 included the recommendation to rebuild the Egyptian village to achieve the minimum services for the rural community (Darwish, 1978).

There was agreement that community development is part of community organisation, whether in urban or rural communities, as the two concepts are similar in their goals that focus on creating appropriate conditions for growth and progress by bringing about intentional social change. Also, both depends on human relations and creating positive co-operation between sectors of society (Ahmed, 1975).

Contemporary Egyptian society believes in an important principle, which is the centralisation of planning and decentralisation of implementation, meaning that development policy in society is based on the action plan of Ministry of Planning which is based on the proposals of the popular and executive bodies from the bottom to the top. As for the decentralisation of implementation, each comuunity has its own circumstances, so local councils were given a degree of freedom to implement or introduce some amendments to the implementation of projects. Egypt combines the advantages of the central and local systems, each of which has its role in development so that they complement each other (Hassan, 1970, p. 134).

Definition and Values of Community Organisation in Egypt

There are many Egyptian attempts to formulate the concept of community organisation, and we will review the most prominent of them in this section.

Shawky (1961) defines community organisation as "the process that is undertaken intentionally and in accordance with the general policy to bring about economic and social development for people and their environments, whether they are in local or regional communities, relying on coordinated governmental and civil efforts" (Shawky, 1961, p. 43).

Ahmed (1972) developed a definition of community organisation as "one of the methods of social work to support joint efforts at various levels of community in accordance with a plan that mobilises current and future resources within the framework of public policy" (Ahmed, 1972, p. 145).

Abdel Aaal (1981) described community organisation as "one of the methods of social work that has special importance in Egypt as a development society, as its objectives are consistent with development objectives, helps bring about change in social systems, and contributes to deepening the sense of social responsibility and confronting the causes and factors of underdevelopment".

Badran (1999) defines community organisation as "a method of social work used by the social worker to influence community decisions taken at all levels to plan and implement social and economic development programs, so that this leads to strengthening the bond between the people of one community and between the local community and the larger community" (Badran, 1999, p. 57).

Social and religious values guide the practice of community organisation in Egypt through the cohesion and redistribution approach. These values include: respecting human dignity and not being subjected to oppression or injustice, providing people with the opportunity to express their opinions, achieving social justice, and obtaining a fair share of services for the benefit of vulnerable groups in community (Abdel Latif, 1998).

Reviews of Literature

In this section of the chapter, the focus will be on the current situation of community organisation and development in Egypt through a review of recent literature. This review aims to highlighting key themes and challenges.

Key Themes

- **Social development:** Community organisation initiatives, projects and programs in Egyptian often focus on addressing social issues such as poverty, health, education, and environmental protection. Studies have explored the role of community organisation in developing the Egyptian country (Decent Life Initiative), detecting diseases (100 Million Health Initiative), and (Dokan Al-Farah) initiative to prepare orphaned and disabled girls about to get married (e.g., Ahmed, 2021; Imam, 2023).

- **Empowerment:** Community organisation empowering many groups of community, such as students, illiterate females, youth, women, and families in need of care. Attention is also given to institutional empowerment (e.g., Halim, 2015; Taher, 2023).
- **Partnership:** Recent studies in community organisation have indicated the importance of strengthening community partnership between various sectors of Egyptian society, such as governmental organisations, civil society organisations, and private sector organisations (e.g., Muhammad, 2016; Amin, 2019).
- **Technology:** ICT has become central to community organisation practices and interventions in Egypt. This includes utilising digital platforms for online advocacy, E-networking, strengthening digital citizenship behaviours and building E-skills capabilities among community members (e.g., Hammad, 2019; Saleh, 2023).

Challenges

Community organisation and development in Egypt face various challenges that can hinder their effectiveness and sustainability. Here are some of the key challenges faced by community organisation in Egypt:

- **Limited Resources:** Funding limitations, lack of skilled personnel. Research by Afifi (2023) pointed out that there are several challenges facing non-governmental organisations working in the field of women to achieve social justice, and these challenges include: lack of financial and human resources, insufficient information about services, the small number of non-governmental organisations in the field of women, and weak efficiency of workers.

- **Sustainability:** Ensuring long-term sustainability remains a critical challenge. Ammar (2023) mentioned that there are challenges facing the training of employees of the educational administration in Bahariya Oasis in the context of community organisation, including: the lack of a future training plan for community crises, reliance on a single training method, and training programs that do not keep pace with global changes.
- **Political environment:** Egyptian society suffers from weak effective participation in political action, restrictions on access to public information, lack of political socialisation, and failure of the elite to form citizens' cultural and cognitive awareness (Salem, 2016).
- **Corruption, bureaucracy and development** often face significant challenges when it comes to navigating intricate bureaucratic procedures and the potential for corruption. Hassan (2022) founded that there are obstacles to the performance of anti-corruption committees in the government sector in Egypt. There are obstacles related to society, followed by obstacles specific to other agencies concerned with anti-corruption, followed by obstacles specific to the committees, followed by obstacles due to coordination.
- **Rapid population growth:** Egypt has struggled to contain the population explosion crisis that has escalated in the past few years. The population problem, in its various dimensions, is considered one of the most important problems facing Egyptian society, with its negative impact on the development processes and progress it seeks. It is also considered one of the biggest obstacles to the community development process (Amer, 2021).

Future of Community Organisation and Development in Egypt

Based on the provided information, here is an analysis of the future of community organisation and development in Egypt:

- **Civic Engagement and Participation:** Encouraging civic engagement and active participation of community members will be crucial for the success of community organisation initiatives. This can involve promoting awareness, education, and training programs that empower individuals to become active contributors to community development. Engaging youth and marginalised groups in decision-making processes can also foster inclusivity and diversity within community organisations.
- **Urbanisation and Informal Settlements:** Egypt's urbanisation process has led to the emergence of informal settlements with inadequate infrastructure and limited access to basic services. Future community organisation efforts will focus on addressing the needs of these communities, including improving housing conditions, access to clean water, sanitation facilities, and healthcare services. Collaborating with local authorities and international organisations can help implement sustainable solutions for urban development.
- **Climate Change and Environmental Sustainability:** The impact of climate change poses significant challenges to community development in Egypt. Rising sea levels, water scarcity, and extreme weather events affect livelihoods, agriculture, and public health. Future community organisation initiatives will prioritise environmental sustainability, including promoting renewable energy, sustainable agriculture, waste management, and climate change adaptation strategies.
- **Technology for Development:** The integration of technology in community organisation and development will continue to expand. Mobile technology, digital

platforms, and data analytics can facilitate communication, information sharing, and monitoring of development programs. E-learning platforms can provide access to education and vocational training, particularly in remote areas. Embracing digital innovation can enhance the efficiency, scalability, and impact of community development initiatives.

- **International Co-operation and Funding:** Collaboration with international organisations, donor agencies, and development partners will continue to play a significant role in community organisation and development efforts in Egypt. International co-operation can provide financial resources, technical expertise, and best practices to support sustainable development initiatives. Building and strengthening partnerships with international stakeholders can help leverage resources and knowledge for more effective community development.
- **Social Entrepreneurship:** The rise of social entrepreneurship is expected to play a significant role in community organisation and development. Social entrepreneurs combine business principles with social impact goals, creating innovative solutions to address community challenges. The future may see a growing number of social enterprises in Egypt, focusing on areas such as education, healthcare, environmental sustainability, and poverty alleviation.
- **Cultural Preservation and Heritage:** Egypt has a rich cultural heritage, and preserving and promoting this heritage can be an integral part of community organisation efforts. Initiatives that focus on cultural preservation, heritage tourism, and the revitalisation of traditional crafts and arts can contribute to community development by creating economic opportunities, preserving local identities, and fostering a sense of pride and belonging.

- **Data-Driven Approaches:** The use of data and evidence-based approaches will become increasingly important in community organisation and development. Collecting and analysing data can help identify community needs, monitor progress, and evaluate the impact of interventions. Data-driven approaches enable community organisations to make informed decisions, target resources effectively, and measure the effectiveness of their programs.
- **Strengthening Local Governance:** Strengthening local governance structures and fostering decentralisation can enhance community organisation and development. Empowering local authorities and promoting participatory decision-making processes can ensure that community development initiatives are responsive to the specific needs and priorities of local communities.
- **Cross-Sector Collaboration:** The future of community organisation in Egypt will involve increased collaboration among various sectors, including government, civil society, academia, and the private sector. Cross-sector partnerships can leverage diverse expertise and resources to tackle complex community challenges holistically. Collaborative platforms, networks, and forums can facilitate knowledge exchange, coordination, and joint action.

Discussion

This chapter has comprehensively explored the history, key concepts, contemporary practices, challenges, and prospects of community organisation and development in Egypt. It offers valuable insights into the evolving landscape of this crucial field, highlighting both the successes and challenges faced in empowering communities and fostering sustainable development.

The chapter effectively traces the historical roots of community organisation in Egypt, from early efforts by foreign communities to the formalisation of government programs and the emergence of social work methods. This historical context provides a valuable foundation for understanding the present state and future directions of community organisation.

The chapter clarifies the concept of community organisation in the Egyptian context, drawing on various definitions and emphasising its core values of social justice, empowerment, and community participation. This helps to establish a shared understanding of the goals and principles guiding community development initiatives.

The review of recent literature sheds light on key themes in contemporary community organisation practices. These include a focus on social development issues, community empowerment, partnership building, and the utilisation of technology. This highlights the dynamic and multifaceted nature of community organisation in Egypt.

The chapter addresses the challenges facing community organisation in Egypt, including limited resources, sustainability concerns, political limitations, and rapid population growth. Recognising these challenges is crucial for developing effective strategies and overcoming obstacles to progress.

The analysis of the future of community organisation and development offers a hopeful outlook. It emphasises the potential of civic engagement, technology, social entrepreneurship, and data-driven approaches to contribute to sustainable development. Moreover, the chapter highlights the importance of international cooperation, cross-sector collaboration, and the strengthening of local governance.

Overall, this chapter provides a valuable resource for scholars, practitioners, and policymakers interested in community organisation and development in Egypt. By fostering dialogue and further research, it can contribute to the advancement of this field and the empowerment of communities in Egypt.

Conclusion

Community development and organisation play vital roles in the socio-economic progress and overall well-being of Egypt. Firstly, it has become evident that community development initiatives in Egypt offer a platform for fostering social cohesion, empowering individuals, and strengthening local networks. Moreover, community organisations in Egypt have been instrumental in mobilising resources, advocating for the rights of marginalised groups, and promoting inclusive development. These organisations serve as catalysts for change, facilitating dialogue between different stakeholders, and fostering collaboration among community members, civil society, and government institutions. Furthermore, it is important to acknowledge the unique cultural context of Egypt, which influences community development approaches. Cultural heritage, traditions, and values play a significant role in shaping community dynamics and influencing the effectiveness of development interventions. It is essential to continue investing in community development, addressing the challenges, and leveraging the strengths of Egypt's diverse communities to drive meaningful and lasting change.

This chapter has provided valuable insights into the importance of investing in community development by providing a valuable foundation for further research into specific aspects of community organisation and development in Egypt. Future studies could explore:

- In-depth analyses of successful community development initiatives and their impact.
- The role of specific actors, such as women, youth, or NGOs, in community organisation.
- The effectiveness of different technology tools and platforms in community development.
- The impact of political and economic contexts on community organisation practices.
- The cultural specificities of community organisation in different regions of Egypt.

References

Aaal, A.H. (1981). "Community Organisation in an Integrated Developmental Social Work: A Field Study". *National Social Journal, 18*(1): 123-41. http://search.mandumah.com/Record/233659

Afifi, N.A.H. (2023). "Contributions of NGOs Working in the Field of Women to Achieving Social Justice". *Cairo Journal for Social Work, 39*(1): 7-51. https://doi.org/10.21608/cjsw.2023.200445.1079

Ahmed, A. K. (1972). *Community Organisation* (second edition ed.). Modern Cairo Library.

Ahmed, A.K. (1975). *Community Organisation.* Anglo-Egyptian Library.

Ahmed, A.K. (1975). *Community Organisation* (*Theories and Cases*). Anglo-Egyptian Library.

Ahmed, K., Ahmed, A. & Suleiman (1963). *Social Work and Community.* Modern Cairo Library.

Amer, A.A. (2021). "The Demographic Variable and Its Impact on the Egyptian Personality". *Journal of Democracy, 21*(84): 70-72. http://search.mandumah.com/Record/1230533

Amin, M.A. (2019). "Community Expectations for Achieving Partnership Between the Community Organisation Department and Civil Society Organisations in Aswan Governorate". *Social Work Journal, 62*(2): 157-224. https://doi.org/10.21608/EGJSW.2019.172378

Ammar, D.A. (2023). "Achieving the Goals of Engineering as a Modern Approach in Community Organisation Method to Training Employees of the Educational Administration in the Bahariya Oasis". *Journal of Education, 42*(198): 528-64. https://doi.org/10.21608/jsrep.2023.310625

Badran, H. (1999). *Community Organisation.* Al-Meligy Press.

Darwish, Y.H. (1978). *Mediator in Community Organisation in Social Work.* Cairo: Dar Al Safa Press.

Fahmy, K. (1997). *All the Pasha's Men: Mehmed Ali, His Army and the Making of Modern Egypt.* Cambridge University Press.

Halim, H.S. (2015). "Empowering Student Unions in Term of Community Organisation". *Social Work Journal, 53*: 239-61. http: //search.mandumah.com/Record/699336

Hammad, S.R. (2019). "Online Advocacy of Clients' Rights within the Framework of Community Organisation". *Scientific Journal of Social Work—Applied Studies and Research, 9*(1): 297-306.

Hassan, A.B. (1970). *Social Development.* Institute of Arab Research and Studies, International Press.

Hassan, A.H. (2019). *Techniques of Community Organisation in Activating Anti-corruption Committees in the Government Sector in Egypt* (Unpublished thesis). Faculty of Social Work, Assiut University.

Hassanein, S.A. (1974). *Social Work Method in Community Organisation.* Anglo-Egyptian Library.

Imam, H.M. (2023). "Community Participation of Rural Women Pioneers in Developing Community Awareness of the Hayah Karema Initiative: Study from the Perspective of Community Organisation Method". *Social Work Journal, 75*(2): 165-205. http://search.mandumah.com/Record/1376848

Iman Abdel-Al Ahmed (2021). "The Contributions of Health Initiatives to Improving the Women Lives from the Perspective of Community Organisation Method". *College of Social Work Journal for Social Studies and Research, 23*(2): 163-95. https://doi.org/10.21608/jfss.2021.158175

Latif, R.A. (1998). "A Framework of Practice in Community Organisation Method". *Journal of Studies in Social Work and Human Sciences, 5*, 13-23. http://search.mandumah.com/record115436

Ministry of Social Affairs (1961). *Evaluation of Associations and Social Institutions.* Information Management.

Ministry of Social Affairs (1964). *Ministry of Social Affairs for 25 Years.* The Technical Department.

Muhammad, S.B. (2016). "The Role of Partnership in Supporting the Ability of Universities to Serve Community: A Future Vision in Terms of Community Organisation". *Social Work Journal, 55*: 83-134. http://search.mandumah.com/Record/763811

Saleh, A.M. (2023). "Digital Skills for University Students from the Perspective of Community Organisation Method". *Scientific Journal of Social Service—Applied Studies and Research, 21*(4): 60-84.

Salem, H.M. (2016). "Challenges of Democratic Transformation After the Arab Spring Revolutions: An Analytical Study of the Egyptian Case". *Annals of Etiquette, Ain Shams, 44*: 13-45. https://doi.org/10.21608/aafu.2016.9671

Shawqi, A.M. (1961). *Community Development and Organisation.* Modern Cairo Library.

Taher, M. (2023). "The Level of Institutional Empowerment in Universities and the Mechanisms for Achieving It : The Perspective of Community Organisation". *Journal of the College of Social Work for Social Studies and Research, 31*(4): 85-112.

8

Faith Based Organisation and Rural Development

The Case of Chinmaya Organisation for Rural Development (CORD), Thondamuthur, Coimbatore

Kanagaraj, S.

Introduction

Traditionally, India has a long history of contributions created by faith-based organisations to cater to the varied desires of society. It plays a significant role in addressing many desires like religious, social, community, etc.; significantly, it strengthens the community and helps it develop holistically. Many faith-based organisations are creating serious efforts for rural development with professional social work techniques for solving issues within the community. Therefore, it is essential to understand the role of FBOs in rural development. Faith-based organisations are unit of grass-roots organisations active regionally but also globally. Their funding is from donations; however, they are additionally eligible for state, national or international grants. Currently, the World Bank readies funds for international faith-based organisations. The main objective of faith-based organisations is to nurture faith where non-secular imaging accompanies serving (Ebaugh, Pipes, Chafetz & Daniels, 2003).

Social Activists have begun looking for temples, churches, mosques, and alternative faith-based organisations to be crucial in strengthening communities. However, very little analysis exists on the role of CORD (Chinmaya Organisation for Rural Development), a faith-based organisation in Rural development with a vision to supply more information about FBOs. Some studies publish very little information concerning the FBOs. Hester (2003) described how spirituality and faith-based organisations could be practical for drug abuse treatment; R. Moss gave information about Faith-Based Social Services: Measures, Assessments then effectiveness and from the studies on Faith-based and secular humanitarian organisations by Elizabeth Ferris, (International Review of Red Cross, 2005), scholars may able to apprehend the partial information of faith non-governmental organisations, their objectives and different activities in several spaces. This study aims to analyse the beneficiaries or recipients of CORD in rural development. Positive association with a spiritual body, predetermined objectives concerning named spiritual values, funding from a religious association or a government organisation, wherever the choice of board members relies on spiritual beliefs, leads to decision-making processes supported by spiritual values (Jayasinghe, 2007).

About CORD

CORD provides a ground for people to perform selfless service. Swami Chinmayananda initiated a rural health care and community development program to facilitate integrated and sustainable development in rural communities throughout India by preaching self-empowerment processes. CORD (Chinmaya Organisation for Rural Development) is a service wing of Chinmaya Mission that operates as a Trust and non-governmental organisation facilitating integrated, participatory and sustainable development in the rural areas of Odisha, Tamil Nadu, Andhra Pradesh and Himachal

Pradesh through steering, financing and monitoring. It's been active within holistic rural development for over 20 years. It facilitates integrated rural development in villages. The involvement of spiritual organisations in welfare and charitable activities has a long history, and they play an essential role in rural development. The vital role of faith-based organisations is to uplift the social conditions of the communities. Ancient donors used to follow a profane approach for social-helping. It has been known that in the past, Christian, Muslim, Buddhist, and alternative faith-based organisations provided native as well as international services to poor and deprived communities, which gave existence to a parallel universe of faith-based evolution.

According to the studies by Berger (2003), faith-based voluntary organisations are often outlined as formal organisations that aim to seek a self-consciously derived identity by practising the teachings of one or more religious traditions and a non-profit making, independent voluntary service to understand collectively articulated concepts concerning general public sensibility on national and international grounds. Although faith-based voluntary organisations operate within a particular legal and political framework of profane civil society institutions, their works and operations are guided by divine thought and the sacred nature of life (Anhelm, 1999).

Faith is essential to a significant section of developing countries, and many local organisations work primarily based on the substantial word "faith". This chapter summarises the present data state and identifies the policy conclusions and role of religion primarily based Organisation in Rural Development. As a result of the research, this report additionally attracts interviews with knowledgeable students and practitioners in community development.

Objectives

The focus is to analyse the contribution of CORD as a faith-based organisation in the field of rural development and the primary objectives are:

1. Investigate CORD's multifaceted approaches to rural development, analysing the spectrum of projects and activities initiated to address diverse community needs.
2. Examine the organisational structure and administrative framework of CORD, exploring how its internal dynamics contribute to efficient project implementation and sustainable impact.
3. Evaluate the significant achievements of CORD across various domains of rural development, highlighting key milestones and success stories that showcase its effectiveness.
4. Identify and analyse the prevalent social challenges prevalent in rural areas that CORD actively addresses, delineating its strategies to tackle issues such as poverty, healthcare, education, and infrastructure.
5. Assess the tangible and intangible impact of CORD's interventions on rural communities, measuring changes in socio-economic indicators, community empowerment, and overall well-being to gauge the organisation's transformative influence.

Research Methodology

The findings of this study have been analysed using both a qualitative and a quantitative approach. The data was analysed under the qualitative data analysis software package of QDA Miner, version 5.0.19. The tools used for Data collection is a Semi-structured interview schedule by using:

(i) Free listing method and key Informant interview (Participant observation method and through the experience of researcher's academic fieldwork).
(ii) Free listing method—Beneficiaries.
(iii) Key Informant Interview—Project Director & Senior Staff.
(iv) Participant observation—Project Director & Senior Staff, Beneficiaries.

(v) Pre-Testing during Field work—Researcher took Preliminary possible information from the respondents. It was Reliable for the study.

Criteria

The main criteria that were followed for this research are: (1) utilised 'faith-based organisations in rural development', (2) included a qualitative and quantitative research design, (3) papers published in English, and (4) papers published in peer-reviewed journals listed in either Sage journals or Scopus. All other studies and articles were excluded.

Process of Searching Documents and Sampling Criteria

This study used a search machine: Scopus. Scopus recorded only 23 documents (articles) between 2001 and 2018 on 'faith-based Organisations'. The Universe is Researcher Collected CORD's (Chinmaya Organisation for Rural Development) beneficiaries list. The universe has 238 beneficiaries of 2 villages. The researcher selected 60 samples by using the Systematic Random sampling method.

Narrowing the Sample

The researcher selected 60 samples. By using the Systematic Random sampling method from the list of 238, the first one was randomly picked at 3; from that onwards, systematically selected 3, 6, 9 and so on up to the 60th beneficiary.

Sample Frames are:
18 Males and 42 females (18+42 = 60)
2 Leaders in the village, three field staff of CORD
Sources of Data Collection
Primary Data from Beneficiaries
Leaders [2], field staff [3]
Project Director
Beneficiaries [18+42=60]

Secondary data

Annual Reports

Project Proposals

Program Notices

Legal and official documents from CORD.

Data Analysis: Theme Extraction and Synthesis

While analysing the different aspects of the cases from respondents that the researcher had gone through while conducting the study, many factors contributed to different objectives' attributes. Through the free listing method and critical informant interviews, the researcher assimilated more information. The data was analysed under the qualitative data analysis software package of QDA Miner, version 5.0.19.

Review Findings and Discussion

Establishment of Chinmaya Organisation for Rural Development CORD

In 1985, Parampujya Gurudev Swami Chinmayananda founded CORD. The organisation started working towards integrated rural development in Sidhabhari in Himachal Pradesh under the guidance of Chinmaya Thapovan Trust as a rural primary health care and training centre. Eighteen years later, in 2003, Pujya Guruji Swami Thejomayananda established CORD as a separate trust to replicate rural development work. It initially started as a primary health care centre and later shifted on to CORD (Chinmaya Organisation for Rural Development).

The Prominent Faces Responsible for the Establishment of CORD

The Pujya Gurudev Swami Chinmayananda, head of the Chinmaya mission, was mainly responsible for the establishment. He motivated others to start the organisation in rural areas to fulfil rural development's primary needs and wants. Dr. Shama Matre, a

Padmashri awardee, is the primary person responsible for starting CORD under Swami Chinmayananda's guidance.

Core motivation for the establishment

Pujya Gurudev saw that the women of Himachal Pradesh, who had been serving the saints and sages in the Himalayas for years, were very backward and needed help. This is the core motivation to begin CORD by Guruji.

CORD: The Historical Perspectives

In 1985, CORD's activities started under the Chinmaya Rural Primary Health Centre and Training Centre, and then CORD was established in 2003 as a separate trust. The CORD work was replicated in areas like Orissa and Tamilnadu in 2005. On 2nd October 2006, CORD Siruvani started. It was started as a means of women's empowerment in all aspects like politics, health, society, and economics. Which are the primary goals of CORD.

CORD, Siruvani was started on 2nd October 2006 in a rented building. It initially started working on a single panchayat, Thenamanlur panchyath, focus panchayat, because CORD work on all aspects in all wards, then we extended to Ikkaraiboluvampatti panchayath (2013) and Vellimalaipattinam (2014). The CORD office shifted as own building in 2015.

The Goals of CORD

The CORD aims at integrated sustainable participatory rural development and women empowerment in all aspects (political, health, social, economic) in the concerned areas. The significant problems addressed by the CORD are especially women-related problems, Alcoholism, Farming problems, Economic problems, Marginalisation, etc.

Beneficiaries of CORDS's Intervention

The beneficiaries of CORD interventions are women in the rural areas where CORD works, especially marginalised women, i.e., underprivileged single deserted by husbands or other sections of society, Scheduled Caste and the overall focus was on all around women development and especially farmers (small and marginal farmers).

Major Services of CORD for Rural Communities

The main service is community-based organisations like Mahila Mandal, self-help groups, farmer's clubs, community-based rehabilitation centres for persons with different abilities, Youth groups, both male and women, Balvihar, etc. Through these, the CORD empowers the people. CORD has an annual plan based on people's requirements. The yearly plan is broken down into quarterly plans and budgets, and the work is executed in the various sectors.

Swami Chimayananda ji's philosophy guides the work of the CORD.

The guruji's philosophy guides the work of the CORD to help the poorest people in the community and the needy through spiritual guidance. Gurudev said, "Everybody has the potential to develop; they all possess the one great gift, the ability to discover and develop the infinite possibilities within us". He feels everybody has the potential to develop, and CORD's job is to help them develop that potential. For women, the empowerment cord will do everything but will only ignite the spark in the people who improve themselves; through that they improve themselves and the people around them. It is like a repelling effect; one person gets empowered, and he empowers other people so that it grows. This is the strategy for empowerment.

Legal Status of CORD

It is legally registered as a public charitable trust with its office at 89, Ruthy Road, New Delhi. Registered under the Indian Registration Act with the Income Tax Act, 1961. CORD mobilises resources for its intervention from the CORD's Head office in Delhi. People participate in CORD interventions through community-based organisations, mainly through Mahila Mandal (Women's group) and its several subgroups. (*Source: CORD administrators, beneficiaries*)

CORD Administration Structure

The efficacy of the CORD is basically the result of good administrative measures. The administrative structure has been derived in a format that facilitates the rural ethnos. Every staff members are provided regular training for upgrading their skills.

Economic, Political & Social Background of the Beneficiaries

There are more Scheduled Castes than the backward caste; around 58 per cent of the Scheduled Caste and the backward caste about 40 per cent are the beneficiaries of the CORD. The CORD focuses on poor people who have to live with a primary livelihood and basic ability to stand up in society. Most people are going for daily wages to meet their daily expenses. From the respondents, the researcher selected beneficiaries, field staffs, non-beneficiaries, and village leaders. From this, the researcher gathered relevant knowledge. Most of the villages are poor; about 55 per cent and 45 per cent (from Scheduled Castes and Backward Castes) have a middle economic status. In this community, all people reside in rural areas and are not affiliated with the political party.

Evaluation about CORD's Initiative

The researcher found that the CORD's services are very relevant to the community's problems, and 96.67 per cent of people are satisfied about the services provided by CORD.

Problems Faced by the People in this Community

The problems faced by the people in the community located in Thondamuthur Block, Coimbatore District, Tamil Nadu, India are: alcoholism is the central issue faced in the mentioned community. Drainage systems and improper waste management are this community's other leading focal issues. From the data, it was identified that 56.70 per cent of the community faces this major problem. There are other problems such as, sanitation, water scarcity, and other issues in public management. The prospect of cultural dynamism, research concludes that 1.70 per cent of people also had less unity in their village.

Activities Undertaken by CORD in this Community

The primary activity was to strengthen Mahila Mandal, i.e., women's group. This women's group leads all CORD activities simultaneously and stays as the nucleus for the flagship program in CORD. About 91.70 per cent of the women in the populace were associated with the Mahila Mandal directed by CORD. Alongside women empowerment, the CORD took initiatives for empowerment of farmer's club. The farmer's club's activity reached the people well, and about 63.30 per cent took benefits of all CORD. Medical Camp initiative is also critical set of activities by CORD Siruvani. Around 37 per cent are got benefit in this noble activity held by CORD. The other significant activity is building toilets. About 70 per cent respondent took benefit in this scheme.

Beneficiaries of the Services of CORD

Women are the highest number of beneficiaries, and precisely 98.30 per cent of women got benefitted from the CORD's service, followed by children and farmers. The CORD's intervention benefited 73 per cent of children and 50 per cent of farmers.

Changes in the Community Because of the Activities of the CORD

The changes came in the community after the intervention of the CORD. A large size of the population are satisfied with changes in the behaviour and usage of toilets in the community. 63.30 per cent of the people avoided plastics because of their awareness of CORD, and they have taken an important role in changes in the community. CORD is also doing waste segregation in the particular community.

Conclusion

This study has widely justified the effectiveness of a faith-based organisation in rural development. CORD Siruvani is one such organisation that implies a substantial developmental model for rural development. The researcher found alcoholism to be a significant issue in the community. So, an exclusive de-addiction centre by CORD could help the people in that community solve this problem. CORD is the light bearer for women empowerment initiatives in Indian realms in rural developmental arena. Women empowerment signifies the authority to make democratic decisions, which has been portrayed in an exemplary manner in CORD via the medium of Mahila Mandal. Results show that Rural development lays its foundation on education. CORD's community has witnessed a substantial growth rate of 31.67 per cent of people attaining high school level education. The same could be remodelled in different rural terrains in India.

Mahila Mandal (Women's Association) is the most vital initiative of CORD. Women's empowerment is widely given consideration and is facilitated to be the nucleus of a milestone achievement by the CORD. The education and development of this community and the reduction of alcohol consumption are closely associated with profound intervention from Mahila Mandal. However, what still renders a challenge that has yet to be addressed is impoverished waste management. The CORD's philanthropic activity has notably contributed to a broader scope of infrastructural development than the waste segregation unit in Boluvampatti. This is not just a high-end achievement but also ideal for rural and urban development. In the present context of India, the farming community has been confronted with a wide range of problems. CORD comprehends the deep-ended need and intervenes with the farmers' club. This again is a notable milestone initiative of CORD Siruvani. As M.K. Gandhi gospels about the rural community as the backbone of India in the same enlightened prospect *Swami Tejomayananda* (*World-wide head of Chinmaya Mission*) renders, "CORD is a bond of love and understanding encouraging a process of sharing which enriches both the giver and the receiver. In giving and serving, the giver grows spiritually, and the receiver is blessed with the power of transformation".

References

Asomugha, C.N. (2011). "Faith-Based Organisations, Science, and the Pursuit of Health". *J Health Care Poor Underserved*. https://doi.org/10.1353/hpu.2011.0008

Bernard R.A. (2008). "Faith-Based Social Services: Measures, Assessments and Effectiveness". *The British Journal of Social Work, 38*(2): 302. https://doi.org/10.1093/bjsw/bcm167

Bradley, T. (2005). "Does Compassion Bring Results? A Critical Perspective on Faith and Development". *Culture and Religion, 6*(3): 337-51. https://doi.org/10.1080/01438300500460401

Candice, N. & Watson, B.S. (2009). *Faith-based Organisations and their Contributions to Society*. Retrieved from http://www.bing.com/cr?IG=DDD3976154D845E88C57A6A352D47D3F&CID=38E7B5CF42C76D471E0ABEFD43C16CFF&rd=1&h=2djbY15bFSxQ4_cZ06MyJ8KNJLuJyxSbNMD0LvNOPnc&v=1&r=http%3a%2f%2fopensiuc.lib.siu.edu%2fcgi%2fviewcontent.cgi%3farticle%3d1397%26context%3dgs_rp&p=DevEx,5066.1

Chikwendu, E. (2004). "Faith-Based Organisations in Anti-HIV/AIDS Work Among African Youth and Women". *Dialectical Anthropology, 28*(3-4): 307-27. https://doi.org/10.1007/s10624-004-3589-1

Erik van Ommering (M.Sc., VU University, Amsterdam), *The Roles of Faith-based Educational Institutions in Conflict Transformation in Fragile States.*

Ferris, E. (2005). "Faith-based and Secular Humanitarian Organisations". *International Review of the Red Cross, 87*(858), 311. https://doi.org/10.1017/s1816383100181366

Flanigan, S.T. (2007). "Paying for God's Work: A Rights-Based Examination of Faith-Based NGOs in Romania". *VOLUNTAS: International Journal of Voluntary and Non-profit Organisations, 18*(2): 156-75. https://doi.org/10.1007/s11266-007-9035-7

From Faith Missions to Churches, 1800s to 1930s. *Pentecostal Churches in Transition*, 27-80. https://doi.org/10.1163/ej.9789004175266.i-250.9

Grills, N. (2009). *The Paradox of Multilateral Organisations Engaging with Faith-based Organisations*. Retrieved from http://journals.rienner.com/doi/pdf/10.5555/ggov.2009.15.4.505

Holenstein, A. (2005). "Governmental Donor Agencies and Faith-based Organisations". *International Review of the Red Cross, 87*(858): 367. https://doi.org/10.1017/s1816383100181391

Jayasinghe, S. (2007). "Faith-based NGOs and Health Care in Poor Countries: A Preliminary Exploration of Ethical Issues". *Journal of Medical Ethics, 33*(11): 623-26. https://doi.org/10.1136/jme.2006.018549

Johnsen, S. (2014). "Wheres the 'Faith' in 'Faith-Based' Organisations? The Evolution and Practice of Faith-Based Homelessness Services in the UK". *Journal of Social Policy, 43*(02): 413-30. https://doi.org/10.1017/s0047279413001001

Lee, D. & Kong, L. (2015). "Effecting Environmental Change: The Challenges of Transnational Environmental Faith-Based Organisations". *The Changing World Religion Map*, 2983-2996.

Levin, J. (2016). "Partnerships between the Faith-based and Medical Sectors: Implications for Preventive Medicine and Public Health". *Preventive Medicine Reports*, 4, 344-350. https://doi.org/10.1016/j.pmedr.2016.07.009

Lunn, J. (2009). "The Role of Religion, Spirituality and Faith in Development: A Critical Theory Approach". *Third World Quarterly, 30*(5), 937-951. https://doi.org/10.1080/01436590902959180

Monsma, S.V. (2003). "Non-profit and Faith-based Welfare-to-work Programmes". *Society, 40*(2): 13-18. https://doi.org/10.1007/s12115-003-1047-3

Pandya, S.P. (2013). "Beneficiaries of Social Initiatives of Indic Faith-Based Organisations". *SAGE Open, 3*(2): 215824401348968. https://doi:10.1177/2158244013489688

Parry, S. (2003). "Responses of the faith-based organisations to HIV/AIDS in Sub Saharan Africa". *Geneva: Ecumenical HIV/AIDS Initiative in Africa*, World Council of Churches.

Patel, P. (2011). "Women Migrants and Faith Organisations: Changing Regimes of Gender, Religion and Race in London". *Feminist Review, 97*(1): 142-150. https://doi.org/10.1057/fr.2010.39

Ronald D. Hester. (November 2002). Spirituality and Faith-based Organisations: their role in Substance Abuse Treatment. *Administration and Policy in Mental Health.*

Samta Pandya, S. (2014). *Seva as a Form of Faith-Based Social Work in India.* Retrieved from https://globaljournals.org/GJHSS_Volume14/1-Seva-as-a-Form-of-Faith-Based.pdf

Samta Pandya, S. (2016). "Seva in Mata Amritanandamayi Mission: Social Service as a Public Face of Faith". *Implicit Religion, 19*(3): 401-23. https://doi.org/10.1558/imre.v19i3.31114

Santiago, R.L. (2009). "Faith-Based Organisations and Public Health". *Igniting the Power of Community,* 93-108. https://doi:10.1007/978-0-387-98157-4_7

Stoecker, R. (2007). "Visions of Development: Faith-based Initiatives". *Community Development Journal, 43*(2): 254-56. https://doi.org/10.1093/cdj/bsn004

Vidal, A.C. (2001). *Faith-based Organisations in Community Development.* Washington DC: The Office.

Zehavi, A. (2008). "The Faith-based Initiative in Comparative Perspective: Making Use of Religious Providers in Britain and the United States". *Comparative Politics, 40*(3): 331-51. https://doi.org/10.5129/001041508x12911362383110

9

Vipassana

The Buddha's Therapeutic Model for Psychiatric and Correctional Social Work Practice

Geetanjali

Introduction

Mindfulness-based practice in the social work domain is getting recognition more widely and very fast. Compatible with social work values, meditation assumes that human nature is good rather than flawed (Keefe, 2011). Uses of meditation effectiveness and use in social work practice were conducted by Wang (2018). The study conducted by Wang, D.S. in 2018 shows its utility in the social work domain. And this study makes it more specific by focusing on meditation at the next level, which is "Vipassana" as a therapeutic model in psychiatric social work practice as well as correctional social work practice. Generally, meditation techniques are frequently connected to spirituality and religion. Though closely related, meditation does not always have to be connected to religion and can be used for purposes that are quite separate from it. Beyond the wall of spirituality and religion, Buddha's meditation technique, *vipassana*, has great potential in the area where intro-inspecting leads to thinking constructively and helps with decision-making that focuses on the present moment, which is not affected by overthinking either about unchangeable pasts or uncertain future thoughts. A well-defined state of undifferentiated awareness can be attained through meditation practices (Keefe, 2011). These practices reduce unnecessary and unproductive "background mental noise" by keeping the focus on the present moment and away from unchangeable past or uncertain future thoughts (Arias, Steinberg, Banga, & Trestman, 2006). Meditation is the best adjunct model for curing social deviance. According to Lee *et al.* (2011), there is a theoretical connection between social work practice and meditation. Besides meditation's neurobiological impacts, self-determination theory and system perceptions are also incorporated into the practice.

Methodology

A desk review study was conducted to examine the applicability of *vipassana* in conjunction with psychiatric and correctional social work in improving mental health and reducing deviant behaviour in individuals. An online portal was used to gather secondary data, which was then examined for its enormous potential in the field of social work. No review has been found on *vipassana*: the Buddha's Therapeutic model for psychiatric and correctional social work practice in a collaborative form which could be a future recommendation.

What is *Vipassana*?

The *vipassana* technique, a hidden practice handed down by Gautam Buddha, has profound implications for human physical, mental, social, psychological, and spiritual aspects.

In one sentence "Vipassana is a way of self-transformation through self-observation". This is a very old technique and non-sectarian technique which provides the art of living. It was rediscovered by Gautama Buddha more than 2500 years ago and was taught by him as a universal remedy for universal ills. At Bodh

Gaya, India, in 589 BC, Buddha affirmed the way to enlightenment and the supreme aim of existence. Buddha taught a number of insights on how to improve society. Buddhism is practiced in several forms today, such as *Theravada, Zen, Vajrayana,* and *Mahayana*. *vipassana* meditation, popularised by Mahasi Sayadaw and S.N. Goenka, is a form of *Theravada* Buddhism, based on Buddha's teachings emphasising self-examination for liberation from the cycle of *Samsara* (birth, death, and rebirth). There are the four objects of attention in *satipatthana vipassana bhavana*, first acts of bodily behaviour;

Second Feelings or sensations; third Acts of consciousness; and fourth is Mind-objects. During *vipassana* three events occur in such meditation in successive order: first Arising of the phenomenon; second Observing or noticing of the phenomenon that arises and What the *yogi* comes to know and "see" (Sayadaw Mahasi, 2016).

More information about *vipassana* can be seen in Mr. Goenka's videos on *vipassana*. Goenka (2014) says, "It is a method of self-transformation through self-observation which focuses on the deep interconnection between mind and body". Goenka concludes that *vipassana* can be practiced by all. It is the only way to reach *Nibbana*—the road of equanimity and is a ten-day silent meditation technique taught by S.N. Goenka under the guidance of assistant teachers.

Psychiatric Social Work and *Vipassana*

Social work is a rainbow practice. Which embark colour of empowerment, liberation, social change and development, social cohesion. (Global Definition of Social Work, n.d.)

In order to help the people to attain their own personal and community well-being, social workers may support them on their path through change by equipping them with the necessary skills, information, and competence. On the mental side, *vipassana* can lead to increased self-awareness, emotional intelligence, improved focus and cognitive function, better emotional regulation, reduced anxiety and depression, and the cultivation of inner peace and happiness (Verma, 2023). Therefore, it is useful in the field of psychiatric social work, persons who are not able to do his or her daily activity suffering from trauma like PTSD or any kind of depression, can channelise their thinking process through the self-actualisation. Buddhist technique of self-observation is also known as *vipassana*. Meditation is an essential part of daily life since it broadens one's viewpoint, lowers stress levels, and increases one's physical and mental well-being, all of which contribute to a more balanced lifestyle and improved psychological well-being. By promoting harmonious, caring, and fulfilling interactions, a greater sense of self-awareness can improve relationships, mental health, and general life satisfaction (Verma, 2023). Before introducing *vipassana* to the client it is very necessary to make proper understanding about the technique and proper undertaking is required otherwise it may be detrimental. Like receiving traditional modes of therapy, there can be difficult moments when things are revealed or strong emotions and reactions arise, and without proper guidance and support, can result in adverse effects (Wang, 2018). For example, individuals with schizophrenia may increase their experience of depersonalisation and self-preoccupation through meditation (Keefe, 2011).

Some formal meditation practices may be daunting or unappealing (or inappropriate at the time) for some individuals for various reasons (Wang, 2018). A social worker can help reduce resistance to meditation practices rooted in Eastern religion and philosophy by providing education, presenting information in an acceptable manner, and reducing misconceptions. Than by proper acceptance only it will help clients to overcome with his or her difficulties.

In a research by De Sousa *et al.* (2022), *vipassana* meditation has shown effectiveness in reducing psychosocial problems among individuals with alcohol dependence syndrome.

In 1994, a research was carried out on 21 inmates of India's Tihar Jail who had suffered from psychiatric disorders. In the jail, they participated in a ten-day *vipassana* residential course.

After the course, depression and anxiety were reported to have significantly decreased, with 70 per cent of participants demonstrating a clinical improvement and not requiring therapy. Similar to this, the PGI well-being scale was used both before and after *vipassana* to 120 prisoners. According to Chandiramani *et al.* (1998), there was also an unanticipated improvement in well-being, including happiness, emotional control, satisfaction, and freedom from disease and worry.

A mindfulness qualitative study by Darby and Bevan (2017) with six Australian healthcare practitioners revealed that five out of six participants improved acceptance skills, interoceptive awareness, self-judgment, anxiety, equanimity, emotional regulation, interpersonal relationships, and enjoyed loving kindness. Five out of six individuals exhibited better emotional regulation, indicating strong interpersonal relationships with family members and close friends (Lama & Aryal, 2022).

Correctional Social Work and *Vipassana*

Vipassana meditation enhances self-awareness, emotional intelligence, interpersonal relationships, and communication skills by encouraging practitioners to observe thoughts, feelings, and bodily sensations without judgment. Self-awareness enhances emotional intelligence, enabling better understanding of reactions and empathy, leading to stronger interpersonal relationships and improved communication skills (Goenka, 2014). Buddha's teachings emphasise the importance of meditation for understanding reality and problem-solving, as it helps individuals understand and address their unique challenges.

Meditation plays the most important role to understand the reality of the facts. Accordingly, meditation is the most effective means of comprehending and resolving human issues (Buddhist Text Translation Society, 1998). *Vipassana* meditation can significantly transform human life by fostering mindfulness, self-awareness, and emotional flexibility, leading to a deeper understanding of oneself and the world (Verma, 2023). Like Tihar

Jail, similar studies conducted in Baroda Central Jail, Chandiramani *et al.* (1994) investigated the effects of *vipassana* meditation on antisocial behaviour, personality, and other psychological factors like well-being, hostility, hope, and nakedness among jail inmates. The study revealed a remarkable reduction in the neurotic tendencies, aggression, hostility, and helplessness mindset among the 120 convicts. Simultaneously, the participants' hope and well-being were enhanced through participation in *vipassana* courses. Jail Superintendent Vora (n.d.) claims that the *vipassana* courses conducted at Baroda Central Jail strengthened the rapport between the inmates and the jail staff (Lama & Aryal, 2022). In 1992, the first *Vipassana* camp was held in Baroda Central Jail, benefiting the entire 1,250-person prison population with its beneficial courses, followed by three more *vipassana* camps which included 310 inmates and 23 jail staff, demonstrated significant changes and success beyond our expectations after the initial course. (*Jail Courses and Vipassana/Vipassana Research Institute*, n.d.). That time Mrs. Kiran Bedi, was Inspector General of Prisons' she said "I was searching for a method which could help in transforming the inmates of the jail. I have found that in *Vipassana*." Another significant change observed in inmates, who participated in *vipassana* have been able to give up their addictions to drugs, intoxicants, smoking, etc.

Rehabilitation for offenders is increasingly becoming an integral part of the future of correctional facilities worldwide (Edward, M., 2021). *Vipassana* make rehabilitation process more easily. The adaptation of classical and response conditioning are enhanced by *vipassana*. It aids in the management of trauma, cognitive distortions, and emotional dysregulation, all of which contribute to maladaptive behaviour. *Vipassana* is recommended as a possible benefit for treatment techniques by Therapeutic Communities, mostly due to its structured therapeutic setting. Therapy-based interventions have shown significant efficacy in reducing recidivism rates, promoting lasting lifestyle changes for offenders. This approach goes beyond incarceration, fostering a more pro-social community. Over time, various therapy styles have been introduced into prison settings. Cognitive Behavioural Therapy (CBT), Dialectical Behaviour Therapy (DBT), Therapeutic Community (TC), and Mindfulness are but a few of the many types of therapies and interventions that have been developed and implemented within a correctional context (Edward, M., 2021). With regular practice of *vipassana,* awareness level increases and social workers are able to intervene easily and able to make positive changes in clients. Meditative practices could focus on moment-to-moment awareness of structural injustice; volunteers could ask participants to consider how one's personal self-improvement could be skilfully combined with efforts toward social or political change, through the lens of Buddhist concepts such as "right speech" and "right action" (Godrej F., 2022). Buddhist-derived interventions (BDIs) for incarcerated populations is conducted by Shonin *et al.,* (2013). Buddhist teachings suggest that a mind filled with unconditional love and compassion is free from negative predilections and incapable of intentionally causing harm. A systematic review of controlled studies on BDIs in correctional settings was conducted. Which results Intervention participants showed significant improvements in five key criminogenic variables: negative affect, drug-related attitudes, anger and hostility, relaxation capacity, and self-esteem and optimism (Shonin *et al.*, 2013).

Way to *Vipassana*

Dhamma centres are running all-over the world. Anyone who is in any mental or physical state if they are not in a critical or emergency situation and able to sit properly and meditate inside the centre for ten days then a person can experience a life changing experience—physical as well as mental. The mental condition will be upgraded to the highest form and purified. This is the process to attain the best version of a person. On 4th December, 1949, Mahasi Sayadaw personally instructed the very first batch of twenty-five meditators in the practice of *vipassana* (Sayadaw Mahasi, 2016). Currently, *vipassana* centres are running all-over the world. There are a total

242 Centres along with 128 Non-centres available all-over the world where anyone can register themselves. In Asia, 182 Centres and 28 Non-Centres and in India 114 Centres along with 14 Non-Centres are available.

Process for enrolment, functioning and routine in Dhamma centres: Through the official website www.dhamma.org, we can get more information about the courses, locations, special site and much more about its vision. By visiting its official website, anyone can get the information related to it and can also get information about where its centres are in the whole world and in different places and can also get information about whatever is being done at the centre. There are courses available from a particular date to a particular date that can be checked whether seats are vacant or not, it can also be checked how many seats are vacant for women and how many seats are vacant for men. And if the seat is vacant then you can submit your application online for the slot time. The application process is very simple, you have to enter some of your basic information and apply for the category under which you want to apply, like Male or Female and the date for which seats are available. And then after a few days you will be informed through email that your application has been accepted and in the same email, you are given complete information about what materials you have to bring with you. So, you should arrange all the required things and all the things and then take the print out of your application and reach the centre on the same date called for. It is necessary to mediate with right method, therefore, teaching assistant give proper instructions. The core concept of *vipassana* is mind and matter are impermanent things. Meditation helps to see impermanent things as sufferings, things that come and go, tormenting us and inspiring fear and anxiety is reduced by meditation. During *vipassana* persons try to see suffering as they really are. They are processes lacking in a personality, a soul, a self. You have to meditate to see that there is no personality, no soul, no self (Sayadaw Mahasi, 2016). *Vipassana* helps in reconstructing mental functioning, thinking process and purification of the mind. The practice of natural breathing helps focus and purify the mind, ultimately leading to the calmness of mind, free from all anxiety and depressions, helps to take right decision, overall helps persons in self-transformation through self-observation. The action is oriented by the order of mind; if the mind is free from anxiety and depression it can direct itself towards positive actions for the benefit of one and all (Lama & Aryal, 2022). 10-day Courses are an introductory course to *Vipassana* Meditation where the technique is taught step-by-step each day. The courses begin after a 2 - 4 pm registration period and orientation, followed by 10 full days of meditation, and end the morning of the 11th day by 7:30 am. *Vipassana* students are required to follow five precepts: abstain from killing, stealing, sexual activity, lying, and intoxication during the course. Like this *sīla* (moral conduct), several codes are listed on the website https://www.dhamma.org/en/about/code from where anyone know about the functional code of conduct in *dhamma* centres. Course timetable starts at 4:00 am and ends at 9:30 pm each day.

Conclusion

We draw the conclusion that the application of mindfulness-based practices in social service contexts holds considerable promise, especially when combined with many of the social work interventions now in use. Meditation teaches people to alter their relationship to their thoughts without specifically addressing and focusing on the difficulties that arise, as opposed to actively addressing and focusing on the content of trauma (Lee *et al.*, 2011). Research shows that the meditation technique "Vipassana" positively impacts physical, mental, social, and spiritual health by promoting focus, purification, and spiritual enlightenment through natural breathing (Lama & Aryal, 2022). The *vipassana* meditation technique is becoming more and more popular around the globe these days, and it is helping people overcome all of their ignorance, sorrow, and suffering (Verma, 2023). Persons as social worker client in psychiatric social work practices adopting *vipassana* meditation technique leads toward healthy, peaceful life and able to do some fruitful outcomes for their family and the society. *Vipassana* has played a significant role in helping prisoners become law-abiding citizens and in the general reform of prisons. It seeks to accomplish the goals of the government, improving the efficacy of inmate welfare and encouraging its broad implementation in other prisons. (*Jail Courses and Vipassana/Vipassana Research Institute*, n.d.). Persons who are in any kind of distress or deviant behaviour are able to make themselves more calm and able to improve their condition. For example, persons in any kind of trauma example heart rate variability, and personal burnout mindfulness in this context can be a more relatable, more practical, and more equitable practice, used to lift up, to heal, and to therefore make positive impacts, such as those found in this pilot study, tools to help improve mindfulness, foster greater emotional capacity, and decrease in burnout (Trammel *et al.*, 2020). If social worker's clients are more mindful and emotionally regulated, clients may sense or benefit more from psychiatric improvements and correctional mindset. It is therefore, regular practice of *vipassana* in psychiatric social work and correctional social work contributes positively to the advancement of happiness, relief, harmony, and peace in society.

References

Arias, A., Steinberg, K., Banga, A. & Trestman, R. (2006). "Systematic Review of the Efficacy of Meditation Techniques as Treatments for Medical Illness". *Journal of Alternative and Complementary Medicine*, *12*(8): 817-32.

Buddhist Text Translation Society. (1998). *Buddhism: A Brief Introduction*. Buddhist Text Translation Society.

Chandiramani, K., Dhar, P.L. & Verma, S.K. (1998). *Psychological effects of Vipassana on Tihar Jail Inmates*.

Darby, M. & Beavan, V. (2017). "Grist to the Mill: A Qualitative Investigation of Mindfulness-Integrated Cognitive Behaviour Therapy for Experienced Health Professionals". *Australian Psychologist*, *52*(6): 491-502. https://doi.org/10.1111/ap.12215

De Sousa, C.A.A., De Souza Vale, R.G., De Oliveira, L.M., Vale, J.K.L., Drigo, A.J., Pernambuco, C.S. & Borba-Pinheiro, C.J. (2022). "Meditação Vipassana sobre o estado de ansiedade, depressão e qualidade de vida de profissionais em isolamento social no período de lockdown-2020/COVID-19 (Vipassana meditation on anxiety state, depression and quality of life of professionals in social isolation in the lockdown period-2020/COVID-19) (Meditación Vipassana sobre el estado de ansiedad, depresión y calidad de vida de los profesionales en aislamiento social en el período de confinamiento-2020/COVID-19)". *Retos: Nuevas Tendencias En Educación Física, Deportes Y Recreación*, *46*: 705-13. https://doi.org/10.47197/retos.v46.93434

Edward, M. (2021). *Mindfulness-based Stress Reduction in a Correctional Facility: A Systematic Literature Review and Meta-Analysis on the Impact of Violent Behaviour* (Doctoral dissertation, The University of Waikato).

Global Definition of Social Work. (n.d.). Retrived from https://www.ifsw.org/what-is-social-work/global-definition-of-social-work/ on 10 February, 2024.

Godrej, F. (2022). "Yoga, Meditation, and Neoliberal Penalty: Compliance or Resistance?". *Political Research Quarterly*, *75*(1): 47-60.

Goenka, S.N. (2014). *Art of Dying*. Pariyatti Publishing.

Jail Courses and Vipassana/Vipassana Research Institute. (n.d.). Retrieved on 20 March 2024. From https://www.vridhamma.org/research/Jail-Courses-and-Vipassana

Keefe, T. (2011). "Meditation and Social Work Practice". *Social Work Treatment: Interlocking Theoretical Approaches*, New York: Oxford University Press, pp. 293-314.

Lama, S. & Aryal, B. (2022, December 31). "Interconnecting Vipassana with Human Health and School Curriculum". *Interdisciplinary Research in Education*. https://doi.org/10.3126/ire.v7i2.50473

Lee, M., Zaharlick, A. & Akers, D. (2011). "Meditation and Treatment of Female Trauma Survivors of Interpersonal Abuses: Utilising Clients' Strengths". *Families in Society*, *9*(2): 41-49.

Sayadaw, M. & Noe, M.T. (2002). *Fundamentals of Vipassana Meditation*. Buddhadhamma Foundation.

Shonin, E.S., Van Gordon, W., Slade, K. & Griffiths, M.D. (2013)."Mindfulness and Other Buddhist-Derived Interventions in Correctional Settings: A Systematic Review". *Aggression and Violent Behaviour*, *18*: 365-72.

Trammel, R.C., Park, G. & Karlsson, I. (2020, September 7). "Religiously Oriented Mindfulness for Social Workers: Effects on Mindfulness, Heart Rate Variability, and Personal Burnout". *Journal of Religion & Spirituality in Social Work: Social Thought*, *40*(1): 19-38. https://doi.org/10.1080/15426432.2020.1818358

Verma, A.K. (2023). "View of Buddhism and Vipassana Meditation: A Scientific Method for Mental and Social Growth in the Modern Age". *Millah: Journal of Religious Study, 22*(2): 583-610.

Wang, D.S. (2018). *Meditation in Social Work Practice: A Systematic Review of the Literature for Applicability and Utility*. www.jswep.in

10

Bhagavad Gita

An Ancient Example of Successful Counselling

Vandana Sinha

Introduction

Bhagavad Gita is a sacred and most worshipped Hindu scripture which gives us deep spiritual knowledge, knowledge of human behaviour, action which is morally right and of good relationship. *Bhagavad Gita* is 5000 years old scripture but the lessons of *Bhagavad Gita* is essential for our lives even today. For whole society there is lesson for human being that greed and lust for kingdom can ruin a man's present but if someone fights for truth and justice then it is permissible and should be appreciated. It is believed that the teachings of the *Bhagavad Gita* present the solutions to many problems of our daily life. It promotes the mental well-being of people. *Gita* teaches us how to overcome emotional turmoil. In *Bhagavad Gita* there are eighteen chapters and 700 verses. Each chapter has some lessons. It is deeply associated with human psyche.

Psychological Problem mentioned in *Bhagavad Gita*

In the first chapter of *Bhagavad Gita,* we see the scene of battlefield of Kurukshetra that begins with an enquiry about the situation of battlefield that was supposed to witness a war between Pandavas and Kauravas or war between *Dharma* and *Adharma.* It means what is right and what is wrong. Arjuna the disciple and friend of Lord Krishna is in the mental state of depression and anxiety, he does not want to fight. In this chapter Krishna listens Arjuna very patiently which is the very first phase of counselling. As a good counsellor or therapist Krishna allows Arjuna to express his feelings. Here the **ventilation technique** of social case work or counselling has been used. In the battle of Kurukshetra when Arjuna looked that his opponents in the battlefield are his near and dear ones and he had to kill his opponent for the victory in the battle (*yuddha*) field, he was very perplexed and could not decide right course of action.

भीष्मद्रोणाप्रमुखतः सर्वेषां च महीक्षिताम् ।
उवाच पार्थ ष्थ्यैतात्समवेतान्कुरूनीति ।। 1.25
तत्रापष्यस्थितान्पार्थः पितृनथपितामहान् ।
आचार्यान्मातुलानभ्रातृन्पुत्रान्पौत्रान्सखींस्तथा ।। 1.26

Meaning: His grandfather Pitamah Bhishm, his most respected teacher Guru Drona, his cousins and so many relatives and friends are there to whom he must fight with.

कृपया परयाविष्टो विषीदन्निदमब्रबीत् ।
दृष्टवेम् स्वजनं कृष्ण युयुत्सुं समुपस्थितम् ।।
सीदन्ति मम् गात्राणि मुखं च परिषुष्यति ।
वेपथुष्च शरीरे मे रोमहर्षच्च जायते ।। 1.28, 1.29

Meaning: After looking the scene of battlefield he become nervous and filled with anxiety. All the symptoms of **anxiety neurosis** can be clearly seen in the above *Shloka* of *Gita*. Arjuna's body was shivering, he was feeling dryness in mouth and goosebumps were there. These all are symptoms of anxiety.

गाण्डीवं स्त्रंसते हस्तात्त्वक्चैव परिदह्यते ।
न च षन्कोम्यवस्थातुं भ्रमतीव च मे मनः ।। 1.30

Meaning: The bow of Arjuna, Gandiva is slipping from his hands and skin was burning even he was not able to stand any longer. He started forgetting himself and his mind was reeling.

After these physical symptoms of nervousness and anxiety Arjuna wanted to skip from battlefield, he didn't have desire to fight and win.

एतान्न हन्तुमिच्छामि घ्नतोऽपि मधुसूदन।
अपि त्रैलोक्यराज्यस्य हेतोः किं नु महीकृते।। 1.35

Meaning: He started saying to lord Krishna who was his friend and driving his chariot, that I don't want to kill my teachers, grandfather, maternal uncles, father-in-law, brother-in-law and all relatives for the wealth and kingdom. I am not prepared to fight with them even in exchange for the three worlds (तीनों लोक), let alone this earth.

Arjuna wants to quit the battle. In other words, we can say that Arjuna doesn't want to perform his duty he disliked his job, as a *Kshatriya* and *Yoddha,* his job was to face the battle bravely but he was in dilemma and he couldn't take the right decision.

Counselling by Lord Krishna in *Bhagavad Gita*

In the above situation Arjuna needs counselling, when a person is in a stressful situation, suffering from anxiety and couldn't take right decision then an expert counsellor can counsel and guide him and make him able to take right decision. Thus, the person can overcome from the dilemma and perform his duty in a right manner.

Here in *Bhagavad Gita* lord Krishna was a great counsellor. He did Arjuna's counselling in such a manner that ultimately Arjuna came out from his *agyan* or ignorance and dilemma. Thus he could perform his duty in Kurukshetra's battlefield with confidence. Lord Krishna enlightened Arjuna with the knowledge of immortal soul. Everyone has soul which is different from his/her physical body. Body decays but soul never decays, body is mortal, it can be killed but soul can't. No one is able to destroy the imperishable soul.

In chapter 2nd of *Bhagavad Gita* in *shloka* no. 17 he says:

> अविनाषी तु तद्विद्धि येन सर्वमिदं ततम् ।
> विनाषमव्ययस्यास्य न कष्चित्कर्तुमर्हति ।। 2.17

Meaning: Know that soul which pervades the entire body is indestructible, nobody is able to destroy the imperishable soul.

> अन्तवन्त इमे देहा नित्यस्योक्ताः शरीरिणः ।
> अनाषिनोऽप्रमेयस्य तस्माद्युध्यस्व भारत ।। 2.18

Meaning: Only the material body of the indestructible, immeasurable, and entered living entity is subject to destruction, therefore, fight, O descendant of Bharata.

Krishna not only convinced Arjuna for *Yuddha* (Fight) but he also took him out of his guilt to kill his near and dear ones.

> य एनं वेत्ति हन्तारं यष्चैनं मन्यते हतम् ।
> उभौ तौ न विजानीतो नायं हन्ति न हन्यते ।। 2.19

Meaning: He who thinks that the living entity is the slayer or that he is slain, does not understand. One who is in knowledge knows that the self neither slays nor is it slain.

In 2nd chapter, Lord Krishna started to clear the situation, why war is inevitable and why Arjuna should indulge into the war. Lord Krishna says that only the material body of the indestructible, immeasurable, and eternal living entity is subject to destruction, therefore, fight, O' descendant of Bharata. For the soul there is never birth or death. Nor having once been, does HE ever cease to be. HE is unborn, eternal, ever-existing, undying, and primeval. HE is not slain when the body is slain. Further Krishna tells Arjuna that this material body is just like a garment. Soul puts on new garment (body) giving up old ones. Soul can neither be cut by any weapon, nor can be burned by fire, nor moistened by water, nor withered by wind. You should not grieve for the body. If you think that the soul is perpetually born and always dies, still you have no reason to lament.

Further lord Krishna told the need of battle and selfless duty. He told Arjuna that fighting on religious principles is duty of *kshatriya*, this is a religious war (धर्मयुद्ध) and if you don't fight then you will certainly incur sins for neglecting you duties and thus lose your reputation. Lord Krishna tells Arjuna about *Sthitprajna*—a person with positive mental health, a person who is totally unaffected from grief, desire or lust and anger, one who has control over his emotions, a person who is conscious of his *Atma* or self and detached from worldly affairs.

In chapter 2nd of *Bhagavad Gita*, verse 54 to 72 is all about *'Sthitprajna'*. Chapters 3rd, 4th and 5th of *Bhagavad Gita* are about *'karma'* (duty or job). How to perform duty selflessly? is the teaching of *karmayog*. *Bhagavad Gita* is mentioned as *nishkamkarma*, by practising this, one should not feel any anxiety related to her/his duty. Further *Bhagavad Gita* gives the concept of *'jnanayog'* (true knowledge) in chapter seven. In chapter 8 to 12 *Bhakti* (devotion) is described. *Bhagavad Gita* teaches us that if someone performs his duty by devotion or devotes reward of his duty to supreme God then he will be free from stress and anxiety related to his duty.

Through the above teaching of devotion or *Bhakti* lord Krishna made Arjuna able to choose right decision. Chapter 14th of *Bhagavad Gita* explains three traits or qualities of human being—they are *Sat, Raj* and *Tam*. A man with a quality of *Sat* is considered as a nice person who is sensitive towards others, he knows what is right. But the main goal of any human being should be salvation or *Moksh* and it can be attained only when a person should free himself from all three *Gunas*. At the end when all the above knowledge was passed to Arjuna in chapter 18, Lord Krishna says to Arjuna that people would think that you have left the battlefield out of fear only, the world would consider you coward. To prevent this you have to fight in the battlefield just for the sake of fighting without considering happiness or distress, loss or gain, victory or defeat.

By the above preaching lord Krishna is trying to resolve the confusion and dilemma of Arjuna and ultimately made him mentally prepared for the battle.

Modern Counselling and Counselling by Lord Krishna

Counselling is a technique in psychology which cures mentally and emotionally troubled people. In the battle of Kurukshetra, Arjuna got emotionally disturbed by looking his grand parent, friends, relatives and his own people in the opposite side and he lost his power. Arjuna was so much confused that he wanted to quit from battlefield. In that type of situation lord Krishna took the role of a counsellor for Arjuna. He modified Arjuna's behaviour and finally Arjuna decides to fight for the truth.

Rogers (1952) defined counselling as a process in which the counsellor-client relationship is basic. Rogers emphasises the process by which structure, the self is relaxed in the safety of the relationship with the therapist, and previously denied experiences are perceived and then integrated into an altered self.

In the Arjuna's case we can see that the above definition is totally implemented. Here the relationship between lord Krishna and Arjuna is friendly relation, thus Arjuna was able to describe his anxiety, his feelings and his dilemma to lord Krishna, the therapist, By the ***talk method*** lord Krishna clarified the situation, developed ***insight*** of Arjuna about his duty and changed his behaviour, i.e., Arjuna's decision of not to fight in battlefield so he altered his personality into an ***altered self*** because at last, after 18 sittings of the counselling, Arjuna took decision not to give up but to fight for truth and *dharma*.

Counselling is concerned with Decision-making Skills and Problem Resolution

The counsellor aids in decision making, in expanding his client's range of alternatives or option open to his, in modifying his behaviour pattern in desired direction.

In *Bhagavad Gita* we found that lord Krishna was able to counsel his friend and disciple Arjuna to take right decision and thus resolve the problem. In chapter 2nd of *Bhagavad Gita*, verses 34, 35, 36 and 37 lord Krishna explains alternatives or the situations when Arjuna will not fight then what would happen? How will people remember Arjuna for long time? He will remembered as a coward, by neglecting his duty (fight for *dharma* and truth), Arjuna will lose his reputation. For a respectable person, like Arjuna these are shameful alternative situations instead of fighting or performing his duty to fight in the battlefield. Imagining these situations enables Arjuna to take decision that is right for him.

Counselling is a Learning Teaching Process

If client is to make meaningful and informed choices, he must know himself the facts of his present situation, and the possibilities as well as the most likely consequences of the choices. Thus, the client gains an understanding of himself to a degree which enables him to take positive steps in the light of his new orientation.

At last in the chapter 18, verse 73, Arjuna said that now with help and your graciousness I am out of my dilemma, I gained my insight and now without any doubt I will obey you. It means I will do my duty. Thus, the **behaviour modification** was done by the proper counselling.

Counselling Techniques used in *Bhagavad Gita*

All the eighteen chapters of *Bhagavad Gita* are full of various counselling tools and techniques used by lord Krishna to counsel Arjuna. It starts from ***ventilation*** technique, then ***clarification*** of situation, ***suggestion of alternatives, insight development*** by ***spiritual guidance and healing.*** And ultimately Arjuna came out of his state of dilemma and took decision to fight for righteous aim, that is *dharma*.

Firstly, Lord Krishna patiently listens all the confusion and causes of anxiety of Arjuna thus the technique of ***Ventilation*** was used. Arjuna tells all his confusion without any hesitation because lord Krishna was his friend, Krishna uses ***talk therapy*** to calm down Arjuna and to release his anxiety and fear.

Arjuna was the counselee and lord Krishna taught him the skill of coping in the battlefield. He taught Arjuna the **awareness of situation**, **job devotion**, **non-duality** and **principle of work detachment.**

Lord Krishna resolves the conflict of Arjuna by enlightening him with spiritual knowledge of existence of soul and used the technique of ***clarification*** by narrating the doctrine of *Karma* or deed. Selfless *karma* or deed (means duty without any expectation of reward) is explained to Arjuna and by these counselling processes lord Krishna **strengthened the ego** of Arjuna, thus he was enabled to take right and wise decision.

Conclusion

Gita's approach to solve the problems is most suitable for Indian psyche and especially Hindu psyche because there is the belief system about immortal Soul, rebirth and doctrine of *Karma* (Deeds) If you are just and stand with truth than any hurdle in the way of truth should be demolished.

Gita encourages to behave with selflessness. The ultimate aim of any soul is '*moksh*' it means free from all greed, lust and any type of negative emotion. Thus, *Gita* takes on the path of righteous knowledge and righteous deed.

References

Dhillon, M. (2023). "Weaving together the Ancient and the Contemporary: Intersections of the Bhagwad *Gita* with Modern Psychology", *Pastoral Psychology, 72*: 525-37. Retrieved from https://link.springer.com/article/10.1007/s11089-023-01070-2

John, W. & Sons (2017). *Counselling Psychology*. Retrieved from https://books.google.co.in/books/about/Counselling_Psychology.html?id=8dgsDwAAQBAJ&source=kp_book_description&redir_esc=y.

Kress, E.V. & Seligman, L.W. (2021). *Theories of Counselling and Psychotherapy.* Retrieved from https://universalbooksellers.com/theories-of-counseling-and-psychotherapy-by-seligman-reichenberg/, Pearson

Mishra, V., Rajpurohit S. & Nebhinani, N. (2023). "*Bhagavad Gita* and Psychotherapy: Relevance and Applications", *Medical Journal of Dr. D.Y. Patil Vidyapeeth, 16*(4): 495-499. Retrieved from https://journals.lww.com/mjdy/fulltext/2023/16040/bhagavad_gita_and_psychotherapy__relevance_and.3.aspx

Mittal, A. & Prusty, B. (2023). "Bhagwad *Gita* from the Lens of Psychotherapy: A Qualitative Comparison Among Three Age Groups". *YMER, 22*(2): 1176-99. Retrieved from https://ymerdigital.com/uploads/YMER2202C9.pdf

Narayan Rao S. and Sahajpal P. (2013). *Counselling and Guidance.* New Delhi. McGraw Hill Education (India) Private Limited.

Pietrofesa John J., Splete Howard H., Hoffman A. and Pinto Diana V. (1978). *Counselling Theory and Practice*, Chicago, Rand McNally College Publishing Company.

Reddy, M.S. (2012). "Psychotherapy-insight from Bhagvat *Gita*", *Indian Journal of Psychological Medicine. 34*(1): 100-4. Retrieved from https://www.researchgate.net/publication/225095885_Psychotherapy_-_Insights_from_*Bhagavad_Gita*

Robern Lewis, G. Mitchell, H. (1995). *Introduction to Counselling and Guidance.* Retrieved from https://books.google.co.in/books/about/Introduction_to_Counseling_and_Guidance.html?id=fHFRAAAAYAAJ&source=kp_book_description&redir_esc=y

Sharma, N. (2014). *Cognitive Behaviour Therapy in Perspective of the Bhagwat Gita, 3*(1): 19-21. Retrieved from https://www.ijhssi.org/papers/v3(1)/Version-2/D03102019021.pdf.

Shreemad Bhagavad Gita (May, 2020). Chapter 2. Retrieved from www.sanatan sanskrit.in bhagwat-geeta-

Shreemadbhagwadgeeta (2019). Gorakhpur, Geeta Press.

Sommers-flanagan, J. & Sommers-flanagan, R. (2018). *Counselling and Psychotherapy Theories in Context and Practice: Skills, Strategies, and Techniques.* Retrieved from https://www.wiley.com/ en-in/Counseling+and+Psychotherapy+ Theories+in+Context+and+ Practice%3A+ Skills%2C+Strategies% 2C+and+Techniques%2C+3rd+Edition-p-9781119473312

Tyagi, S. and Khan, M.A. (2018). "Counselling Implications of Shrimad *Bhagavad Gita*", *Zenith International Journal of Multidisciplinary Research, 8*(9): 236-46. Retrieved from http://www.zenithresearch.org.in/images/stories/pdf/2018/SEP/ZIJMR/22_ZIJMR_VOL8_ISSUE_9_SEPTEMBER_2018.pdf

11

Dharma in Dialogue

Blending Counselling Techniques with *Bhagavad Gita* Wisdom

Arunima Dhar

Introduction

Hindu philosophy is regarded as one of the earliest forms of philosophy (Flood, 1996). The *Gita*, a sacred Hindu scripture nestled within the *Mahabharata*, is the colloquial name for the *Bhagavad* (or *Bhagvad*, depending on spelling). It is considered a cornerstone of Hindu philosophy due to its exploration of fundamental concepts like duty, righteousness, and spiritual paths, providing ethical guidance and universal wisdom that resonates across cultures. Through its dialogue between Arjuna and Krishna, it integrates diverse philosophical ideas and paths to spiritual realisation, serving as a revered scripture that continues to inspire seekers on the spiritual path. Many of the Hindu scholars consider the Hindu scripture "The *Gita*" to be a summary of important Vedic ideas (Robinson, 2005). It is also regarded as an invaluable guide to incorporating Vedic insights into everyday life (Rosen, 2006). In the ancient verses of the *Bhagavad Gita* , profound wisdom unfolds as a guide to life's intricate dilemmas. Beyond its spiritual significance, the *Gita* offers timeless insights that resonate with the human experience, providing a philosophical foundation for navigating the complexities of the mind and soul (Hall, 2007).

Essentially, comprehending and following one's *dharma* enables individuals to establish definite goals and objectives for themselves and their organisation. By harmonising their endeavours with a higher purpose, individuals can ignite greater dedication and commitment from others within their organisation. Moreover, this concentration can aid individuals in making difficult decisions by prioritising the collective benefit. Furthermore, engaging in the practices of *yoga* and meditation as delineated in the *Bhagavad Gita* can facilitate the cultivation of enhanced self-awareness and emotional intelligence in individuals. Through these methods, individuals can acquire the ability to regulate their responses to stressful circumstances and gain deeper insight into the requirements and motivations of those they lead and even the organisation. Finally, the *Bhagavad Gita* underscores the significance of serving others. This principle can be translated into managing an organisational culture that esteems community contribution. For instance, individuals can motivate the other members or subordinates to volunteer or contribute financially for noble endeavours. By nurturing a sense of altruism, individuals can foster a more favourable and efficient work atmosphere (Srivastava, 2016). Around the world, the text has been applied to improve management knowledge, business practices, and leadership paradigms (Hee, 2007). Numerous forms of management, leadership, and administration have been outlined based on the *Gita* (Sharma, 1999). Contrastingly, the relative significance of different philosophical concepts that are highlighted in the *Gita* (such as dedication to work versus love of God), there are scholars who disagree on a few points (Gambhirananda, 2003). Yet the *Bhagavad Gita* has sparked a tremendous degree of curiosity beyond India's borders and across diverse cultures. It has been translated into more than 75 languages worldwide, and more versions are constantly being released (Venkatesh, 2022).

Review of Literature

Most Hindu religions regard the *Gita* as sacred (Miller & Moser, 1986). The *Bhagavad Gita* presents a dialogue between Prince Arjuna and Lord Krishna, taking place on the battlefield of Kurukshetra. As Arjuna grapples with moral dilemmas, existential questions, and the turbulence of his own emotions, Krishna serves not only as a divine guide but as a counsellor, offering solace, guidance, and profound insights into the nature of the self and the intricacies of human existence. A psychological interpretation of the *Gita* involves drawing parallels between the conversation between Lord Krishna and Arjuna and contemporary psychotherapy techniques (Reddy, 2012). The *Gita* portrays what might serve as one of the first known instances of cognitive behavioural therapy (CBT), with Lord Krishna serving as the client and Arjuna acting as a psychotherapist-type role. Arjuna is said to have a variety of automatic negative beliefs at that point, in addition to cognitive distortions such personalisation and catastrophising. Lord Krishna's speech could be considered as a means of confronting Arjuna's cognitive biases and akin to psycho-education for individuals coping with anxiety symptoms (Bhatia, Madabushi, Kolli, Bhatia, & Madaan, 2013). A further connection between CBT and the character of Lord Krishna and Arjuna's discourse is proposed by Sharma (2014). According to him, just as the primary goal of CBT is to positively transform patients' thoughts and the interpretations they provide; here Lord Krishna tries to alter Arjuna's understanding of the causes behind the conflict, rather than the actual state of affairs. The analogy between the *Gita* and psychotherapy methods to humanistic-existential therapy is expanded by Phogat *et al.* (2020). They contend that the *Gita* discusses self-knowledge that results in the realisation of peace, much as existential and humanistic perspectives emphasise the significance of self-awareness and self-understanding to facilitate personal development. According to Bhatia *et al.* (2013), the *Gita* features aspects that could be related to interpersonal therapy (IPT), such as the emphasis on rekindling relationships and interests that can aid in the healing process for bereaved patients. The emphasis on developing self-esteem and changing roles. There are further parallels between IPT and Lord Krishna's method with Arjuna that have been noted. Simultaneously, some scholars (Bhosale, 2015) believe that the *Gita* represents the earliest recorded instance of rational emotive behaviour therapy (REBT). It has been suggested that the *Gita* and REBT, which Albert Ellis introduced to psychology in 1957, both encourage people to pursue happiness. Moreover, the *Gita* and REBT believe that the *Gita* exhorts people to seek happiness and believes that although people have constraints, they can still flourish. Additionally, both hold that each person is autonomous and shapes their own mental health.

Although scholars have juxtaposed the *Gita* with many therapeutic approaches, there is no definitive. Regardless of the therapy that the *Bhagavad Gita* most closely resembles, Lord Krishna's method of therapy shares many similarities with contemporary psychotherapy. The chapter explores and uncovers the parallels between counselling techniques and the teachings of the *Bhagavad Gita*, highlighting how this ancient scripture provides a nuanced understanding of the human psyche. From active listening and empathy to mindfulness and cognitive restructuring, the *Gita*'s verses echo the essence of therapeutic approaches aimed at fostering self-awareness, resilience, and inner balance. Against this backdrop, this chapter delves into the rich tapestry of counselling principles embedded within the verses of the *Bhagavad Gita*, revealing a harmonious convergence of ancient wisdom and modern therapeutic practices.

While the *Bhagavad Gita* is a religious and philosophical text, its teachings can resonate with individuals seeking guidance and support in the realm of mental and emotional well-being. Some people may find inspiration and therapeutic value in the timeless wisdom offered by the *Gita*, integrating its principles with contemporary counselling approaches. Gandhiji, the Father of the Nation and a renowned Indian social activist thought that the *Gita*'s contents included quotes not to justify violence nor does it describe a war. He believed that the text instead conveyed a message of non-violence. He read the *Gita* as highlighting the necessity of achieving a state in which the person is insusceptible to the three *gunas* (characteristics or traits) and so unable to experience rage. A person would not go to battle if they had no fury (Desai, 2012). Hence, it is essential to approach the integration of *Bhagavad Gita* with sensitivity to diverse cultural and religious backgrounds as it recognises that counselling should be inclusive and respectful of individual beliefs and values.

Bridging Ancient Wisdom and Modern Counselling

In the multifaceted landscape of counselling, practitioners are increasingly recognising the significance of integrating diverse philosophies and wisdom traditions into therapeutic approaches. One such profound and holistic approach emerges from the dialogue between counselling techniques and the ancient wisdom encapsulated in the concept of "Dharma" as found in the *Bhagavad Gita* . Here the synthesis of the counselling techniques and ancient wisdom, the two realms elucidate how "Dharma in Dialogue" serves as a bridge between the two and offers holistic and transformative framework in the field of counselling that can be explained under the following aspects—

- *Understanding Dharma:* In the *Bhagavad Gita*, *dharma* is something that goes beyond the idea of duty. It represents moral values, upright behaviour, and the universe's inherent order. In order to apply this idea to therapy, one must acknowledge that each person possesses an innate moral compass and assist them in finding a harmonic balance between their true selves and the outside world (Reddy, 2012).
- *Dialogue with the Self:* The *Bhagavad Gita* promotes self-awareness and reflection, which are essential components of counselling. "Dharma in Dialogue" starts with an introspective discussion that invites people to consider their moral compass, core values, and beliefs. Through

self-dialogue, clients can traverse their internal landscapes and discover guiding principles that might influence their decisions and actions. This self-dialogue becomes a therapeutic process (Dhillion, 2023).

- *Counselling Techniques Aligned with Dharma:* The use of different therapeutic strategies is essential to counselling. "Dharma in Dialogue" combines counselling techniques that are consistent with the *Bhagavad Gita*'s precepts. Many counselling techniques, such as active listening, empathy, and unconditional positive regard, resonate with Lord Krishna's compassionate and understanding guidance to Arjuna (Frankel, Rachlin, & Yip-Bannicq, 2012).
- *Mindfulness and Detached Action:* A common feature of modern therapy is mindfulness, which fits in well with the *Bhagavad Gita*'s emphasis on being in the present moment. The *Gita* also presents the idea of detached activity, in which people carry out their tasks without any regard for the results. As a result, this integration becomes a pillar of "Dharma in Dialogue", encouraging acceptance and fortitude in the face of uncertainty (Bhatia, Madabushi, Kolli, Bhatia, & Madaan, 2013).
- *Holistic Well-being:* "Dharma in Dialogue" reaches beyond the conventional objective of alleviating symptoms. By treating not only psychological issues but also spiritual and existential aspects, it promotes people's holistic well-being. By acknowledging the connection between the mind, body, and spirit, this method promotes balance and a sense of wholeness (Mishra, Rajpurohit, & Nebhinani, 2023).
- *Cultural Sensitivity and Inclusivity:* A holistic counselling approach should be considerate of different ethnic and religious origins in this age of cultural diversity. While recognising the universal principles of morality and the distinct cultural settings that influence individual perspectives, "Dharma in Dialogue" promotes respect for other belief systems (Bhargava, Kumar & Gupta, 2017).

In counselling, the integration of diverse philosophies, such as the *Bhagavad Gita*'s concept of "Dharma", offers a holistic framework. This approach combines counselling techniques with ancient wisdom to foster self-awareness, align actions with moral values, promote mindfulness, encourage detachment, address holistic well-being, and embrace cultural diversity for inclusive and effective therapy.

Analysis and Discussion in the Context of *Bhagwad Gita*

Analysing how counselling methods and approaches fit with the philosophy and teachings found in the *Bhagavad Gita* entails doing a comparative analysis. Examining ideas like responsibility (*dharma*), mindfulness, detachment, and moral behaviour as they are portrayed in the *Gita* may be part of this study. The conversation also centres on how counselling methods might be combined with the *Bhagavad Gita*'s wisdom to create a cogent and successful therapeutic strategy. This entails investigating the ways in which the spiritual and intellectual insights offered by the *Gita* can enhance a variety of notions. Following is the discussion of the practical application of counselling techniques in light of the *Bhagavad Gita*:

- *Inner Conflict and Decision-Making:* In the *Bhagavad Gita*, Arjuna wrestles with his morality and inner conflict over participating in combat. In a similar vein, people who seek counselling frequently struggle with internal conflicts and making decisions. The *Gita* offers guidance on resolving these disputes by highlighting the significance of mindfulness, self-awareness, and knowing one's responsibility (*dharma*).
- *Mind Management:* The nature of the mind and the difficulties in managing it are concerns covered in the *Bhagavad Gita* . It offers advice on controlling the thoughts and feelings. In order to enhance mental health, counselling frequently entails assisting clients in comprehending and controlling their ideas and feelings.

- *Detachment and Equanimity:* The *Gita* imparts the idea of detached action, which is carrying out one's tasks without regard for the outcome. This concept is in line with several therapeutic philosophies, such mindfulness-based cognitive therapy, which places a strong emphasis on being in the present moment without being overly attached to results.
- *Spiritual and Existential Issues:* The *Bhagavad Gita* provides an understanding of the meaning of existence, the essence of the self (*atman*), and the idea of divine consciousness (Brahman) by addressing significant spiritual and existential issues. During therapy, people in counselling may examine their existential or spiritual issues.
- *Self-Discovery and Personal Growth:* Understanding one's true nature and reflecting on oneself are two ways that the *Bhagavad Gita* promotes self-discovery and personal development. A comparable process of self-examination and personal growth is frequently included in counselling.
- *Mindfulness and Self-awareness:* Counselling technique that contribute to people becoming more conscious of their thoughts and emotions include self-awareness exercises and mindfulness activities. The *Gita* places great emphasis on the value of mindfulness and self-awareness. It inspires people to develop awareness of their ideas and deeds and to comprehend the nature of the mind.
- *Cognitive Restructuring*: With a view to encourage more positive thinking, cognitive restructuring entails recognising and correcting harmful thought patterns. The *Gita* rectifies Arjuna's misguided beliefs and offers a conceptual framework for reassessing his outlook on life and responsibilities.
- *Goal Setting:* A popular counselling strategy to assist clients in working toward constructive transformation and personal development is goal planning. The *Gita* helps Arjuna comprehend his *dharma*, or duty, and establish a goal that is in line with his life's purpose.

- *Acceptance and Commitment:* Individuals are encouraged by Acceptance and Commitment Therapy (ACT) to embrace their thoughts and feelings and make a commitment to behaviours that are consistent with their values. The *Gita* emphasises the value of acting with detachment, meaning carrying out one's responsibilities without being attached to the results.

Analysing how counselling aligns with *Bhagavad Gita* philosophy involves comparing concepts like responsibility (*dharma*) and mindfulness, and exploring how counselling methods can merge with the *Gita*'s wisdom for effective therapy. Practical applications include guiding clients through inner conflict, promoting mindfulness and self-awareness, restructuring negative thought patterns, and setting goals aligned with personal growth, all while emphasising detached action and acceptance of outcomes.

Conclusion

"Dharma in Dialogue" represents a convergence of ancient wisdom and modern therapeutic practices, offering a holistic approach to counselling that addresses the complexities of the human experience. As counselling continues to evolve, this synthesis becomes a guiding light, fostering self-discovery, resilience, and the pursuit of a life aligned with one's authentic principles. In the dialogue between *Dharma* and counselling, individuals embark on a transformative journey towards inner harmony and a meaningful connection with the world. Even while the discussion between Lord Krishna and Arjuna and the contemporary therapeutic technique shares many parallels, it is important to recognise the distinctions as well. It is imperative to remember while comparing the *Gita* to person-centred therapy. Lord Krishna took a very directive stance, making it very evident what Arjuna should do. Although the plethora of concepts found in the *Gita* is now recognised by psychologists, no single coherent treatment technique based on the *Gita* has been shown to be beneficial. It should be crucial to carry out more research even though the *Bhagavad Gita*'s core ideas are more widely accepted as a text in psychology. Also, while "Dharma in Dialogue" offers a comprehensive approach to counselling, it is essential to acknowledge potential challenges. These may include ethical considerations, the need for cultural competence among counsellors, and the delicate balance between spiritual guidance and professional boundaries. The *Gita* does, however, seem to offer a time-tested, culturally approved method of addressing life's challenges, thus it seems worthwhile for psychologists to keep researching the ways in which it can support mental wellness.

References

Bhargava, R., Kumar, N. & Gupta, A. (2017). "Indian Perspective on Psychotherapy: Cultural Issues". *Journal of Contemporary Psychotherapy, 27*(2): 95-103. doi:10.1007/s10879-016-9348-1

Bhatia, S.C., Madabushi, J., Kolli, V., Bhatia, S.K. & Madaan, V. (2013). "The *Bhagavad Gita* and Contemporary Psychotherapies". *Indian Journal of Psychiatry,* 55(Suppl 2): S315.

Bhosale, S. (2015). "Rational Emotive Behaviour Therapy in Perspective of *Bhagavad Gita* research". *International Journal of Current Research, 7*(11): 22612-13.

Desai, M. (2012). *The Bhagavad Gita according to Gandhi.* Radford VA: Wilder Publications.

Dhillion, M. (2023). "Weaving Together the Ancient and the Contemporary: Intersections of the *Bhagavad Gita* with Modern Psychology". *Pastoral Psychology, 72*: 525-37.

Flood, G.D. (1996). *An Introduction to Hinduism.* Cambridge, UK: Cambridge University Press.

Frankel, M., Rachlin, H. & Yip-Bannicq, M. (2012). "How Non-directive Therapy Directs: The Power of Empathy in the Context of Unconditional Positive Regard". *Person Centred & Experiential Psychotherapies, 11*(3): 205-14.

Gambhirananda, S. (2003). *Bhagawad Gita.* Kolkata, India: Sixth Impression.

Hall, S. (2007, May 6). "The New Middle Ages: The Older and Wiser Hypothesis". *The New York Times, Sunday Supplement.*

Hee, C.C. (2007). "A Holistic Approach to Business Management: Perspectives from the *Bhagavad Gita*". *Singapore Management Review, 29*(1): 73-85.

Miller, B.S. & Moser, B. (1986). *The Bhagavad Gita: Krishna's Counsel in Time of War.* New York: Columbia University Press.

Mishra, V., Rajpurohit, S.S. & Nebhinani, N. (2023). "*Bhagavad Gita* and Psychotherapy: Relevance and Applications". *Medical Journal of Dr. D.Y. Patil Vidyapeeth, 16*(4): 495-99.

Phogat, P., Sharma, R., Grewal, S. & Malik, A. (2020). "The Overlapping Principles of *Bhagavat Gita* and Contemporary Psychotherapies". *International Journal of Indian Psychology, 8*(3).

Reddy, M.S. (2012). "Psychotherapy—Insights from *Bhagavad Gita* ". *Indian Journal of Psychological Medicine, 34*:100-104.

Robinson, C.A. (2005). *Interpretations of the Bhagavad Gita and Images of the Hindu tradition: The Song of the Lord.* London: Routledge.

Rosen, S. J. (2006). *Essential Hinduism.* Westport, CT: Greenwood Press.

Sharma, N. (2014). "The *Bhagavad Gita* as a Complimentary Tool to Cognitive Behavioural Therapy". *International Journal of Applied Psychology, 4*(2): 45-49.

Sharma, S. (1999). "Corporate *Gita*: Lessons for Management, Administration and Leadership". *Journal of Human Values, 5*: 103-123.

Srivastava, P.S. (2016). "Ensuring Personality Development Through *Bhagavad Gita*'s Teachings". *International Journal of Research in Social Sciences, 6*(11): 230-42.

Venkatesh, M. (2022). After *Bhagavat Gita*, Tokyo Professor translating Hanuman Chalisa for Japanese Readers. *Indianarrative.* Retrieved from https://www.indianarrative.com/culture-news/after-bhagavat-gita-tokyo-professor-translating-hanuman-chalisa-for-japanese-readers-85048.html.

12

Srimad Bhagavad Gita as a Text of Counselling and Sri Krishna as the Best Counsellor

Venkatesha Murthy, S. and *Padmaja, D.S.*

Introduction

In the *Bhagavad Gita*, Lord Krishna was the therapist and Arjuna was the Victim/Client. The way Lord Krishna eliminates the cognitive distortions from the mind of Arjuna and motivates him to fight the battle is depicted in *The Gita*. A good relationship between Krishna and Arjuna is maintained through unconditional positive regard, the basic acceptance and support of a person regardless of what the person says or does, just like the client- therapist relationship. It involves active participation from both the sides just as the Krishna-Arjuna and their parallel enthusiasm. Similarly, Cognitive behaviour therapy emphasises on the present, just as Krishna focused on solving the distress related to the battle and explained how perfection can only be achieved through Action.

Cognitive Behavioural Therapy (CBT) is a talking therapy that can help you manage your problems by changing the way you think and behave. Cognitive behavioural therapy is a problem-oriented strategy. It focuses on current problems and finding solutions for them. CBT emphasises on how to change these negative patterns to improve the way you feel. It looks for practical ways to improve your state of mind on a daily basis. CBT aims to teach the client to be his/her own therapist, just as Krishna taught Arjuna the way to calm himself and how to realise his duties.

Lord Sri Krishna is as empathetic to Arjuna as a therapist is to a client in distress. Arjuna unfairly holds himself accountable for the destructions which reflect his depressed state of mind. The way CBT tries to work with patients to identify, evaluate and respond to their dysfunctional thinking, Krishna makes Arjuna understand his delusional thinking. In conclusion, the above-mentioned analogy is just a small-scale example of how our ancient Indian Scripture *Bhagavad Gita* enlightened us about the modern Psychotherapy techniques. We in this era have to acknowledge, appreciate, study and propagate this ancient historic inheritance globally.

Srimad Bhagavad Gita—A Power for Positive Life

Arjuna, just like any other client portrays the act of self-blame, guilt and blames himself for whatever is happening. Krishna explains that all this is not true, just like a therapist consoles the client about his/her false beliefs. Krishna explains the importance of *Karma Yoga* by telling him not to expect any rewards in return and just keep doing *karma* which helps relieve one from stress or guilt which in turn emphasises on not to think of unreal goals, as mentioned in the cognitive behaviour therapy.

For instance, Arjuna experiences significant tension and worry while on the battlefield, causing him considerable stress. He is worried about how is he going to stand against his own family. At this point, Krishna explains how this stress is not permanent and will resolve soon. Krishna helps to calm his mind through imparting the knowledge of importance of Duty and *Karma Yoga*, which is the most important concept of *The Gita*. Krishna says that this stress is very temporary just like the therapist explains it to the client, that the anxiety is not long-lasting.

There is no shortage of spoken and written commentary on the *Bhagavad Gita*, which is considered the distilled spiritual essence of the Vedas and Upanishads. We all know that whenever we have a problem, *Bhagavad Gita* offered an answer and the solution. For a student of psychology, *Bhagavad Gita* offers a valuable case study for lessons in psychotherapy—resolution of conflict and successful resumption of action from a state of acute anxiety and guilt laden depression that precipitated in action. This presentation makes a humble attempt to discuss the therapy process involved in *Bhagavad Gita* in which Lord Krishna helped the grief-stricken Arjuna through dialogue and discussion. The focus would be on the conflict and diagnosis of patient, the background setting of the situation, personality of patient, technique of therapy, underlying psychological concepts/principles/theories, the *Guru-Sishya* concept, etc.

Bhagavad Gita—An Eternal Pathway to attain *Moksha*

Bhagavad Gita is part of the great epic *Mahabharata*, dialog between two individuals Lord Krishna and Arjuna on the battlefield of Kurukshetra for control of the kingdom of Hastinapur (Reddy, 2012). The conflict in *Mahabharata* is between two groups of cousins, Kauravas and Pandavas. The *Bhagavad Gita* is a discourse by Lord Krishna, who guided Arjuna during the war, toward the course of action which was necessary to fulfil his duty. Arjuna, mounted on a chariot steered by Lord Krishna, prepared to confront an army comprising his own relatives, teachers, and mentors. Despite his formidable prowess and unwavering character as a warrior, Arjuna initially hesitates to engage in battle, fearing the potential loss of his loved ones. Overwhelmed by feelings of guilt, attachment, and uncertainty, he contemplates withdrawing from the battlefield (Bhatia *et al.*, 2013). Trying to answer queries and elucidate the distress of his clients, a comparison is being done between the task of a mental health professional to that of Lord Krishna in guiding his disciple as detailed below in line with different types of psychotherapy. One of the most renowned discourses in psychotherapy and philosophy comes from the scripture of Hinduism—*Bhagavad Gita* (Balodhi, 2011).

Bhagavad Gita is part of the great epic *Mahabharata*, a widely popular mythological story in Hindu philosophy; part of *Bhishma Parva*, *Gita* is almost in its entirety the dialogue between two individuals, Lord Krishna (considered as incarnation of Bhagawan Vishnu, Narayana) and Arjuna (the Pandava prince, Nara) in the battlefield (war between the Pandavas and the Kauravas, the cousins, for control of the kingdom of Hasthinapur) of Kurukshetra. It has 18 *yoga*s (chapters), with about 701 *shlokas* (short poems), the first one being "Arjuna Vishada Yoga" (Sorrow of Arjuna) and the last one "Moksha Sanyasa Yoga" (*Nirvana* and Renunciation).

Readers must comprehend the *Bhagavad Gita* in a manner that resonates with their individual belief systems and cultural-religious backgrounds. A fiction story or a piece of history dating back to about 4000-5000 B.C. or part of mythology dictated by Sage Veda Vyasa and written by Lord Ganesha! What is more important and relevant is *NOT WHAT IT IS BUT WHAT TRANSPIRED* in those 18 chapters of *Bhagavad Gita*; the process and content of the dialogue; its usefulness as a model of counselling and possible contemporary application value to current day psychological therapies, specially, but need not be limited to, in the Indian context. The fact of interest for the student of Psychology lies embedded in the dialogue between these two *shlokas*:

- *Sishyasthe Aham Sadhi Mam Tvam Prapannam*
  (I am your disciple, Guide me, Help me) [*Bhagavad Gita*, Gorakhpur Press] II chapter….3rd *shloka*
- *Nasto mohah Smrtir labdha Tvat Prasadan mayachyuta Sthithosmi gata-Sandehaha Karishye Vachanam tava*
  ("Clouds" have cleared; my senses are back, all your gift with my doubts vanished, Ready to act as you direct) XVIII chapter…..73rd *shloka*

The 3rd *shloka* of 2nd chapter is depiction of the helpless state of Arjuna praying Lord Krishna for help. The 73rd *shloka* of 18th chapter is reflection of dissolution of anxiety, worry, depression and guilt and preparedness for action with confidence and vigour. Whatever transpired between the 3rd *shloka* of 2nd chapter and the 73rd *shloka* of the 18th chapter is the matter of scientific curiosity for every student of psychology as it resulted in the total relief from the distress.

Bhagavad Gita **and Counselling: An Insight to Internalise Individuals**

Counselling and Psychotherapy play vital roles as integral components of psychiatric interventions for patients experiencing psychological distress or illness. The available psychotherapeutic models have been developed primarily from Western literature and imported for use in diverse cultural contexts. The applicability and usefulness of these models in the Indian context was discussed with some scepticism keeping in mind the varying cultural, religious, spiritual, societal attitudes (broadly described as eastern/oriental culture) by psychiatrists in the past (Varma *et al.*, 1976; 1975; 1964). The *Guru-Shishya* concept, as a model in psychotherapy, popularised by Neki (1975) is widely debated in the Indian context. The very first word in *Bhagavad Gita* is "Dharma" and the last word is "Mama". "Mama Dharma"—My duties, responsibilities, rights, ethics, morals, attitude, action, activities and so on. Some commentators recommend *Gita* as an elaborate detailing of *MAMA DHARMA* (Swamy, 2022).

In the analysis of perception, feeling and behaviour, the *Bhagavad Gita* may be a source of psychological insights. But it is more than that: The *Bhagavad Gita* is called a talk therapy. The Krishna, after recognising the cause for Arjuna's fear, taught him skills to cope with this issue by teaching the awareness of job devotion, reflection, the endless spirit, the non-duality and work detachment principle. The counselling sessions have been focused on Arjuna's present dilemma and problems. In CBT (Cognitive

Behavioural Therapy) understanding of the case, the way of thought and context offered to the event is more significant than the event itself. The primary focus in treatment is on the positive changes in the patient's thinking.

Srimad Bhagavad Gita adopts the teacher-taught relationship in the process of counselling with such features as complete state of surrender, questioning endowed with devotion and exercise of free-will. The cognition and effect of mind are elevated to the status of first six chapters known as *Jnana Yoga*; another six chapters known as *Karma Yoga* which focuses on the consequences of actions. The final three chapters, the *Bhakti Yoga* focus on doing good deeds.

The first chapter, *Arjuna Vishada Yoga*, narrates the expression of Arjuna's sorrow, anxiety, fear and guilt leading to a state of inaction after seeing his kith and kin (*Gurus*, cousins, uncles, nephews, friends...) lined up in the enemy camp in the battlefield—Fighting this war, to win the kingdom, means killing all these people whom Arjuna respected and loved; a sin of commission from any angle. Overwhelmed by the acute state of sadness and guilt, Arjuna drops his weapons (Gandiva) and turns to Lord Krishna, his charioteer, for help and guidance.

- *Sishyasthe Aham Sadhi Mam Tvam Prapannam* (I am your disciple, Guide me, Help me) II.......3

Srimad Bhagavad Gita and Counselling: Some Glimpses

In Chapter I, 10th and 11th *shloka* talk about psychology of Duryodhana. Through this Lord Krishna is telling how narrow-minded people think. The 21st to 23rd *shloka* talks about Arjuna's enthusiasm for war; this is the usual attitude of all the people before they start any kind of work for that matter. The 28th *shloka* serves as a precursor, indicating the emotional impact of seeing all the relatives. Following this, the 29th and 30th *shlokas* delve into the psychological effects experienced. In the 31st *shloka*, a judgment is passed on what is inaccurate or untrue. The subsequent verses, from the 32nd to the 34th *shlokas*, impart teachings on mistaken beliefs and various types of fallacies.

In Chapter II, the 11th *shloka* identifies the root cause of delusion, while the 26th to 30th *shlokas* address the inevitable realities of life. Moving to Chapter III, the 21st *shloka* emphasises the influence of individuals in higher positions, while the 25th and 26th *shlokas* illustrate the actions of a wise person. Further, the 33rd to 35th *shlokas* highlight the importance of *svadharma*. The 37th *shloka* discusses *Kama* and *Krodha* as the real enemies underlying all sins, whereas, the 40th and 41st *shlokas* focus on desires and methods to manage them. In chapter IV, 36th *shloka* is about inclusivity of a sinner and a simile of a boat which is compared to the ups and downs of life, 37th *shloka* is about the simile of fire which is referred to the purification process in life, 39th *shloka* is all about competency of a well-qualified aspirant.

In chapter V, 13-16th *shloka* highlight on practical functioning of a wise man, 23rd *shloka* covers enjoying one's life with healthy dispassion and self-control, 25th *shloka* points out unconditional love to all beings, 28th is all about insistence on self-control and consistent meditation. The Chapter VI talks about developing a contemplative mind, self-confidence and self-control of the person, moderation in all aspects as key to *yoga*, Krishna acknowledges the fickle nature of the mind and insists on dispassion and practice of *yoga* and meditation, inconsistence on integrity and regular practice of *dhyana*. In Chapter IX, the emphasis is on the principle that what one desires ultimately manifests. The Chapter X highlights the importance of possessing three qualities: curiosity, absorption, and nourishment. It suggests that every individual should dedicate half an hour each day for self-care. Moving to Chapter XIII, it underscores the significance of values such as humility, simplicity, non-violence, and forbearance, which prepare the aspirant's mind to receive and reflect upon self-knowledge.

Chapter V describes a process of unlearning to relearn, which aids in personal growth and performance. This process involves steps such as the holy dip, churning, transformation, and examination, engaging both the conscious and subconscious mind.

In the Chapter XVI, Krishna sums up the entire *asuri sampat* as the three basic materialistic traits of desire, anger and greed. Shastra is the *pramana* in determining what is right and wrong. The Chapter XVIII, containing the five factors namely – body, doer, sense organs, various efforts and the ultimate supreme person involved in every action and their uniqueness is spoken about. It also covers *Satvika*, *Rajasika* and *Tamasika* types of action, enumeration of the will and happiness, also about the knowledge, the scholar and the *karma*. The important highlights in view of process of *Bhagavad Gita* are; Arjuna is the patient and Lord Krishna the therapist, Single session therapy, No specified "Time limit of 45-60 minutes", Counsellor is a relative of the patient, Therapist stays with the patient throughout the crisis, and Patient has immense belief in the therapist and considers him a friend, philosopher, guide (*Guru-Sishya* Relationship)

Single Case Report—level 5 evidence in the current day terminology. Blind application of this approach may run the risk of overgeneralisation, a commonly found overenthusiastic error in psychology, too obvious in the history of psychoanalysis.

Personality of Arjuna: Pandava Prince, no significant neurotic traits, maladjustments or faulty coping pattern; a great warrior and veteran of many battles, in the recent past he fought against the same army and won the battle (Uttara Gograhanam). Proactive role in the preparation for the current war and he drove into the battlefield with great enthusiasm to fight and win.

Lord Sri Krishna as a Best Counsellor and Therapist

Counselling is a cure for troubled minds. To describe Krishna as the Supreme Counsellor, the Supreme Psychologist certainly appropriate. His knowledge of all psychological matters is infallible, just as He Himself is infallible (Padma, 2011). Arjuna, a great fighter who was emotionally ill while he was fighting with parents, instructors, peers and all his own citizens in the battlefield of Kurukshetra in *Mahabharata*. Arjuna was unable to take a decision and lost both his spirit and power. Arjuna requested the guidance of Lord Sri Krishna as he had in confused mood during the war. Sri Krishna had this sense in which Arjuna would advise him of awareness in different aspects, from which he might correct his mind and decide correctly. In this case, Sri Krishna can be considered the psychiatrist, Sri Krishna's counsellor Arjuna or Lord Krishna, the attacker can be regarded as his client or counsellor, the place is Kurukshetra, where the fighting between both the two adversaries of the same governing clan is waged between the two sides (the Kauravas and Pandavas). A long-time friend, relative, well-wisher of the patient, highly respected in the community, supposedly with supernatural powers, legendary mediating skills, mischievous lover boy in his younger days, with tons of common sense and in the contemporary language a kind of Go-Getter (Rhythma Kaul, 2017).

Sri Krishna also imparts knowledge on the behavioural tendencies of persons with different natures. In the Sixteenth Chapter of *Bhagavad-Gita,* Krishna describes people endowed with either divine or demoniac natures, including their consciousness, how they think, act, and the consequences of their actions. For example, Krishna says that people with demoniac natures are attracted by impermanence, or in other words, they are attracted to the material world. He explains that although they consider themselves to be progressing in life, such attraction causes them to indulge in materialistic life while they gradually glide down toward hell. To avert the disaster of succumbing to the demoniac nature, Krishna advises that one should give up the behavioural tendencies of anger, lust, and greed, which he describes as the three gateways leading to hellish, or demoniac, life (*Bhagavad Gita,* 16.21).

Descriptive Psychopathology of Arjuna

Anxiety

- *Seedanthi mama gatrani mukham cha parisushyathi vepathus cha sarire me roma-harshas cha jayate* (Weakness of limbs, Dryness of mouth, Shivering of the body, Goose skin) I........29

- *Gandivam sramsate hastat tvakchaiva paridahyate na cha saknomy avasthatum bhramati va cha me manah* (Gandivam slips from the hand, "Burning" of skin, Unable to stand, "Dizziness"/Confusion of Mind) I.........30

Depression

1. **Negative thoughts**: *Na kankhse vijayam Krishna na cha rajyam sukhani cha Kim no rajyena Govinda kim bhogairjivitena va.* (Do not desire victory, Neither kingdom nor pleasures why kingdom, why luxuries, why this war, why...) I.......32
2. **Guilt:** *Ahobatha MahatPAPAM karthum vyavasatha vayum Yadrajya sukhaobhena Hanthum Swajana mudyatham* (Preparing for the sinful act of killing our own kin...) I........44
3. **Death wish:** *Yadi Ma Mapratheekaram asastram Sastrapanayah Dhartarashtra rane hanusthanme KSHEMAtharam bhaveth* (Even if I get killed in the war by my enemy it will be good) I......45

- **Therapeutic Process**
  Cognitive/Rational Emotive Approach
  Discussion on the natural inevitability of birth and death of life cycle, immortality of soul, performance of your own *Dharma* (duty) otherwise running the risk of shame and public defame. Goal of therapy is removal of guilt and remotivate for action.
- *Asochyan anvasochastvam Pragna-vadams cha bhashase gatasun agatasumscha n anusochanti panditah*
  (You worry about events you are not supposed, and speak like a learned man, Wise people do not worry about things that are perishable, or immortal) II.......11
- *Vasamsi jirnani yatha vihaya navani grhanti naro parani tatha sarirani vihaya jirnany-anyani samyati navani dehi* (As you remove torn clothes and wear new ones ATMA also leaves... and occupies new bodies) II.........22

- *Nainam chindanti sastrani Nainam dahati pavakah na chainam kledayanty apo na soshayati marutah* (*Atma* can never be torn by arrows (bullets), Burnt by fire, Washed away by floods (Tsunami) lifted by winds (Typhoon, Hurricane) II........23
- *Jatasya hi dhruvo mrtyuh dhruvam janma mrtasya cha tasmaad apariharye rthe na tvam sochitumarhasi* (Everything born must die, Everything dead must get born again and you should not worry about these events) II........27
- *Atha chethva mimam dharmyam sangramam na karishyasi Thatha swadharmam keerthin cha hitva Papamavasyasi* (Your "Dharma" is to participate in war, If not You lose your *dharma*, fame and Commit a Sin) II..........33
- *Sambhavitasya Chakeerthi hi Maranadathirichyathe* (For a noble man disgrace is worse than death)II......34
- *Hathova prapsyasi swargam jitva va bhokshyase mahim thasmad utthistha Kaunteya yuddhaya krta-nischayah* (If you die you will go to heaven, winning will get you kingdom. So get up and decide to fight) II.........37
- **Action and Renunciation**

  The one concept in *Bhagavad Gita* that received exceptional respect and applause from several great scholars is the emphasis on *Karma* (Action). Intelligent action (*Gnana Karma*) without performance anxiety and without the greed for the fruits of the work (*Nishkama Karma*) and never to have the choice of non-performance of duty (*Akarma*) emerges as a key point in the teaching of *Bhagavad Gita*.
- *Karmany evadhikaras te Mma phalesu kaddacana Ma karma-phala-hetur bhur Ma te sango'stv akarmani* (You have the right only on Action, Not on the fruits of your work Never own responsibility to the result, Must never lose interest in work) II..........47

  Humanistic School: Emphasis on the power and capabilities of individual self, and how the person alone will be responsible for his actions, growth or otherwise. "You are your choices". "You are your destiny".

- *Uddharedatmana'tmanam atmanam avasadayet atm'aiva hy atmano bandhur atm'aiva ripur atmanah* (Self-Empowerment, No inferiority, Your "Self" can be your friend or your own enemy) VI.........5
  Viswarupa-Darsanam-? Hypnosis: Is the therapist inducing a state of hypnotic trance at this point!
- *Vedanam Samavedosmi... Indriyanam Manasyasmi... Naranam cha Naradhipam....*
  I am the best of everything - Omnipotent, Omnipresent... X chapter
- *Pasyame Pardha Rupani Sathasotha Sahashrasu...* (Arjuna, Look at my Hundreds and Thousands of forms...) XI...5
- **Trust (Bhakti):** Trust (Faith) remains a single most important element in the therapeutic relationship; not just in psychology but the medical practice in general.
- *Sarvadharman Parithyajya Mamekam Saranam Vraja Aham Thva Sarvapapebhyo Mokshaishyami Ma Suchah* (Leave everything and Trust me, I will rescue you from all the problems, Do not Worry) XVIII.......66

Guru-Sishya Relationship: _Gurukul_ Tradition

Imparting wisdom with devotion to learn and teach, dialogue and discussion being the process, bound by relationship of trust is the ancient tradition of *Gurukul.* (Swamy Dayananada, 1978)

Therapeutic Components:

- Satisfactory Premorbid Personality of the patient with adequate coping skills.
- Therapist is a trusted Friend, Philosopher, Guide.
- Catharsis, Ventilation!
- Cognitive and Rational emotive approach! Cognitive Distortions, Misinterpretations (*Sankhya Yoga*)
- Emphasis on Work with renunciation (*Karma Yoga*), Smart Action without performance anxiety (*Gnana Karma Sanyasa Yoga*)

- Behaviour Therapy – Flooding!—Prolonged, continuous exposure to the anxiety provoking situation as the therapy was in the battlefield itself.
- Insight Oriented! (*Gnana Vignana Yoga*)
- Viswaroopam – Hypnosis! (*Viswaroopa Sandarshan Yoga*)
- Trust (*Bhakti Yoga*)

The *Bhagavad Gita* holds profound significance, offering vast intellectual depth as it delves into and elucidates various life experiences. Its reach extends to individuals with diverse intellectual and philosophical backgrounds, aiming to resonate with everyone, regardless of their worldview (Chalam, 1966). The therapeutic model appears eclectic, as the therapist appears unrestricted by any singular theoretical approach. The primary focus is on achieving the end goal of alleviating guilt and reinvigorating the individual to engage in the battle. Throughout the dialogue, a practical and common-sense approach is evident in addressing impediments. Emphasis is placed equally on various aspects including logic, action, renunciation, the power of self, knowledge, wisdom, trust, universality, and the immortality of the human spirit. This appears to be the model of "Person-centred Therapy" in the little sense. Lord Krishna seems to have succeeded in making Arjuna rediscover his emotional balance and power as described in the last *shloka* of *Bhagavad Gita*.

> *Yathra Yougeeswarah krishno Yatra Partho Dhanurdharah*
> *Thathra Sri Vijayo bhuthi dhruva neethirmathirmama.*
> XVIII....... 78

(......Where Arjuna stands with his Gandiva [Bow] there certainly will be wealth, victory and justice—so I believe). "It is not this approach gives power to the person; it never takes it away" (Carl Rogers, 1977).

As is the case with any successful model of therapeutic intervention, which needs to be individualised for maximum benefit, the psychotherapeutic approach practiced in *Bhagavad Gita* also will have its place in the repertoire of psychotherapeutic models and remains a useful tool in the hands of an experienced therapist when applied judiciously for some patients with specific problems of distress.

***Bhagavad Gita* and COVID-19:** The term moral injury is characterised by the conflict arising from being compelled to act, observe, or fail to intervene against one's deeply held convictions of personal morality and societal ethics (Menon *et al.*, 2021). Within the context of a healthcare worker (HCW) during the COVID-19 pandemic, a moral irony emerges when certain principles inherent in fulfilling one's duty directly clash with contemplations for personal well-being, such as self-sacrifice and altruism. So here concept of 4 "D" is being introduced, namely Detachment, Doership, Duty, and *Dhyana* (Zgierska, *et al.* 2018).

Detachment: It means that one should detach themselves from repercussions of his actions that they do in any phase of their life or in any situation they are put in by fate.

Doership: Lord Krishna enlightens us by stating the fact that we are not the actual doers of any job. There is an ultimate power above us who channelises our energies with his powers for us to perform any job. Hence, we should not take pride in whatever we are doing.

Duty: The concept of *dharma* as explained by Lord Krishna states that one should trust his inner self depending on his own duties, however imperfect those may be.

***Dhyana*:** Meditation is stated to be a spiritual practice that results in better well-being of the person, physically, mentally, and spiritually. Suggesting patients meditate, there was a significant improvement in their mental health, alertness, and self-efficacy. A similar concept is also described in the form of three paths or *yoga*, the first being of knowledge (*Jnana yoga*) promoting awareness about self, and reframing our thinking from an "I" to a "we mode," which is needed on a collective basis for prevention of spread of the coronavirus. The *Karma yoga* (path of action) teaches the art of selfless action to healthcare providers, with providing framework for continuing efforts in unforeseen situations. The *Raja yoga* (path of meditation) suggests to have healthy lifestyle and mindful meditation to improve resilience (Keshavan, 2020).

Bhagavad Gita and Management: An Overview

Management includes leadership, coordination, planning, direction, communication, and motivation, all of which are very much evident in the entire discourse of *Bhagavad Gita*. The management focused theme of *Bhagavad Gita* is about man's defined duties and their efficient accomplishment or the path they choose to help attain the ultimate goal. So again, efficient management is to accomplish the goal in a manner, which includes transforming each person into an entrepreneur to undertake his own defined duties. Over the whole discourse, we get to witness Arjuna under the guidance of Lord Krishna overcoming his doubts and guilt and getting ready for the battle. Thus, through the learnings of the management techniques mentioned in *Bhagavad Gita*, we can say that *Bhagavad Gita* is capable of inspiring, one to be motivated to deliver duties which are defined for oneself, further revolutionising the worshippers of idleness into warriors of action (Jayamani, 2013).

Conclusion

Spirituality is a time-honoured concept in healing, which is more of a subjective experience and exists both within and outside the traditional religious system. Incorporating the teachings of the *Bhagavad Gita* into daily practice can aid in the development of a culturally relevant form of psychotherapy, potentially enhancing its appeal and effectiveness in the Indian context. This narrative review aims to explore the utility of the *Bhagavad Gita* in everyday counselling and psychotherapeutic practices. The chapter outlines various psychotherapeutic approaches evident in the dialogue between Lord Krishna and Arjuna in the *Bhagavad Gita*. These psychotherapeutic approaches which are evident when one reads the *Bhagavad Gita* have been compared to modern psychotherapies like cognitive behavioural therapy and psychoanalytic therapy. It aims to show the similarities between them and further postulate how psychotherapeutic principles from *Bhagavad Gita* can be used to develop a more indigenous model of therapy which takes this scripture into account. Considering current psychotherapeutic approaches, average Indian has influence of authority, spirituality, dependence on elders, belief in soul transmigration, and social structure. This signifies a need to increase awareness of developing more indigenous therapeutic models. It also emphasises that the first Counsellor Bhagavan Sri Krishna has proved himself as a best counsellor and became role model to many counsellors in the modern days.

References

Aggarwal, K.K., *Hindustan Times, Indian English-Language Daily Newspaper*, New Delhi, July 26, 2017.

Balodhi, J.P., Keshavan, M.S. (2011). "*Bhagavad Gita* and Psychotherapy". *Asian Journal of Psychiatry*, *4*: 300 2.

Bhagavad Geeta (1927). Gorakhpur Press.

"*Bhagavad Gita* as a Text of Counselling—A Methodical Study with the association of Counselling and Psychotherapeutic Techniques". Main Authors—Deepshikha Thakur & Satish and Corresponding Author —Subodh Saurabh Singh, *Turkish Journal of Physiotherapy and Rehabilitation, 32*(3), ISSN 2651-4451 | e-ISSN 446X

Bhatia, S.C., Madabushi, J., Kolli, V., Bhatia, S.K., Madaan, V. (2013). "The *Bhagavad Gita* and Contemporary Psychotherapies". *Indian Journal of Psychiatry, 55*(Suppl 2): S315.

Carl Rogers, C. (1977). *Carl Rogers on Personal Power.*

Chalam Gudipati Venkata (1966). *Bhagavad Gita.*

Govindaswamy, M.V. (1959). "Surrender-not to self-surrender". *Transaction. 2*: i–x.

Gangadhar, B.N. (2011). "The Indian Treatise on Mental Health Care and Promotion". *Asian Journal of Psychiatry, 4*: 303.

Jayamani, C.V. (2013). "*Bhagavad Gita* and Management". *Commer Spectr, 3*: 60-5. https://commercespectrum.com/uploads/ article/13-02-2013-108. pdf. [Last accessed on 2022, October 10].

Keshavan, M.S. (2020). "Building resilience in the COVID-19 era: Three paths in the *Bhagavad Gita*". *Indian J Psychiatry, 62*: 459-61.

Menon, B., Narayan, S.K., Bhade, S. (2021). "COVID-19, Moral Injury and the *Bhagavad Gita*". Barrett, B., Hayney, M.S., Müller, D., Rakel, D., Brown, R., *Journal of Religious Health, 60*(8): 654-62.

Neki, J.S. (1975). "Psychotherapy in India: Past, Present, and Future". *Journal of Psychotherapy, 29*: 92-100.

Padma Devi Dasi, Krishna, (Jan 1, 2011). *The Supreme Psychologist, Back to Godhead, 45*(1).

Ramachandrarao, S.K. (1983). "The Conception of Stress in Indian Thought: The Practical Involvement in *Gita* and *Ayurveda*". *NIMHANS J, 1*: 123–31.

Rao, A. Venkoba, Parvathidevi, S. "The *Bhagavad Gita* treats body and mind". *Indian Journal of Psychiatry.*

Rao, A.V. (2002). "The Mind in Indian Philosophy". *Indian Journal of Psychiatry, 44*: 315-25.

Reddy, M.S. (2012). "Psychotherapy Insights from *Bhagavad Gita*". *Indian Journal of Psychology, Med, 34*:100-4.

Rhythma, Kaul (2017). "Krishna was World's first Counsellor", *Indian English-Language Daily Newspaper, Hindustan Times*, New Delhi.

Satyananda, D. (1972). *Psychology of the Gita of Hinduism*. London: Oxford and I.B.H.

Swamy Chinmayananda (2002). *Holy Geeta*, Central Chinmaya Mission Trust.

Swamy Dayananada (1978). *Bhagavad Gita.*

Varma, V.K. & Ghosh, A. (1976). "Psychotherapy as Practiced by Indian Psychiatrists". *Indian Journal of Psychiatry, 18*:177-86.

Zgierska, A.E. *et al.* (2018). "Meditation or exercise for preventing acute respiratory infection (MEPARI-2): A randomised controlled trial". *PLoS One, 13*: e0197778.

13

Religion, Spirituality and Social Work

A Study on Buddhism

Sheuli Dutta

Introduction

The relationship between religion, spirituality and social work has been closely linked throughout the contemporary human history. It has often been observed that there is no nation or society without religion. But what is meant by religion? According to Cicero, religion means repetition of prayers or attachment of a continual binding. But the most prevalent conception of religion is that it is a law-abiding scrupulously conscientious frame of mind. Early law was based on tradition and moral obligation to uphold social structure, implying an ascetical attitude towards the gods, rather than legislation. On the other hand, spirituality is an aspect of religious traditions and also of existential value system. A spiritual belief holds that there is a transcendent, spiritual dimension to life and that the universe is unfolding in a meaningful, purposeful way. However, religion and spirituality are manifestly overlapped and interrelated in terms of their culture, theological and historical origins (Koenig, 2009). The integration of spirituality and religious element in social work practice has grown, a shift from a charity-oriented approach to a more professional and secularised field. The National Association of Social Workers' Code of Ethics emphasises the importance of considering individuals' religious beliefs and practices in ethical decision-making. Social workers must be aware of conflicts between personal and professional values and deal responsibly with them. According to the IFSW (2014), social work emphasises that treating people holistically necessitates taking into account their belief systems.

Contemporary social work scholars differentiate spirituality and religion as distinct concepts (Canda, 2008), with spirituality expressing through religious or non-religious forms, while religion is an organised system of values, beliefs, and traditions (Canda, Furman, 2010). Scholars argue that distinguishing spirituality from religion is crucial in spiritually sensitive social work practice (Canda & Furman, 2010; Handler & Pargament, 2014), as religion is a visible faith expression, while spirituality is a broader concept (Zapf, 2005). According to Canda, a person with to understand respect to the environment, it is necessary to learn about the role of religion and spirituality growth and in the development of a person (Canda & Furman, 2010). Surveys show social workers value the spiritual dimension and believe it's crucial for clients (Bullies, 1996; Canda & Furman,1999; Joseph, 1988; *et al.*). The NASW Code of Ethics lacks specific standards for spirituality-oriented activities, as it depends on practice context, practitioner training, spiritual perspective, and client situation (Canda, Nakashima & Furman, 2004). Social workers' religious/spiritual beliefs and practices are intertwined, making it difficult to separate their beliefs from their professional practices (Kawan, 2020). Scholars suggest mindful usage of spirituality (Furness & Gilligan, 2010), incorporating spiritual sensitivity into cultural competence models (Vaddhanphuti, 2013), making religious spirituality a standard topic in social work classes (Dudeley, 2016), and focusing on spiritually sensitive social work practice (Canda & Furman, 2010). Therefore, the integration of spirituality in social work literature has grown, despite the lack of adequate discussion in the earlier phase. Social work practices in various societies are rooted in spiritual and religious ideologies, with Indian spirituality being a prime example of this integration.

Indian Spirituality in the Light of Hinduism and Social Work

The spirituality teachings in Indian tradition points to the fact that Hinduism is associated with humanism and human welfare. Canda and Furman (2010) highlight Hindu oriented views in social work literature, primarily addressing *yoga* a based on Swami Vivekananda and other *yogic* traditions. Klaus Klostermaier (2010), a prominent scholar of Hinduism, asserts that the Hindu tradition is open to new ideas and scientific thought, and many elements share humanism values. *Manu Smriti* (Manu, VI, 92) prescribes the tenfold system of virtuous duties: contentment; abstention from injury to others; active benevolence and returning good for evil; resistance to sensual appetites, abstinence from theft and illicit gain; purity, chasity, and cleanliness; coercion of passions; acquisition of divine wisdom; veracity, honesty and fidelity; and freedom from wrath and hatred. There is a prominent commonality between Hinduism and Social Work practices. Schools of social work commonly teach that the origin of the profession lies in the humanistic principles of the many world faith traditions. Many social workers, regardless of their religious affiliations, are taught that their religion doesn't significantly impact their professional practice (Cnaan, 2004). Many Indian practitioners argue that professional social work is a Western concept, but Hinduism reflects its core values. Social work addresses human needs, enhancing adjustment and understanding clients' concerns. The Code of the National Association of Social Workers outlines core values like Service, Social Justice, Dignity, and Competence.

The fundamental tenet of Hinduism, "Dharma", places a strong emphasis on social responsibility, truth, non-violence, compassion, and regard for others. Verse 32 of Chapter 6 of the *Bhagavad Gita* describes how perfect "yogis" see equality and respond to the happiness and sorrows of others (*atma upamyena sarvatra samam pashyati yo'rjuna sukhava yadi va duhkham sa yogi paramomatah*). The verse advocates for social justice and equality, with non-violence being the highest form. The moral precept known as "*karma*" encourages social responsibility and recognises the result of one's deeds. In chapter 2, verse 47 of *Bhagavad Gita* states, "*karmayevadhikaraste ma phalesu kadacana, ma karma-phala-hetur bhur ma te sangostvakarmani*", which means "your right is to work only"' but never to its fruits. Do not let your attachment to inaction or the results of your actions serve as your drive. Finding your moral obligation is the main focus. According to Hindu scriptures, good deeds are credited toward the law of *karma*. The verse 49 of chapter 2 highlights how crucial it is to seek out divine knowledge and fulfil moral obligations. As social workers assist clients in mobilising their resources and acknowledging the inherent dignity of human beings, they are embodying the Hindu concept of the law of *karma*. Hinduism's concept of "Atma" places a strong emphasis on the equality of all living things, including people, animals, and plants. It also declares that all living things are entitled to dignity and respect as God dwells there. (verse 20 of chapter 10; verse 11 of chapter 9; *Bhagavad Gita*). In the *Vedic* phase, charity being the most potent way to earn "punya". The *Rigveda* and *Bhagavad Gita* emphasise generosity and charity without contempt towards recipient, referred to as "saatvik" (without craving for result) or 'taamasik' (craving for pleasure or impure aim), and poor are considered "Daridra Narayana". Professional social workers' training focuses on developing core values and cultivating compassion, controlled emotional involvement, and human dignity. The ideal of *Nishkam Sewa* in *Bhagavad Gita* involves offering help without self-gain or praise(verse 47, chapter 2; verse 4, chapter 3).

Buddha and His Teaching

Born in Lumbini, Nepal, Siddharta Gautam, the founder of Buddhism, grew up in Kapilavastu. At the age of 29, he became aware of the suffering of his people and sought spiritual solace through ascetic practices. Turning away from asceticism, he devoted himself to meditation and mindful breathing. Eventually, he attained a state of supreme vision, awareness, knowledge, and clairvoyance without any supernatural assistance. He later known as "*The Buddha—The Enlightened One and taught Dharma throughout his life*" (Thomas, 2019). According to T.W. Rhys while Gautama was initially regarded as a Hindu, he eventually recognised as the greatest and most wise figure among Hindus (Rhys: 78-79). Buddhism is more a system of philosophy and practical ethics than a religion. It focuses on the existence of sorrow and suffering, not just for the poor and wretched but also for those in luxury (Narasu: 20). Therefore, Buddha's supreme knowledge was realised by himself alone. He referred himself by the terms *Tathagata* (The Accomplished One), *Araham* (The Worthy One), *Samma Sambuddha* (The Fully Enlightened One), and *Bhagava* (The Exalted One). Buddhism is a religion that promotes generosity and compassion, debunking knowledge without benevolence and promoting peace by discharging war, capital punishment, and crime against humanity.

In the sixth century B.C., a global awaking and spiritual unrest led to reformists addressing social issues. This period in India as well as globally resulted in the emergence of various reformist schools, among them Buddhism and Jainism were the most influential. Gautam Buddha, the founder of Buddhism, wrote nothing but his teaching were handed down through his disciples. It is a psycho-ethical tradition that involves gradual pacification of thought (*Pariyatti*) and practical application (*Patipatti*). It aims to eradicate ignorance and visualise truth, addressing suffering and achieving a state of bliss through a tri-steps path such as *Dukh*, *Nirvana* and *Magga*. Buddha's teachings emphasise non-violence, mutual attraction, and rightness. He opposes the caste system and believes no person is superior or inferior based on birth. The Buddha discovered and revealed the *Dharma*, which consists of "The Four Noble Truths". The first truth is that misery or pain and suffering. According to the second truth, selfish desires are the root cause of misery, which exists throughout all stages of life. The third truth asserts that eliminating selfish cravings is the path to liberation from suffering. "The Noble Eightfold Path" is the fourth truth.

While Buddhist teaching emphasises the development of ethical character, Indian religions frequently practice the doctrine of release (*moksha, vimukti*) from the evils of existence. The Buddhist perspective bears a strong resemblance to the Upanishadic doctrine, which states that release holds on certain types of knowledge (Thomas, 1953). *Nirvana*, or *nibbana*, is therefore the opposite of release. The nun Dhammadinna is reported to have responded to the layman Visaka in this way (Majjh: 304). Thus, the Buddhist doctrine of *Nibbana*, or *Nirvana*, differs from other schools of thought in its belief soul's immortality. This belief was prevalent in ancient cultures, including Egyptians, Greeks, Romans, Jews, and pre-Buddhist Indians. *Vedanta*, a non-dualism system, believes that the universe is maya and governed by *Brahman* (an invisible agency), and union with *Brahman* through *yoga* leads to salvation. The doctrine of *Nibbbana*, taught by Buddha, contradicts the idea of the soul's immortality in all other religions. By avoiding extremes such as indulgence of sense gratification and self-mortification, the Tathagata gains Enlightenment through the Middle Path, leading to *Nibbana*.

The *Lankavatara-sutra* is a significant canonical text for subjective idealism and has a unique literacy character. It was translated into Chinese around A.D. 430 and A.D. 443, but may have existed earlier in a simpler form. The full title of this *sutra* is "*Saddharma*-lankavatara", which means Ceylon, but here it is a city on the peak of Mount Malay and the fortress of Ravana. With the opening of *sutra*, it was taught to Ravana the two fundamental truth that is the external things are external due to wrong interpretation of inner experience, and reality is apprehensible through sudden revulsion (Thomas, 1953). *Lankavartara* has a psychological basis. It is based on early Buddhism which identifies six consciousness states; eye, ear, nose, tongue, touch, mind-consciousness. Professor Suzuki distinguishes between mind-consciousness and *manas*. Therefore, former involves memory, judgement, and imagination and later is the deeply-seated consciousness in the soul that ignorantly clings to the ego-conception and reality of an external world. Mind-consciousness arises from attachment to external objects, and it is nourished by *vasanas*. It is a reflection on the ideal of oneself. It has no separate body or mark, through attachment to objects, the system of thought-construction is mutually conditioned. So, when mind-consciousness is got rid of, the seven consciousnesses are also got rid of.

Decline and revival of Buddhism

The decline of Buddhism in India is often linked to royal persecution, including attempts by Brahmin ruler Pushyamitra Sunga to destroy monasteries and reward Buddhist heads (Mitra, 1954). Taranath, a Tibetan Buddhist chronicler, identified this period as the first of three attacks against Buddhism, during which many monasteries were destroyed and learned monks were slaughtered (Chimpa, Chattopadhya, 1980). However, some scholars argue this is false and absurd. Musalman invaders' brutal massacres were more effective than orthodox Hindu persecutions, contributing to the decline (Smith, 1924). Even later, Ambedkar also acknowledged it. However, Brahmanism survived due to state support, the death of the Buddhist priesthood by Islam, and persecution by Brahmanic rulers (Ambedkar: 230). Basham's study reveals that the decline of Buddhism in India was primarily due to the rise of Hinduism, a reformed religion that transformed worship of Shiva and Vishnu into fervent devotion. Buddhism, a separate religion challenging caste and denying Vedas, failed to base itself on popular life, with Brahmans handling Buddhist families' rituals. Thus, Muslim invasions nearly vanished Buddhism (Basham, 1958).

"I will not die a Hindu"—Dr. B.R. Ambedkar's life is entwined with the history of new Buddhism or the rebirth of Buddhism. His exceptional role in bringing Buddhism back to life is astounding and demonstrates its applicability in today's world. Ambedkar's extensive study of Indian history and Buddhist texts, including essays like "Who Were the Sudra?" and "The Untouchables", influenced his evaluation of Buddhism as an alternative to the Brahmanical social order, emphasising morality. B.R. Ambedkar initially did not view Buddhism as an alternative to Hinduism due to its association with Hindu-reformist Arya Samaj. However, he later compared Buddhism to Marxism and believed that it could attribute by teaching ethical responsibility and changing attitudes (Ambedkar: 441). He believed that religion should relate facts of life and morality, rather than God or salvation. Ambedkar interpreted Buddhism as an ideology for social equality and justice, particularly for the oppressed, especially *Dalits* or Untouchables. He converted to Buddhism on 14th October, 1956, rejecting Hinduism for its inequality and oppression, and instead following the eight-fold path of Buddha (Keer: 499-500). Ambedkar's conversion aimed to make it part of a larger political movement addressing the material contradiction in Indian society (Guru, 1989: 419-20).

Buddhism and Social Work

Buddhism's relevance to social work practice is growing globally in secular contexts. In recent years engaged Buddhism and mindfulness are gaining prominence throughout the world. Social work is a practice-based profession promoting social change, development, and empowerment, based on principles of social justice, human rights, collective responsibility, and diversity (IFSW & IASSW: 2014). Buddhism's philosophy of *Dhamma* focuses on man-to-man relationships, teaching, training, community development, and political activity for a better society. It is an ancient Indian religion, practiced in many countries such as Japan, China, Burma, Thailand, South Korea, Vietnam, Mongolia, Sri Lanka and India. Buddhism is a pragmatic teaching that transcends sorrow into wisdom through ethics, meditation, philosophy, science, art, and poetry. Early Buddhists created social conditions conducive to individual values, such as the 'Welfare State' of king Ashoka. Buddhism emerged in

India as a spiritual force against social injustices, caste tyranny, and emancipation of women (Rahula, 1978).

The Concept of "Social Karma"

The development of conditioned behaviour patterns within a culture—known as "Social Karma"—is the outcome of many wills rather than the accumulation of individual *karma* (Ken, 2009). *Karma*, which in Buddhism translates to "action", is impacted by one's intentions. It suggests that we are a product of our past, present, and future deeds by embracing both. *Karma* refers to deeds, while *Vipaka* denotes outcome. Buddhism posits that *karma* is a natural law that operates independently, without external intervention. It says that regardless of human justice, every action has its own rewards and consequences. Therefore, *karma* is not a divine force but rather one's actions, allowing for self-driving and a struggle against nurture and nature. The central idea of social work, "service", and the Buddhist concept of "karma" or "social *karma*" are closely related. Social workers are ethically obligated to put the needs of others before their own interests. They do this by applying their knowledge, morals, and expertise to solve social issues and assist the underprivileged. They frequently give their professional services freely and without expecting payment in exchange. Buddhism holds that while an individual cannot alter the conditions passed down from earlier generations, they can allow themselves to be guided in the direction of self-improvement by choosing the morally upright path.

Giving, Helping and Teaching

Giving is a crucial initial step in Buddhist practice, fostering merit and morality, and leading to liberation from the cycle of *samsara* (Jootla, 2011). It combats greed, the first unwholesome motivational root, and helps cure egoism and selfishness (Silva, 2011). Giving is the way to overcome miserliness, according to the *Devata samyutta*. Alms given from wealth is highly praised in the *Suttas*, which list fourteen items for charity. Public generosity is especially important for recluses, Brahmins, destitutes, way-farers, wanderers, and beggars (Silva, 2011). The *Magha Sutta* asserts that when one is established in generosity, hatred is eradicated, and it fosters social cohesiveness and solidarity. David Brandon emphasises respecting others as acknowledging their Buddha nature, despite superficial positions, and recognising their purpose and autonomy as well. As Brandon (1976) puts it, "He is another form of nature".

The act of giving and helping is a necessary social service in the field of social work. Whether it is a direct giving act, which we call charitable action from UNICEF, or the destitute relief camp from the local government or non-government social workers, help people in need and address social problems, challenging negative discrimination and providing services indiscriminately are the prime responsibilities of a social worker. Both Buddhism and social work provide social service in an act of 'giving and helping' to the members of the society to enable them to develop optimally, function effectively, and lead, a life with decency, dignity, and liberty. These services have been rendered to all irrespective to their religion, caste, race, language, culture etc.

The Buddha's teachings emphasise discipline, meditation, and wisdom. The *Tripitaka* categorises these teaching into *Sutra*, *Vinaya* (precepts or rules), and *Sastra* (commentaries), emphasising meditation, discipline, and wisdom respectively. The four Universal Vows of Buddhas and Bodhisattvas are:

1. Sentient beings are innumerable, I vow to help them all;
2. Afflictions are inexhaustible, I vow to end them all;
3. Ways to practice are boundless, I vow to master them all;
4. Enlightenment is unsurpassable; I vow to attain it.

Our goal is to help others break from delusion and awaken, leading to true happiness and a cessation of suffering. This involves cultivating good virtue, ending greed, anger, ignorance and arrogance, and upholding precepts to guard against harmful consequences created by speech, body and mind, i.e., words, deeds, and thoughts. True wisdom arises from cultivation of high moral character, from a pure, non-discriminatory and compassionate mind (Kung, 2010). Buddhism, a self-help discipline, aims to meet the needs of the underprivileged and improve human well-being which requires morality and ethical obligations.

Compassion

Buddhism is called a religion of compassion. A well-known line from the sutra of contemplation on the Buddha of immeasurable life is-

"The Buddha's mind is great compassion. It is with this unconditional compassion that they embrace all beings". According to this scripture, comprehending the teachings of Buddha imply entails knowing what his infinite compassion entails (Haseo, 2010). *Karuna* is the Pali word translated as compassion. *Anukampa* and *daya*, often translated as "sympathy" are closely allied to it (Aronson, 1980). The five precepts are the cornerstone of all Buddhist spiritual development. In Buddhism, morality takes precedence over rituals, offerings made in devotion, and austerities. A way of life based on values and deeds is what the Buddha, also known as *Dhamma*, called his own. Ashoka Maurya also used the term *Dhamma* in his inscription as compassion. Alongside Buddha's compassion for oneself and others, the Four Noble Truths and Eightfold Path emphasise Compassion. The noble truth is mercy and hope for the abolition of suffering. It is the embodiment of compassion.

The Eightfold Path is a Buddhist teaching that emphasises compassion, understanding, intent, speech, action, livelihood, effort, mindfulness, and concentration. It emphasises accepting reality, recognising truth, ethical behaviour, respect for agreements, non-harmful occupations, mindfulness and concentration. Compassion is the dominant feature of Buddhist teaching, guiding individuals towards the cessation of suffering.

The Buddhist way of life is full of compassion, equality, tolerance, self-reliance and individual responsibility, similar to social work. The compassion of a social worker is a precondition for effective social work both Buddhist and social workers have compassion for others. They like to deal with distress people and problems. Both believe in self-sufficiency and dignity of each individual; cultivate a spirit of openness, cooperation, goodwill, and equality. E.R. Canda (2020) expresses his view on compassion in the relationship with social work and Buddhism. He states that compassion is a combination of qualities, such as sincere empathy, clear unbiased mind, and skilful response. In social work, a social worker combines with the empathetic care, listening, and skilful means to help clients. The Buddhist ideal of Bodhisatva of compassion, represented by a thousand eyes and hands, ready to help in need. Buddhist idea of "Upaya" which refers to skilful response to reach out in many ways and different directions according to the client's (individual) need. Therefore, compassion is not just a feeling of pity, it is heart-to-heart connection and skilful response.

Role of Socially Engaged Buddhism in Contemporary Society

Socially engaged Buddhism or engaged Buddhism, a modifiable approach to practicing Buddhism in the contemporary world. It was first introduced in the 20th century by notable figures like Thich Nhat Hanh, Sulak Sivaraksa, and the Dalai Lama. This movement reinterprets traditional Buddhist doctrines and applies them to social, political, and environmental concerns. Engaged Buddhists participate in activism and community service, aiming for compassion and non-violence (King, Winston L., 1994). The term was coined by Ven. Thich Nhat Hanh, who believed that Buddhism is inherently engaged. During the Vietnam war in the mid of 1950s, Hanh argued that Buddhism should help the needy and impoverished. He established Buddhist courses and became the chief editor of *Phat Giao Vietnam* magazine and wrote about Engaged Buddhism. However, pro-catholic president Ngo Dinh Diem's anti-Buddhist decrees in 1963 led sparking protests and causing the Buddhist crisis in south Vietnam when he outlawed Buddhist flags and celebrating Buddha's birthday. It resulted in civilians deaths and detentions of nuns and monks as well as contributed decline of Wu's regime's popularity (Miller, 2015). Hanh and his follower's combined non-violent meditation techniques, promoting active non-violent resistance and establishing Engaged Buddhism in the historical context (Wang, 2023).

With distinct historical, cultural, and geographical characteristics, each country is unique. People in every nation therefore have unique mental development and value systems. Each society thus has its own social structure and problems. For India as well, it is justified. India faces various social issues such as population explosion, casteism, poverty, unemployment, and lack of independence of making decision as a girl child. Buddhism can help to address these problems by providing philosophical, spiritual, social, and moral lessons. Buddha's teachings are eternal and can be applied to various circumstances. India has a history of applying Buddhism for social justice, with Dr. B.R. Ambedkar fighting against caste-based discrimination and incorporating principles of equality into Indian Constitution. Engaged Buddhism can promote social change and address these unique challenges. Even it emerged as a response to modern trauma in Asian Buddhist countries, including colonialism, war, social injustice, environmental degradation, genocide, and religion suppression in wide range. Though the Buddhist scholars are divided into two groups, few maintain continuity between present and past Buddhism, while others argue that Traditional Buddhism has no interest in society (Ven Dhammavamso, 2009). But Thich Nhat Hanh's "Fourteen Guidelines" aim to overcome oppression by considering contemporary society's changing scenarios (Hanh, 1998; Edelglass, 2009).

Conclusion

Religion and spirituality have long been intertwined in social work. The integration of spirituality and religious elements in social work practice has evolved from charity-oriented approach to a professional and secularised field. There is a significant influence of Hinduism and Buddhism in social work practice in providing services to the mankind. The concept of *Nishkam Sewa* in *Bhagavad Gita* involves offering help without self-gain or praise which is ideal in social work practice. The teachings imparted by the Buddha remain just as pertinent in today's world as they did during his lifetime. Engaged Buddhism, a dynamic and responsive approach to contemporary society, actively tackles many issues, is shaping a more compassionate and equitable world. Therefore, scholars suggest mindful usage of spirituality and focusing on spiritually sensitive social work practice. Indian society and spirituality are multidimensional, offering innovative possibilities for social work practice. Understanding these principles in a secular context and having good skills in professional management of negative impacts can guide holistic social practice. Spirituality is considered an essence of life, focusing on interconnectedness with oneself and others. Therefore, it is crucial in social work assessments and interventions, influencing healing, transcending suffering and providing philosophical and moral lessons to balance material and transcendental worlds.

References

Ambedkar, B. (1987). *Dr. Babasaheb Ambedkar: Writings and Speeches.* Dr. Ambedkar Foundation, Vol. 3.

Basham, A.L. (1954, reprint 1990). *The Wonder that was India.* Rupa & Co., Calcutta.

Bhagavad Gita., The Song of God—Swami Mukundananda. https://doi.www.holy-bhagavad-gita.org/chapter/2/3/6/verse/47/49/4.

Buddha Net—Worldwide Buddhist Information and Education Network. https://doi.www.buddhanet.net/27/2024.

Bullies, G.R. (1996). *Spirituality in Social Work Practice.* Washington DC: Taylor & Francis.

Canda, E. (2020). *Buddhism and Social Work: On Religious and Spiritual Issues*, part 2. ARIISW written and edited by Inagaki, Kikuchi & Gohori. https://doi.www.researchgate.net/publication/344526962.

Canda, E., Nakashima, M., Furman. L. (2004). "Ethical Considerations About Spirituality in Social Work : Insights from a National Qualitative Survey". *Families in Society: The Journal of Contemporary Social Services. 85*(1): 27-34. https://doi.www.familiesinsociety.org.

Canda, R.E., Furman, D.L. (2010). *Spiritual Diversity in Social Work Practice: The heart of Helping*. Oxford University Press, 59-62; 70; 89-90. https://doi.ndl.ethernet.edu.et/bitstream/123456789/20904/1/17.pdf.

Dhammavaso, Ven (2009). *Buddhism—A Balancing Factors for Current World Developments*. https://doi.www.academia.edu/189470.

Dudley, R.J. (2016). *Spirituality Matters in Social Work: Connecting Spirituality, Religion, and Practice*. Routledge Taylor & Francis Group.

Ebimgbo, S., Okoye, U., Agwu, U.P. (2019). "Spirituality on Social Work". *Research Gate*. https://doi.www.researchgate.net/publication/330926888.

Edelglass, W. (2009). "Engaged Buddhism: Thich Naht Hanh's Interbeing". *Research Gate*. https://doi.www.researchgate.net/publication/309534352.

Gilligan, P., Furness. S. (2014). "The Role of Religion and Spirituality in Social Work Practice: Views and Experiences of Social Workers and Students". *Research Gate*, July. https://doi.www.researchgate.net/publication/27313730.

Harris, J.E. (1997). *Detachment and Compassion in Early Buddhism*. Buddhist Publication Society, No. 141. https://doi.www.accesstoinsigh.org/lib/authors/harris/b/141.html.

Haseo, T.D. (2010). *Learning the Buddha's Great Compassion*. A Talk delivered at the International Buddhist Association, Jan 30. https://doi.bschawii.org/3/2012/05/haseo-learning.pdf.

Jones, K. (1981, 2009). *Buddhism and Social Action: An Exploration*. The Wheel Publication, No. 285-86.

Jootla, E.S. (2011). *The Practice of Giving*. The Wheel Publication, No. 367, 368, 369 (Selected Essays), 10-24. https://doi.www.bps.lk/olib/wh/wh367-bodhi-Dan-The-Practice-of-Giving.

Joseph, M.V. (1988). "Religion and Social Work Practice". Social Casework: *The Journal of Contemporary Social Work, 69*: 443-452.

King, W. (1994). "Engaged Buddhism: Past, Present, Future". *The Eastern Buddhist, 27*(2): 14-29.

Kwan, C. (2020). "The Impact of Religion/Spirituality on Social Workers' Daily Practice". *Research Gate*, April. https://doi.www.researchgate.net/publication/351111908.

Miller, E. (2015). "Religious Revival and the Politics of Nation Building: Reinterpreting the 1963 'Buddhist Crisis' in South Vietnam". *Modern Asian Studies, 49*(6): 62.

Mitra, R.C. (1954). *The Decline of Buddhism in India*. Viswa Bharati, Calcutta.

NAPSWI (2015). *Code of Ethics for Professional Social Workers in India*.

Narasu, L.P. (1907). *The Essence of Buddhism*. Asian Educational Services, New Delhi.

NASW, *Code of Ethics.*

Rahula, W. (1978). *Zen and the Taming of the Bull: Essays.* Gordon Fraser.

Rhys, T.W. (1952). *The History and Literature of Buddhism.* Susil Gupta (India) Ltd., Calcutta.

Silva, D.L. (2010). *Giving in the Pali Canon.* The Wheel Publication, No. 367-69 (Selected Essays), 25-44. https://doi.www.bps.lk/olib/wh/wh367-Bodhi-Dan-The-Practice-of-Giving.

Smith, V. (1924). *Early History of India.* Oxford Publication.

Thero, P.M. (2017). "The Role of Buddha as a Teacher". *Asia Pacific Journal of Advanced Business and Social Studies, 3*(1), 157-69. https://doi.www.apiar.org.au.

Thomas, J.E. (1933). *The History of Buddhist Thought.* Routledge & Kegan Paul Ltd., London.

Wang, Y. (2023). "The Role of Engaged Buddhism in Contemporary Society". *Research Gate,* 21. https://doi.www.researchgate.net/publication/375794572.

Zapf, M.K. (2005). "The Spiritual Dimension of Person and Environment: Perspectives from Social Work and Traditional Knowledge". *International Social Work, 48*: 633-642.

Vincent, M.S. (2019). "The Approach of Indian Spirituality towards Social Work: Integrating Swami Vivekananda's Teaching in Social Practice". *International Journal of Research in Engineering, IT and Social Sciences. 9*(2): 62-66. http://doi.indusedu.org.

14

Aid giving and taking from Indian Social Work Perspectives and Practices

Arasu, K.T.

Introduction: Aid Giving and Taking Scenarios in India

In India, service to humanity and nourishing human beings through charity and philanthropy, which are called aid instruments, aimed at individual, group, community and societal well-being. The ideas of charity and philanthropy are interconnected, interrelated and interface with each other in theory and practice of Social Work. Charity and Philanthropy are regarded as private initiatives and interventions for public or common goods. These are part of old, new and emerging streams of private giving of aid, which gained momentum in recent times due to new richness and use of disruptive technologies. There is dynamic change in Indian charity, philanthropy and social work after the advent of COVID-19. Yet, the inter-connections, complexities and nuances for a well-informed giving are yet to be captured from Indian and indigenous social work perspectives and practices (Sriram & Varma, 2022).

Giving aid in India, according to Agarwal, S. (2010) is strongly rooted in Indian culture, heritage, religion and social ethos. One concrete example of aid is Bhoodan Andolan (1951) of Vinoba Bhave, whose power of persuasive leadership and peaceful transformative actions resulted in donation of 5 million acres of land for the landless.

In India, charitable giving is rooted in concepts such as *Daan* (charitable offering) and *Sewa* (service to humanity) with diverse range of giving traditions exist in India, according to Agarwal, S. (2010). *Daan*, which denotes, different forms of donations and offerings—cash and in-kind have been part of Indian religious, cultural, social and humanitarian traditions. *Daan*, therefore, is the fountain head of pooling, providing and distributing resources that drives the *Sewa* and Social Work ahead to serve the humanity. Both, therefore are complementing and supplementing each other in human and humanistic services.

Yet, every day giving in India is not structured like corporate and Western philanthropy. In India, every day giving by individuals and families—be it giving as alms to alms-seekers, hand-outs to friends, neighbours, charities and offerings on special days have been part of Indian system, custom, tradition and civilisation. Nevertheless, according to Cantegreil *et al.*, (2013), philanthropy in India failed to capture the reality of the ground.

On the motive of giving, Cantegril *et al.*, (2013) cited Erskine K.'s (2006) seven reasons why people give: altruism, appreciation, competitions, devotion, guilt, self-interest and tradition. In India, micro-charitable giving is still in an informal and anonymous way and therefore, its rhythm and ramifications are yet to be fully gauged.

Despite long legacy of charitable and philanthropic giving, as per National Foundation of India (2013), social justice philanthropy that aims to address systemic causes of underdevelopment, as against charity approach, that merely addresses immediate outer manifestations of a deeper problem. Therefore, social justice philanthropy is fully aligned with the ethos of philanthropic Social

Work with focus on empowering people to attain equal and just society.

Towards Decolonised Philanthropic Social Work

As per Holland (2014), philanthropic organisations are striving to decolonise giving, as part of innovation in giving aid. Banerjee *et al.* (2022) raised questions about coloniality and colonial hangovers of charity and philanthropy. The need for decolonisation of systems and philanthropic social work services and practices using decolonisation lens has been the new breeze of change evident. This is intended to undo the colonising practices by way of de-learning, re-learning, deconditioning and deconstructing the colonial practices to make giving more humane, empowering, free, independent, sustainable and resilient, rather than perpetual dependence on donors.

Pfeifer (2020) views micro philanthropy as an excellent way to "democratise" donations at the grassroots level, in which, everyone has the opportunity to donate for common good. This is aimed at refining, indigenising and localising the practices of charitable giving within the country context of redistributive justice and democratic framework.

The practices of "pro-active", "reactive", "directive", "strategic and responsive" styles of philanthropic giving and grant making were flagged by Laugharn, P. (2008). The need for co-creative and cooperative philanthropic overtures, as part of strategic philanthropy was proposed as solutions from philanthropic social work perspectives and practices. In pursuance of it, philanthropic social work is regarded as an organised and systematic effort to indigenise giving. This is an effort to find sustainable and win-win solutions to create resilient families and communities using the power of philanthropy and social work.

Micro Philanthropic Giving Scenario in India

Based on the study on domestic giving in India (OECD, 2019), it is evident that the entire spectrum of retail giving remains largely unknown, unaccounted and undocumented in India. Therefore, little is understood about the quantity, quality, intend, accountability, manner and different modes of micro giving and taking at the national, regional and local levels in India. The domestic philanthropic giving in India highlights the absence of level playing field and skewed distribution of philanthropic resources within India, which calls for the need for creating a level playing field in philanthropic giving.

Reflecting the Indian context, the charitable giving and taking have diversities and pluralities. After the advent of COVID-19, there is further change in the trend of physical to electronic mode of giving, which is evident from the Global Study on Emerging Ways of Giving (2023) in India carried out by Charity Aid Foundation, India. This study explored existing and emerging vehicles of aid such as crowd funding, online giving, mobile giving, workplace giving, online volunteering and social impact interventions. The shift to digital mode of giving resulted in ease of giving practices.

Studies on Charitable Philanthropic Giving in India

According to the research study, India Philanthropic Report-2023 and 2024 of Sattva Consultancy carried out by Sheth, A. *et al.*, (2023 & 2024), philanthropy grew 10 per cent for financial year 2023. The family philanthropy grew 15 per cent and retail philanthropy increased to 12 per cent. There is notable increase in corporate giving. Nevertheless, India continues to fall short of NITI Aayog's estimated spending of 13 per cent of GDP needed to meet the 17 UN Sustainable Development Goals (SDGs) by 2030.

Only a small percentage of India's everyday giving goes towards non-governmental organisations. Around Rs. 3,500 crores go to NGOs, making it a mere 6 per cent contribution to total philanthropic giving in India (*The Hindu*, 24 April 2019). 90 per cent of it is from informal sources, which is going mostly to religious and community causes (Sattava Consultancy: 2020).

Shresth and Varma (2022) pursued a household longitudinal study of How India Gives for the year 2020-21 with a sample of

81,000 households by Centre for Social Impact and Philanthropy (CSIP), Ashoka University. The study noted that "cash" donations towards 'religious organisations' was estimated to be INR 16.6 thousand crore, which constituted 70 per cent share of the market. This was followed by contribution to 'beggars', with an estimated share of 12 per cent (INR 2.9 thousand crore), 'family and friends' at 9 per cent (INR 2 thousand crore) and 'non-religious organisations' at 5 per cent (INR 1.1 thousand crore).

Verma, S. (2023) on the Report of How India Gives for the year 2021-22 of CSIP, Ashoka University noted a 14 per cent percent increase in household donations in 2021-22, as compared to 2020-21. The total donations made by Indian households during 2021-22 is estimated to be INR 27 thousand crores, an increase from INR 23.7 thousand crores in 2020-21.

Need for Indigenous Research on Philanthropic Social Work

Chopra, D. (2022) noted that retail or micro giving in India remained an under-researched topic. Viswanth, P. (2010) Co-Founder of Dana Asia in a foreword to the book *Daan and other giving traditions in India* states, "As a philanthropic practitioner, one of the gaps, I have felt (and continues to feel) is the absence of credible research and writings on philanthropic giving in India". The spirit of generosity and the "joy of giving" traditions in various milieus remain invisible and therefore requires an exploration to fill the gap in the scholarly and practitioner literature from indigenous perspectives and practice of social work.

Sidel (2010) in the foreword to the book *Daan* noted the need to understand its own terms, which is practiced in India. From the shrinking financial resources from foreign shores, it makes sense to turn to citizens/private aid for philanthropic social work purposes.

Being a trained social worker with long legacy of working with Civil Society Organisations (CSOs) since the middle of eighties and having gained greater insights into fund raising at the international, national and regional levels, I have privy to information on outpouring of aid both at the institutional and individual levels through evocating fund-raising campaigns during tsunami. Yet, the underpinnings and understanding of philanthropic giving and its connections with social work remains a gap. This requires a thorough review and relook from practitioner's perspectives to get more clarity and rounded view of philanthropic social work, a new arm of Social Work within the socio-political economy of India.

Social Work practitioners often hold the view that charity is not social work. Social work is primarily of helping people to find enduring solutions through trained persons. Philanthropy is a practice pursued largely by good hearted and good spirited individuals, politicians, religious people and by corporates. Charity and philanthropy, in all likelihood may make the receiver dependent on the giver. Yet, to avoid this happening, the services of trained social workers could be deployed, as they are armed with technical know-how by placing the recipients of aid in "person-in environment" perspectives and practices. Philanthropic social work, therefore focuses on assisting the poor and indigent with a view to improve the well-being in a sustainable way using philanthropic capital.

Charity, Philanthropy and Social Work Connections

According to Olawale *et al.* (2022), philanthropy is being carried out by pubic spirited individuals who look more from satisfying the recipients by their offerings. On the other hand, Social Work is all about placing the users, as the centre of gravity, by way of empowering and evolving sustainable solutions by the users of services. Yet, philanthropy intersects and complement with social work. By the right use of philanthropic offerings, it may be possible to find sustainable solutions of human and community problems. In this matter, giving fishing is regarded as charity and teaching how to catch fish is all about social work. Philanthropy is a practice prior to or at the first level in social work value chain. If right interventions with regular follow ups, philanthropy turns out to be transformative, reformative and renewable act of helping, which is all about philanthropic social work.

Having taking cognisance of conceptual and experiential insights and wisdom, this documentation's focus is exclusively on retail giving and receiving, which is grounded in Indian realities. This is an attempt to document giving and receiving aid in our own native context from indigenous and decolonising perspectives and practices of philanthropic social work. This may contribute towards new mode of fund raising and finding solutions within philanthropic social work.

Purpose and Methodology Pursued for this Documentation

1. This documentation is primarily done to draw practice and reality oriented social work insights and analysis of giving and receiving of aid in India, by relating and correlating with prior studies reflecting World Giving Index-2020-2021 and 2021-2022 of Charity AID Foundation and India Philanthropy Reports-2023 and 2024.
2. This chapter is intended to clarify and amplify the ideas of giving and taking aid and its intricate connections and intersections with Social Work (SW) in general and philanthropic social work in particular from Indian indigenous perspectives and practices.
3. This is an effort to document Indian way of giving and taking retail aid from decolonisation social work perspectives and practices.

The documentation primarily used qualitative grounded theory, based on facts, evidences, anecdotal data, personal life journey and lived experience. Added to it, my engagement in fund raising, visits to various charitable institutions, interactions held with givers and receivers and analysis of various funded philanthropic interventions. I also used social and news media content analysis and reviewed published literature and studies on the theme.

Practitioner's Perspective of Charity and Philanthropy

Based on grounded practice in Odisha Super Cyclone in 1999,

Tsunami (2004), Chennai flood in 2015 and 2023, I am of the view that philanthropy is for social good, which is a good deed of humanism, humanistic and religious and social tradition. It is an expression of kindness, magnanimity, munificence, generosity and doing good for the humanity in desperate need. Charity and philanthropy are human expressions of relieving the human sufferings, which may be an instinctual and instantaneous act of passion to serve humanity in an empathetic or sympathetic way.

Drawing from experience, philanthropy may be arising out of charitable impulse and instincts, which may give a sense of pride, prestige and privilege in view of better economic and social status and material wealth. Reactive philanthropy is a form of aid giving to respond to crisis to tide over the trauma caused by disasters with little follow-up. Pro-active, organised and formal philanthropy are intended to bring about durable differences in the life of suffering humanity.

Charitable giving may be one-off or short-term offerings, as per the interest and choices in times of natural or manmade disasters. Philanthropy may be an expression of human flourishing and outpourings and inner cravings of the givers by serving the unserved, help the un-helped, feed the unfed, cloth the un-clothed, care the uncared and shelter to unsheltered or any other type of help including mitigation of adverse effects of climate change and natural and man-made disasters. Beyond the temporary solace or respite to the receivers of aid, aid has long continuum too, which, may start from rescue of human life in time of disasters, rendering relief during emergencies, provide reconstruction and recovery services.

Aid may be rendered directly by givers or through institutional services to fix problems in a durable way, which is all about social work. On the other hand, charitable donors may withdraw from the scene of disasters, once, the relief and aids were delivered. Here, regular follow-up support may be beyond their capacity. Social Work in general and philanthropic social work in particular can make philanthropic offerings more humane way to make huge differences in the life of users. Therefore, aid has two sides—positive and negative sides. For the trained social workers, philanthropy is a big opportunity as transformative and problem-solving instrumentalities in converting aid into sustainable social work practices. The good intentions of philanthropists were metamorphosed into doable plan reflecting immediate, medium and long term needs of receivers. This was made possible through participatory and sustainable social work practices for the benefit of suffering humanity. I have seen the values of philanthropic social work during the intervention cycle.

Global and Indic Perspectives and Practices of Aid

It is time for us to relook at aid givers and takers from Indic perspectives and practice. It is evident that Indian way of giving and receiving is different from Western countries. In this respect, it is worth relating and correlating with World Giving particularly with World Giving Index 2022 and 2023 of Charity Aid Foundation (CAF). This report documented post-pandemic period insights of global giving around the world. The report acknowledges the value of helping others across border. Yet, the report stated that charity and generosity vary across cultures.

As per the CAF report, India was ranked 57 out of 121 countries in 2022, which made a slide further to 44 in 2023. Indonesia is rated as the most generous country in the world with a score of 68 in terms of donation and volunteering in 2022 and 2023. The study took three variables—helping a stranger, donating money to a charity and volunteering time for an organisation to do good to those in need. It is evident that we respond instinctively by way of aid to kith and kin and known persons who are in need of help.

The culture of giving aid to strangers is not common in India, as has been the case in Western world, where the tradition of giving increased 10 per cent in 2022. Further, in Western world, there are little personal and family interaction, kinship relations and connections with their neighbours and local community. The charitable giving is also different in rural India comparing urban settings, in terms of kinship and existence of community systems. Yet, increased wealth generation among rich families, entrepreneurs and technocrats, new crop of givers emerged within India. They want trusted and credible agency to reach out the last mile and last person.

The concept of donating time in the form of volunteering for charitable purpose is also different in India. The reason is the informal and personal system of volunteering and mutual support system. In India, sparing time by young and adults for religious and community services is quite common. Yet, the time spent for voluntary services are never taken on board. Therefore, this form of volunteering is invisible, unaccounted and unacknowledged. The rationale of volunteering service to humanity is different in India in view of religious, cultural and social reasons.

India Philanthropic Reports 2023 and 2024

In India, the authentic benchmark of giving aid is reflected in the Indian Philanthropic Reports 2023 and 24 brought out by DASRA and Bain & Company. The salient features of the report are given below.

1. Private philanthropy grew 10 per cent in Financial Year (FY) 2022-2023 to 2 lakh crore ($15 billion). Women givers form small share indicating continuing inequality in giving system.
2. India's social sector spending as percentage of GDP growth rate is 8.7 per cent for Financial Year (FY) 2021, which is increased to 9.6 per cent for FY 2022 due to 35 per cent growth in public spending.
3. Corporate Social Responsibility (CSR) spending has grown at 13 per cent over the last five years. It reached 5 billion (Rs. 27,000 crore) in the FY 2022. It grew at a slower pace in FY 2022. It is estimated that CSR growth may reach 6.4 billion (Rs. 52,000) by FY 2027.
4. For the FY 2022, private giving is totalled about $13 billion (Rs.1.05 lakh crore). The family philanthropic

contributions by Ultra-High Net Worth Individuals (UHNWI) accounted for Rs. 1,000 crore. High Net Worth Individuals (HNWI) donated Rs. 200-1,000 crore. The affluent individuals contributed about 7-200 crore. The retail giving cumulatively contributed about 86 per cent of private philanthropy in India.

5. The family philanthropy has grown at 12 per cent over the last five years, reaching to 3.6 billion (Rs. 27,000 crore) in FY 2022. While it grew at slower pace in FY 2022, the report expect that the growth may reach 6.4 billion (Rs. 52,000 crore) by FY 2027.
6. Retail giving in India continues to be community driven with just over 22 per cent of contribution coming from formal giving. It has grown at a modest rate of 6 per cent annually for the FY 2017-2022 with contributions reaching $4 billion (Rs. 32,700 crore). Retail giving is expected to grow at 9 per cent annually.

Yet, ground level reality of formal and informal giving aid is qualitatively different in India with more evidences are given below.

Cinematic and Heroic Mode of Indian Aid

Here, aid giving scenario by film icons is described to understand the real mode of giving in India from social work perspectives. The givers distribute money, clothes, food, medical aid, medical services etc. amidst glitz, glamour, fanfare and flamboyance with wide media publicity. The motives of the givers and recipients are different, wherein, the giver is placed on an iconic and heroic status, who is viewed on a higher pedestal. The recipients are invariably viewed in a lower pedestal by the givers. There is absence of level playing field between the givers and the takers of aid. Here, the dignity, sensitivity and worth of the recipients are not taken on board and mostly, power, prestige, pride and publicity of the givers are manifestly exhibited and marketed using aid as a means of instant band aid solutions.

The givers' offerings are mostly part of the visibility drive to project them in public. Service to the people is their "feed" to boost up the image of heroism among film stars. For some film stars and megastars, charity is a pathway to enter into politics and to become popular with the masses and followers. M.G. Ramachandran, the iconic film hero and former Chief Minister of Tamil Nadu is an illustration, who has been regarded as messiah and mascot of the poor by virtue of his charitable giving. He used charitable and humanitarian acts both in real and film world. MGR projected him as saviour of distressed in films and thereby won the hearts of the people of Tamil Nadu in general and women in particular. It paid political dividends to him.

M.G. Ramachandran's service to the humanity, which is still a model and pathway to enter into politics using cinema medium as powerful tool to enthral common masses. This was replicated by N.T. Rama Rao (NTR), who became the Chief Minister of then composite Andra Pradesh State. Many other Indian film actors used MGR and NTR styles of cinema and aid giving to become popular with the masses. Yet, winners and losers are in the film world.

Invariably, in this mode of giving, the recipients of aid are shown in poor light with smiling faces to send a positive signal of aid. This form of mesmerising charity is used to increase the visibility and interests of donors. It is a form of band aid and tokenistic solution to meet the immediate needs of the receivers. Here, the interests of giver are the prime driving force without any systematic follow-up, which is a big gap in this mode of glamourous giving to humanity.

The donors may use aid for a buy-in to consolidate their fan following of film actors and the recipients are treated as mute forces/cadres. For them, service to humanity is a smokescreen to advance their personal and political interests in the name of service to humanity. This is not part of social work in general and philanthropic social work in particular. Here, charity is used as a tool and instrument to get publicity, popularity, political and business dividends of the giver.

Giving Aid: A Political Act

Charitable giving has been also used as a political tool and gimmick to attract the poor masses, particularly voters. These are part of the scenario and reality of political aid giving in India, which are less talked about in Social Work literature. This is different from the Western mode of aid. Politicians in Tamil Nadu has long legacy of giving various forms of political offerings, which are mainstreamed in our political system by way of offering material, welfare and social services through political party outfits. These were used mainly to harvest votes and to lure the voters to their side. Political parties enter into the fray during disasters by way of providing material aids as relief. The recent case of providing aid in December 2023 floods was a clear instance of water supply, distributing clothes and material support to the victims of flood as part of humanitarian aid.

The intent of this aid is mostly political to secure political loyalty. This is a form of political investment and aid is to keep an eye on the elections. Here, the long-term interest is absent and the real problem solving is remote possibility. This form of muscular aid and freebies are part of the political strategy. Here, aid is a cover for the political parties to expand the rank and file of political cadres of the bottom of the pyramid. In this aid, there is no follow-up after aid is delivered and therefore, providing sustainable solutions to human problems is a remote possibility.

Social Philanthropy in India

In recent times, few conscientious people questioned the mode and model of individual or family charitable giving in times of birth days, marriage and death anniversaries and during festivals and important celebrations. The donors may spare times with the recipients by sharing their desired charitable offerings. This may be an expression of their commitment for the poor. This is regarded as a benevolent act of the giver of aid.

The motives of this charity in this case may be arising out of religious belief and faith that giving aid to poor is service to God or as a form of cleansing the sins and bad deeds of the donor. For the giver, retail aid may be a form of salvation and solace with the hope that aid may relieve and release them from evils/wrongs committed knowingly or unknowingly. This form of aid is fully donor driven in nature.

This form of offerings may be arising out of their genuine belief in helping others, doing it as socially responsible beings and a form of sharing of their wealth and prosperity for lesser beings. Whatever may be the motive, the recipients are beneficiaries of their holy act of giving. Among the donors, taking selfies, videos and photos, which are products or by-products of their charity, which may be used to share in social media to project their image, exhibiting their compassion and mercy towards the poor. Herein, the donor may view the donee as objects, rather a subject of their charity.

At times, aid may be counter-productive in the form of overfeeding with negative health consequences on the receivers of aid. It is evident that, this form of aid has limited accountability from the receiving organisation. Yet, if it is used prudently and productively, the results may be transformative. This form of aid gives more liberty to the recipient organisations, as these funds are free from any strings, comparing the institutional, CSR and government funding.

The key words—alms giving, donation, gifting, altruism, humanitarianism, benefaction, benevolence, do-goodism, dole, freebies and hand-outs denote different forms of charitable offerings. Here, the recipient's need and long-term interests are hardly taken note of and the problem may remain as it is, and the services never and ever strike the roots of the problem. This may be regarded as cosmetic relief, rather than a sustainable help.

It is time for us to examine the pros and cons of patronising way of retail aid objectively, ethically and philanthropic social work perspectives and practices to evolve Indian way of giving and taking. This is an effort to indigenise and localise the concepts and practices of philanthropy by blending giver and receiver perspectives to decolonise aid from Philanthropic Social Work perspectives. We have to go a long way to provide enduring solutions to humanity, in view of nascent stage of philanthropic social work practice.

Mutual Support and Aid Giving in India

Based on experience in Eastern India, I can vouch and validate that in tribal areas, mutual aid and help systems still exist in times of crisis by way of sparing time for volunteering, which is much different from the developed countries. I have seen the system of grain exchange in times of hunger in tribal areas, which is woven into the cultural and social system of the tribes.

On the other hand, in Europe, America, Canada and Australia cohesive communities are absent and individualism is predominant. Therefore, person-to-person and family-to-family links and interactions are weak. We have limited system to count and account mutual aid and volunteering in India, which made it a challenging task to measure aid. Here, aid is being reciprocated, as part of social and economic exchange. Even, in times of marriage and deaths, natural, social, cultural/mutual support system is manifestly visible. Rather than extrapolating foreign system of philanthropy, we need to value and revive our good philanthropic practices.

Institutional and Corporate Mode of Giving and Receiving Aid

Corporate and government giving may be called CSR/government grants, which may be utilised to strike the roots of the problem. The institutional and corporate forms of aid giving may be arising out of policies of an institution. Here, individual interest is moderated by an institutionalised system to serve the humanity in a sustainable way. It is a form of professional help to co-evolve solutions by, for and with those in need in a planned way. However, the institutional services and corporate funding are regulated by contracts between the donors and the intermediary agency. These institutional players serve as a bridge between the aid giver and aid taker and their mission is to find sustainable solutions.

It is a fact that for many CSR entities, branding is part of the contract. The same applies to other institutional donors as well.

Therefore, the conventional religious dictum of left hand should not know what the right hands gives, an Indian religious thinking is not practically doable and workable in CSR and official fundings. This thinking is antithetical to transparency, accountability and open and good governance.

Yet, the ethical and fair way of giving and serving the poor is the desirable way. Good CSOs go by the value system, value framework and value orientation, while receiving aid from the donors. The donations are aligned with the ethos of the recipient organisation. Yet strings attached to corporate/institutional funding, which is integral to the CSO system and practice.

Religious Moorings of Indian Giving

The dictum "charity begins at home" may be arising out of personal, religious and moralistic way of services to families. Being the case in India, religious mode of giving aid is predominant form of services to the humanity in India. Temples, Churches, Mosques and Gurudwaras are the voluntary service hubs in India. For instance, in the case of the Sikh religion, providing *langar* (food) in Gurudwaras is a humanitarian and religious service. Similar system exists in many Hindu Temples, Churches and Mosques as well. Here, the donors are invariably devotees and their offerings have been used to serve to the humanity and devotees, which is called *Sewa*. These religious places also serve as buffer zones for many hungry people. Sustainable practice of philanthropic social work is constrained by the dominance of their belief system. Yet, many religious establishments created separate CSOs to practice philanthropic social work.

Community Mode of Giving

In Tamil Nadu, the customary mode of community giving has been part of the culture and tradition. The clear example is the Moi Virundhu—a form of crowd-funding to bail out families with dire financial strains. In this form, a family hosts community feast and in return, cash and gifts are provided by the invited families (guests). This practice is common in central and western Tamil Nadu. Families take turns to organise the feast to raise money to tide over economic crisis.

It is a form of customary practice of mutual aid to families in need of financial help. Contrary to the Western mode of giving, this practice is confined to community circles. It is a form of pooling community resources for the sake of a family well-being. These are localised versions of community giving. This form of giving was not being captured by the CAF World Giving Index-2022 and 2023. It is a form of social exchange system between the host and guest families.

In recent times, crowd funding is getting institutionalised in India to pool money for specific causes from known and unknown families using the power of information technology coupled with human compassion. Many CSOs use crowd funding for water conservation, tank renovation, watershed development, climate adaptation and mitigation purposes. In recent times, by the use of technology, money is raised from unknown families for help.

Value of Philanthropic Social Work

Here comes the role of trained social workers and philanthropic social work, who are real agents of change in a win-win mode of service to the humanity. In philanthropic social work, service users are taken along for their empowerment and convert them as real agents of change to solve their problems on their own. The power of social work interventions plays a pivotal role in transforming philanthropic offerings as concrete outcomes as solutions.

Philanthropic social work may be seen as silver bullet to bring about social justice. In this matter, social work is seen as a vehicle of services to provide sustainable human development interventions. Social Work is also seen as an instrument to harness the power of aid to serve the humanity. In this form of aid, sustainable returns are possible and feasible.

Key Take Away Based on the Grounded Analysis of Practice-oriented Philanthropy

Based on the evidences of aid practices narrated above, the key take aways are documented below:

1. It is evident from the grounded analysis that Indian philanthropic giving is different from Western mode. Therefore, there is need to capture and co-evolve local and indigenous version of philanthropic social work knowledge system and practices in reality with the India ethos of giving and taking.
2. In this documentation, diverse traditions of philanthropic giving rooted in Indian geography and culture are mapped. Relating and correlating with social work theory and practice within the framework of Indian philanthropic tradition would add greater value in terms of renewal, rejuvenation and enrichment of philanthropic social work.
3. The micro-giving bears greater testimony, relevance and potentials to draw new insights to raise funds for Philanthropic Social Work to meet the domestic and SDG funding gaps and needs, as part of the expanding service to the humanity.
4. We need to rework and relook into the connections of philanthropy from the dynamic and practical perspectives of social work and its value chain. We need to rethink and re-evaluate earlier perspectives of compartmentalised services—relief, social service and welfare and to rework from philanthropic social work perspectives and practices. The lesson drawn is that we need an integrated and intersectional view of philanthropic social work by anchoring in local geography and culture. This may enrich philanthropic social work concept and practice with continuous production and updating of social work knowledge and practice drawn from indigenous wisdom. We need to give a signal that imported and extrapolated

ideas of philanthropy/social work alone may not serve domestic interest. We need to co-evolve our own model derived from Indian reality and ethos.

5. It is evident that decolonisation is a new instrument of analysis to rejuvenate social work theory and practice compatible to the context of India.
6. Another take away from charity is that it is a double edge weapon. It can be used for social transformative actions as well as for political, business and religious purposes. Therefore, charitable and philanthropic giving has darker and brighter sides too. The Philanthropic Social Work has the potential and power to harness the darker side into brighter side in a non-partisan way to solve human problems.
7. It also sheds new light on the relevance of strategic and social justice philanthropy, which are fully compatible with the philanthropic social work theory and practice. The key lesson is that philanthropic social work is a win-win strategy for the common benefits of humanity.
8. The best way forward is to harness and customise aid for empowerment and to spark human happiness in the face of poor. To make it happen, we need a cadre of trained Philanthropic Social Workers to serve as real harbingers of change in the life of ordinary people.

Conclusion

To conclude, Indian philanthropy is different from abroad. We have our own strands and genie of aid. Pooling voluntary giving of aid through formal way calls for organised effort, in which, trained philanthropic social workers can pitch in, pluck, and play in making aid as powerful tool to solve chronic human problems. In pursuance of United Nation's Sustainable Development Goals (SDGs) and the targets sets and to meet the home-grown needs, we need more trained philanthropic social workers to make sure that "no one is left behind" for want of funds. In this respect, charity and philanthropy are effective means to fill the distinct funding gaps. There is greater need to pool philanthropic capital to meet the development challenges. In this matter, mapping of Indic model of aid is the best way forward to serve the suffering humanity by the power of social work.

References

Agarwal, S. (2010). *Daan and other Giving Traditions in India—The Forgotten Pot of Gold (09-17)*. Published by Accounts Aid India. p. 9, para 2, p. 13, para 3, p. 15, para 4, p. 21, para 6, p. 78, para 3. https://sanjayaditya.com/wp-content/uploads/Daan-and-Other-Giving-Traditions-in-India.pdf

Banerjee, S., & Sriram, U. (2022). *Decolonising Philanthropy: From Conceptual Apprehension to Functional Progress*, September 2022, Alliance Magazine. p. 1, para 2. https://www.alliancemagazine.org/feature/decolonising-philanthropy-from-conceptual-apprehension-to-functional-progress/

Cantegreil, M., Chanana, M. & Kattumuri, R. (2013). *Revealing Indian Philanthropy*, London School of Economics, p. 15 para 1. chrome https://eprints.lse.ac.uk/50924/1/ Kattumuri_ Revealing_ India_ philanthropy_2013.pdf

Charity Aid Foundation (2022). *World Giving Index Report: 2022*, (pp. 4, 6, para 1) (https://www.cafonline.org/about-us/publications/2022-publications/caf-world-giving-index-2022,https://www.cafonline.org/docs/default-source/about-us-research/uk_giving_2023.pdf

Chilkoti, A. (2024). "Super-rich are trying new approach to Philanthropy". *The Economist*, 23rd March, 2024, p.1, para 3, https://www.economist.com/special-report/2024/01/10/the-super-rich-are-trying-new-approaches-to-philanthropy

Chopra, D. (2022). Gaining Deeper Understanding of Philanthropy in India Through Research Fellowship, Centre for Social Impact and Philanthropy (CSIP), Ashoka University, p. 1, para 1. https://csip.ashoka.edu.in/gaining-deeper-understanding-of-philanthropy-in-india-through-research-fellowship/

Digital Good, Global Study of Emerging way of giving (2022) (p. 4, para 1), Indiana University Lilly Family School of Philanthropy, https://www.cafonline.org/about-us/publications/digital-for-good-a-global-study-on-emerging-ways-of-giving/#:~:text=Digital%20for%20Good%3A%20A%20Global%20Study%20on%20Emerging,hybrid.%20...%204%20About%20the%20Global%20Study%20

"Emerging Philanthropy in India—Analysis of Gaps and Recommended Interventions". *National Foundations of India* (2013), p. 2, para 1. https://www.nfi.org.in/sites/default/files/publication/NFI%20-%20Emerging_Philanthropy_ Report_...pdf

Holland, A.H. (2024). "Key Trends in Philanthropy are at Odds". *India Development Review*, January 2024, p.1, para 3. https://idronline.org/article/philanthropy-csr/key-trends-in-philanthropy-are-at-odds/

Laugharn, P. (2008). "Proactive *vs.* Responsive Philanthropy". *Alliance Magazine*, 1st September 2008, p. 1, paras 1 & 5 https://www.alliancemagazine.org/feature/proactive-vs-responsive-philanthropy/

Olawale, A. *et al.* (2022). Significance of Philanthropic Social Work—A Focus Intervention Practice in Times of Crisis. p. 10 paras 1-4 https://www.researchgate.net/publication/357182857_SIGNIFICANCE_OF_PHILANTHROPY_AND_PHILANTHROPIC_SOCIAL_WORK-_A_FOCAL_INTERVENTION_PRACTICE_IN_TIMES_OF_CRISIS

OECD (2019). *Indian's Private Giving: Unpacking Domestic Philanthropy and Corporate Social Responsibility*, p. 7, para: 3, p. 8, para 1. https://t4.oecd.org/development/philanthropy-centre/researchprojects/OECD_India_Private_Giving_2019.pdf

Pfeifer, D. (2020). "The Rise of Micro philanthropy: Small Donations With a Large Impact", *E-Philanthropy*, May 2020, p.1, para 2. https://www.nonprofitpro.com/article/the-rise-of-microphilanthropy-small-donations-with-a-large-impact/

Sattva Consultancy (2020). *Matching Contributions in India*, p. 4, para 4. https://www.sattva.co.in/wp-content/uploads/2020/04/Sattva_Publications_ATECF-Matching-Contributions-in-India-report.pdf

Sheth, A., Batabyal, J., Nundy, N., Misra, A., Pal, P. (2024). DASRA and Bain & Company—India Philanthropy Report-2023, p. 6, paras 1 and 2 https://www.bain.com/insights/india-philanthropy-report-2023, https://www.bain.com/insights/india-philanthropy-report-2024/

Sheth, A. *et al.* (2024). "India Philanthropic Report 2024". *DASRA*, p. 1, paras 2 and 3. https://www.bain.com/insights/india-philanthropy-report-2024/

Shresth, S. & Verma, S. (2022). *How India Gives—2020-21*, Cenre for Social Impact and Philanthropy, Ashoka University, p. 10, para 2. How-India-Gives-2020-21-Report.pdf

Sriram, U. & Varma, S. (2022). "From Charitable Giving to Social Justice: Reimaging the Role of Philanthropy in India". *Times of India,* 15th March 2022. Para 3. https://timesofindia.indiatimes.com/blogs/voices/from-charitable-giving-to-social-justice-reimagining-the-role-of-philanthropy-in-india/

Sundar, *et al.* (2019). "'Moi virundhu': How Tamil Nadu's Traditional Crowd Funding Feast Evolved Over the Years", *The Hindu*, August 25, 2019, p.1, paras 1-17. https://www.thehindu.com/news/national/tamil-nadu/moi-virundhu-how-tamil-nadus-crowd-funding-feast-evolved-over-the-years/article29248971.ece

The Hindu, 24th April, 2019. Para 1, https://www.thehindu.com/news/cities/bangalore/indias-everyday-givers-are-motivated-by-impact-andurgency/article26935947.ece

Verma, S. (2023). *How India Gives—2021-22,* Centre for Social Impact and Philanthropy, Ashoka University. p. 11, paras 1 and 3. How-India-Gives-2021-22-Report-1.pdf

Varma, S. *et al.* (2023). *How India Gives—2021-22,* Centre for Social Impact and Philanthropy (CSIP), Ashoka University, p. 11, paras 1 & 3, https://csip.ashoka.edu.in/how-india-gives/

15

Swami Vivekananda's Social Philosophy

An Indian View of the Social Work Principles

Pratheesh, P.

Introduction

Social work aims to enable people to develop their full potential, enrich their lives, and prevent dysfunction by focusing on problem-solving and change. Social workers are change agents in society and the lives of individuals, families, and communities they serve. Mahatma Gandhi, a prominent social reformer, emphasised the importance of social reform over political work, acknowledging that missions have indirectly contributed to India's development. Social work is the professional activity of helping individuals, groups, or communities enhance or restore their capacity for social functioning and creating societal conditions favourable to this goal. It requires knowledge of human development, behaviour, social, economic, and cultural institutions, and the interactions of these factors. From this angle, the Indian socio-religious reformers—particularly Swami Vivekananda—were real social workers who concentrated on advancing social justice, combating societal ills, and addressing poverty in India.

Background of the Study

Renowned religious scholar Swami Vivekananda had a big impact on contemporary Indian society and philosophy. Since criticism of his social thought, particularly from radicals, has criticised his principles as more fundamental Hindutva teachings than enlightened social principles, it is felt necessary to assess the social significance of his philosophy of social service inclusively (Muralidharan, 1994). Therefore, it is imperative to examine Vivekananda's social philosophy in light of Indian conceptions of social work for secular reasons. In addition to helping readers and academics comprehend India's ideological foundations, this study attempts to investigate the numerous interpretations of his social philosophy and contribute to the concepts and philosophy of modern social work.

Methodology

This study employs a historical method to methodically re-enact the socio-religious reform movements of the 19th century and the role played by Swami Vivekananda. The main focus of this study is how his social philosophy is analysed in relation to contemporary social work concepts and principles. Since it is a historical study, it mainly draws from primary and secondary sources, including unpublished materials. The chapter has developed arguments and assessed the theoretical assertion that Vivekananda's social philosophy is crucial to comprehending the unique viewpoint on social work by analysing these texts.

Review of Related Literature

An essential research tool for expanding on previous findings, identifying best practices, and drawing lessons from mistakes is a literature review. The review of literature for this study focuses on two topics: the social work philosophy of Swami Vivekananda and the chosen studies on social work principles.

The principles and methods of social work have been

proposed by many authors, but the most common are the Principles of Acceptance, Individualisation, Self-determination, Non-judgmental Attitude, and Confidentiality. These principles emphasise the importance of understanding and welcoming clients' points of view. Arthur Dunham (1958), Fanshel (1980), Roseblum *et al.* (1996), Reid (1997), Barker (1995), Zander (1993), and Gangrade (2001) supported this perspective. Ramkrishna Raju (1972), Bhatt (1982), Kulkarni (1993), Majumdar (1994), Singh (1995), Pathak (1997), Desai and Narayan (1998), A. Desai (2000) and Pathak (2004) have contributed to the perspectives on the philosophy and principles of social work.

Uzuegbu *et al.* (2017) in "Values, ethics and principles of social work" discusses the importance of social work values, ethics, and principles in ensuring competent and ethical practice. It outlines six values, seven principles, and various categories of social work ethics that are binding on social workers worldwide.

"The literature review on social work and theory" (2016) highlights the gap between theory and practice, with some social workers viewing theory and practice as separate or incompatible worlds. Social workers draw from various sources of knowledge and guidance, and future research should explore the origin of this divide and examine what continues to perpetuate it.

Amulya (2010) provides a detailed analysis of Swami Vivekananda's philosophy, focusing on his social dimensions and sociological implications. Chandrakantha (2015) states that Vivekananda played a significant role in shaping modern India, advocating for social and spiritual reforms, emphasising compassion, universal literacy, and women's liberation. Baruah Debajit (2017) examines Vivekananda's social philosophy and concept of religion, arguing that for India to rebuild its society, social service and spirituality were essential.

Nawaz Sarif (2019) discusses Swami Vivekananda's philosophical teachings and his thoughts and ideas, arguing for universal brotherhood, religious tolerance, and education. Nizia Husain (2023) deems him the leader of Indian nationalism and believes in human welfare to inspire self-confidence and pride. This chapter examines the relevance of Swami Vivekananda's social philosophy in the present context.

Vivekananda's Social Philosophy

Swami Vivekananda, born in Calcutta in 1863, was a religious leader who aimed for the spiritual and material advancement of the people. Inspired by Western knowledge and culture, he developed qualities of open-mindedness, questioning spirit, and uprightness (Banerjee, 2014). He opposed the caste system and developed a universal outlook and principle of equality. Vivekananda believed that the source of Hindu religion and cultures were Vedas, and the philosophy of the Upanishads prepared the way for human salvation. The teachings of Gautama Buddha also influenced Vivekananda, as they established a strong bond of fellowship and love between different groups of people.

He emphasised the importance of religious harmony, teaching that all religions should teach love and mutual tolerance (Nikhilananda, 1964). He rejected fanaticism, rivalries, and heated discussions, and believed that the message of unity in human society would have made significant progress without sectarianism, fanaticism, and violence. Vivekananda considered the Vedanta Philosophy as the best basis for establishing religious harmony, emphasising love and universal self-hood.

He expressed outrage over rights exploitation and advocated for social reform using Western ideas and technology without imitating Western ways of life (Frederic, 2012). He proposed an education system for all-round development, emphasising the empowerment of the people through education, collective thought, and action. He worked for women's educational rights and introduced a new orientation of social service.

Neo-Vedanta and the Principle of Social Work

The Neo-Vedanta philosophy, led by Sri Ramakrishna and Swami Vivekananda, emphasises the practical nature of Vedanta and is constantly undergoing self-renewal. Vedanta has always been new and adaptable to changing circumstances, integrating the best elements of other religions and cultures (Olson, 1998). The central ideal of Vedanta is oneness, with no two in anything or two lives. The difference is in degree and not in kind. Through his Neo-Vedanta, he argued that service to the poor is equivalent to service to God. This axiom was based on his personal experience of the lower classes in his country. Vivekananda called feeding the poor "Narayana Seva" and preached for "Daridra Narayana Seva", which translates to service to the poor as service to Lord Narayana, the Supreme Being in Vaishnavism (Mukherji, 2012).

He spread the message of "divine unity of existence and unity in diversity" throughout British India. He travelled the country, confronting poverty and deprivation, and believed that the only way to help the poor was through the spirit of *Niskama karma* of the *Gita*. He coined the term euphemism "Daridra Narayana" in front of the poor Santals, whom he considered as manifestations of Narayana. The term was popularised by Mahatma Gandhi, who worked for the betterment of poor and distressed people throughout his political career. In 1972, the Swami Vivekananda Medical Mission was established, with the motto "To reach Narayana we must serve the Daridra Narayana, the starving millions of the land. Feel for them, pray for them. Strive for the relief and uplift of the suffering and miserable brethren".

Later, Satya Sai Baba explained that God is worshipped in two forms: Lakshmi-Narayana and Daridra-Narayana. Most people worship Lakshmi-Narayana seeking blessings for their personal prosperity and well-being, while only a handful choose to worship Daridra-Narayana (the Lord in the form of the poor and the forlorn). Baba urged devotees to think only of service to Daridra-Narayana, as it is the highest form of *sadhana* and should be rendered without regard to caste, creed, race, or nationality.

Criticism has been raised by A.C. Bhaktivedanta Swami Srila Prabhupada, who believes that Daridra cannot be Narayana because Narayana is always accompanied by Sri Laksmiji. He believes that a devotee sees everyone and everything in relationship with *Narayana*, and that single out the daridra-*Narayana*, or poor *Narayana*, and rejects the *dhani-narayana*, or rich *Narayana*, is an imperfect vision of a devotee. However, Vivekananda's teachings on Daridra Narayan Seva have had significant impact on Indian social work and various aspects of Hinduism, including medicine, religion, and the concept of Daridra Narayana.

Discussion

Let us begin with the modern principles of social work. Modern Social work principles include the Principle of Acceptance, Principle of Individualisation, Principle of Self-Determination, Principle of Non-judgmental Attitude, and Principle of Confidentiality. These principles emphasise understanding clients' perspectives and welcoming their views. The Principle of Acceptance requires social workers to treat clients humanely, acknowledging their perspectives and creating a respectful environment. The Principle of Individualisation emphasises understanding each client's unique needs, beliefs, and experiences. Social work addresses contemporary social problems like the Best Interest of a Child, Social Welfare in the Public-Private State, and the Me Too Movement. Social conflict theory can be applied to mental health, immigration, and global citizenship.

Vivekananda's social philosophy focuses on various aspects of human existence, including social welfare, progress, education, culture preservation, and religion harmony (Monto, 2010). He believed that the extreme poverty and backwardness of the masses impacted the nation's progress. He believed that the general public needed to hear life-giving principles like the doctrine of the *Atman* found in Vedanta. Despite their poverty, the masses clung to religion but were not taught how to apply these principles. Vivekananda distinguished between secular knowledge to improve their economic situation and spiritual knowledge to strengthen moral sensibilities and inspire faith. He employed education to propagate the Vedic message and improve socio-economic standing.

The seven tenets of contemporary social work are now re-examined in light of Swami Vivekananda's corresponding philosophical position in order to verify the study's hypothetical claim that Vivekanada's social philosophy is crucial for comprehending the peculiar perspective on social work.

Principle of Acceptance: To achieve optimal results in social work, both the client and the social worker must accept each other. The client must accept the social worker as they are assisting the client in overcoming their problem condition. The social worker should acknowledge the client as a person with a problem, regardless of their appearance or history. Personal experiences, such as being abused by an alcoholic father, may hinder acceptance. The social worker should not be influenced by their past experiences or demonstrate hatred or indifference to the client. Mutual acceptance is the first step in creating a good professional relationship to resolve the client's social dysfunction.

> "All the powers in the universe are already ours. It is we who have put our hands before our eyes and cry that it is dark."

Swami Vivekananda emphasised the importance of self-belief in order to change the world. He emphasised that being different doesn't mean being wrong. Therefore, one should believe in themselves and continue on their path without accepting others' opinions or letting go of their beliefs.

> "The great secret of true success, of true happiness, is this: the man or woman who asks for no return, the perfectly unselfish person, is the most successful."

In a world where personal gains are prioritised, Swami Vivekananda's teachings should be incorporated. He believed that if one has resources, they should contribute them for others' well-being. Engaging in selfless acts of kindness can lead to immense happiness.

When viewed from the standpoint of social work, the combined meaning of the two aforementioned philosophical statements is that every person should reach their full potential and provide selfless service to others. Since everyone is inherently a part of the divine spirit, the person in need of assistance must accept the assistance or help from others to overcome the difficult situation. Because of the aforementioned Vedantic viewpoint, the person offering assistance should accept the person who needs it, regardless of their appearance or background. Realising divine unity begins with mutual acceptance, which leads to the development of social relationships that address mass social dysfunction.

Principle of Individualisation: The principle of individualisation in social casework involves recognising and understanding each client's unique features, as well as applying diverse concepts and approaches to assist them in reaching better adjustment. Individualisation is based on the right of humans to be recognised as individuals with unique characteristics, which stems from the fundamental realisation of each person as a distinct entity. Each person encounters unique life situations and develops various interpersonal relationships, and their thoughts, feelings, behaviours, and capacities are distinct and distinct from one another. The success of a helping relationship relies on the worker's individualisation of each case, addressing each person as a unique individual with distinct difficulties. This involves being aware of personal biases, possessing human behaviour knowledge, and maintaining perspective.

> "Soul has no sex; it is neither male nor female. It is only in the body that sex exists, and the man who desires to reach the spirit cannot at the same time hold sex distinctions."

Swami Vivekananda's teachings on equal human rights, based on God's creation, are crucial for a better world. He believed in no right to discriminate based on religion, caste, or gender, advocating for women's rights and lower castes' position in society as social reformers.

> "So long as the millions live in hunger and ignorance, I hold every man a traitor who, having been educated at their expense pays not the least heed to them."

He posited that the world's nature is determined by its inhabitants, and if humanity is empathetic and works for the well-being of others, the world will be kinder to us. This teaching emphasises humility, helpfulness, and helping those in need, making it a powerful tool in understanding and guiding human behaviour.

When viewed from the perspective of social work, the two philosophical statements above have a similar overall meaning. Social well-being is really about appreciating each person for who they are and using a variety of ideas and methods to help them. Since every human being is essentially a unique entity, we ought to acknowledge their right to be treated as individuals with distinctive qualities. Healthy relationships between people are the result of this understanding being successful.

Principle of Communication: Effective communication is crucial in social work, involving verbal and non-verbal means. Miscommunication can occur when the sender cannot articulate their feelings or thoughts, and other impediments include distance, noise, temperament, attitudes, past experiences, and mental capacity. The social worker must understand the client's verbal and non-verbal communication to maintain effective relationships. The setting of the conversation may change, providing opportunities for miscommunication. The worker's primary job is to create an environment where the client feels comfortable expressing their feelings, based on trust, confidence, and acceptance.

Through his speeches, Vivekananda emphasises the importance of communication in all areas of human endeavour, as well as its role in the growth of individuals and the establishment of beliefs and ideologies. The Vedic narrative of God's communication is noteworthy for being an unambiguous record of God's love, mercy, and judgment towards his people. Religious ideas like revelation, incarnation, prophecy, and logos are all forms of communication, and the sacred scripture is the manifestation of divine communication in human language.

> "God's divine communication proceeds from the divine initiative and the content of divine communication lies in the revelation of God himself."

According to him, communication is essential to human existence and its significance cannot be emphasised. It is essential for social interaction, personal development, and the survival of our species and culture. Every person should have the divine ability to communicate on their own and be able to comprehend what others are saying. People will therefore be able to recognise their own divinity and the essence of the *atman* through the freedom of expression and open communication.

The principle of confidentiality: In social work, it is crucial for establishing a strong worker-client relationship. It requires providing information, ranging from factual to highly confidential, to the worker, who must be trustworthy and not use it to cause discomfort or damage. The worker faces difficulties in adhering to this principle, such as sharing confidential information with other agency officials or colleagues, and handling information about the client's criminal activity. In these situations, the worker may reveal the information in the client's best interests, but withholding it is difficult due to confidentiality.

> "Talk to yourself once in a day, otherwise you may miss meeting an intelligent person in this world."

His teaching emphasises the importance of self-awareness and self-introspecting to understand one's true desires and find personal growth. He believes that only one has the potential to correct them, so it's crucial to maintain self-control and continually understand one's innermost desires. This teaching is applicable in all aspects of life.

> "Everything can be sacrificed for truth, but truth cannot be sacrificed for anything."

He underlined the value of maintaining confidentiality and being honest in all situations, saying that while deeds have repercussions, they shouldn't be twisted or lied to make life easier. He felt that the only way to lead a happy and meaningful life is to follow a path that is founded on integrity, faith, and secrecy.

The Principle of Self-Determination: The idea emphasises the client's right to self-determination, stating that social workers should not force decisions or solutions on clients merely because they seek assistance. They should promote and guide clients in making good judgments, helping them realise their potential and feel independent. This is achieved through social responsibility, emotional adjustment, and personality development, which are essential for personal growth and self-worth.

> "Uttisthata jagrata prapya varan nibodhata": "O living entity, you are sleeping in this material world. Please get up and take advantage of your human form of life."

He used the stanza of *Katha Upanishad* that ignorance and unconsciousness are the result of the conditioned soul dozing off in the material world. A snake bite or other venomous snake-bite induces this deep sleep, a state of unconsciousness. Often, people are unaware that they are unconscious and without spiritual awareness while they sleep in the material world. Even on higher planets, the illusory energy captivates individuals, causing them to lose interest in the true meaning of life (Sil, 1993). The state of sleep known as *kala-sarpa* keeps the soul ignorant and causes loss of pure consciousness. Thus, self-determination and awakened consciousness are necessary for the welfare of society and individuals.

Principle of Non-judgmental Attitude: The non-judgmental attitude principle suggests that social workers should approach clients without prejudice, treating them as if they have come for assistance (Zastrow, 2010). This fosters a strong professional relationship, allowing both parties to express understanding. However, this does not mean they cannot make professional judgments about the problem scenario and solutions being evaluated.

In his social philosophy, Vivekananda presents a progressive view of man as a divine spirit, revealing the Infinite self-consciousness through every individual. The difference between *Jivas* lies in their psychological and physiological structure, not in the nature of the indwelling self. The inner self of all *Jivas* is pure, luminous, free, and identical with Brahman. The manifestation of Pure Consciousness varies through individuals, as it is imminent in the universe. Man is more than his psychophysical constitution, with consciousness being the real essence, and the eleven organs serving as instruments.

> "Don't look on the fault of others; you cannot judge a man by his faults."

Vivekananda emphasises the importance of understanding and addressing one's own feelings and behaviours rather than focusing on others' faults. This habit can lead to negative consequences such as limiting happiness, perpetuating depression, isolating oneself from important relationships, turning people off from wanting to get close to one, creating negative energy around oneself, and killing cells in the body with negativity.

Principle of Controlled Emotional Involvement: Regulated emotional engagement safeguards social workers from over-investment or objectiveness in their clients' problems. Over-identification due to parallels between problem and life situations can harm professional relationships and judgments, while sympathising with clients may infringe on their self-determination and independence.

Vivekananda's philosophy emphasises the importance of Pure Consciousness, Pure Bliss, and Pure Existence in humans. He believes that the bright body within the gross body remains intact even after death. Vivekananda emphasised the unity of all beings, despite physiological and psychological differences, as they are part of the same Universal, Brahman. He aimed to boost self-confidence and arouse service in the minds of educated and higher-class people, promoting practical *Vedanta*, religion, universal religion, and education.

Vivekananda emphasises the importance of faith in oneself and in God, as it is the secret to greatness. He believes that if one has faith in all gods but lacks faith in them, there is no salvation. Vivekananda believes that failure only occurs when one fails to manifest their infinite power. To achieve success in life, one must have perseverance and tremendous will. He encourages people to not think of themselves as weak, as this is the greatest heresy. Strength is life, while weakness is death. Strength is happiness, life eternal, and immortal, while weakness is constant strain and misery (Dubey, 2015). Vivekananda urges youths to have faith in themselves and bring out their dexterity. He believes that the spirit of self-reliance, immovable fortitude, and dexterity in oneself is crucial for success.

The client may feel disinterested due to the social worker's objective and aloof manner, which could keep them from sharing sensitive information and reinforce feelings of worthlessness. This could result in an early end to the professional relationship. Similar to this, Vivekananda's social philosophy emphasised the contemporary values of social work in its embedded form. He called feeding the impoverished "Narayana Seva" and advocated for "Daridra Narayana Seva", which translates to "serving the poor as serving Narayana." Thus, it is confirmed that Vivekanada's social philosophy is crucial to comprehending the unique viewpoint on social work.

Conclusion

In conclusion, the principles and methods of social work are essential for providing effective and compassionate care to clients.

By understanding and applying these principles, social workers can better serve their clients and contribute to a more inclusive and equitable society. Swami Vivekananda's social philosophy, focusing on social welfare, progress, education, culture, and religion harmony, can be incorporated into social work to promote self-fulfilment and selfless service to others, promoting happiness and self-belief has a direct implication in the modern principles of social work.

References

Amiya, P.S. (2003). *Swami Vivekananda.* ISBN: 9780198095156, Oxford University Press.

Amulya, R.M. (2009). *Social Philosophy of Swami Vivekananda.* Readworthy Publications. http://www.readworthypub.com

Ashman, K.K. (2010). *The Social Work & Social Welfare: Critical Thinking Perspective* (3rd edn.) Belmont CA: Brooks/Cole.

Banerjee, P. (2014). "Between the Political and the Non-political: The Vivekananda Moment and a Critique of the Social in Colonial Bengal, 1890s-1910s. *Social History,* 39(3): 323-39. http://www.jstor.org/stable/24246487

Baruah, D. (2017). *Social Philosophy of Swami Vivekananda.* Wisdom Library Online. https://www.wisdomlib.org/hinduism/essay/social-philosophy-of-swami-vivekananda/d/doc419376.html

Bennur, H.Y., Dilip, K. (2013). "Mahatma Gandhi and Professional Social Work". *Indian Journal of Research, 3*(5), https://www.worldwidejournals.com/paripex/fileview/mahatma-gandhi-and-professional-social-work_June_2013_9180969135_8609553.pdf

Borden, W. (2010). *Reshaping Theory in Contemporary Social Work: Toward a Critical Pluralism in Clinical Practice* (pp. xi-xviii). New York: Columbia University Press.

Chadha, Y. (1997). *Rediscovering Gandhi,* London: Century.

Chandrakantha, K.M. (2015). "Role of Swami Vivekananda in Social Reforms—A Study", *International Journal of Research and Analytical Reviews, 2*(4), www.ijrar.org.

Complete Works of Swami Vivekananda, Advaita Ashrama, Kolkata 1989, Vol. VII, p. 162.

Dhar, S.N. (1976). *A Comprehensive Biography of Swami Vivekananda* (2nd edn.), Madras, India: Vivekananda Prakashan Kendra.

Dubey, R. (2015). "New Hindu Religious Movements in Contemporary India: A Review of Literature". *Sociological Bulletin, 64*(2): 152-70. http://www.jstor.org/stable/26290776

Ezeh, C.A., Ezeah, P.C. & Aniche, A. (2000). *Fundamentals of Social Work.* Nsukka: Liberty Printing & Publishing Co.

Frederick, N. (2012). "William James and Swami Vivekananda: Religious Experience and Vedanta/Yoga in America". *William James Studies, 9*: 37-55. http://www.jstor.org/stable/26203754

Monto, G. (2010). "Swami Vivekananda's Use of Science to Communicate Spirituality". *Current Science, 98*(5): 711-12. http://www.jstor.org/stable/24111832

Mukherji, G. (2012). "Thinking Community and Nation: Relevance of Vivekananda". *India International Centre Quarterly, 39*(1): 20-29. http://www.jstor.org/stable/41804016

Muralidharan, S. (1994). "Patriotism without People: Milestones in the Evolution of the Hindu Nationalist Ideology". *Social Scientist, 22*(5/6): 3-38. https://doi.org/10.2307/3517900

Nazia Husain (2023). "Relevance of Swami Vivekananda's Social Philosophy in the Present Context". *International Journal of Advanced Research in Science,* 3(3): 46-48. https://ijarsct.co.in/Paper11407.pdf

Nikhilananda, S. (1964). "Swami Vivekananda Centenary". *Philosophy: East and West, 14*(1): 73-75. https://doi.org/10.2307/1396757

Olson, C. (1998). "Vivekānanda and Rāmakṛṣṇa: Face to Face—An Essay on the Alterity of a Saint". *International Journal of Hindu Studies, 2*(1): 43-66. http://www.jstor.org/stable/20106536

Paul, S. (2003), *Great Men of India : Swami Vivekananda.* Sterling Publishers Pvt. Ltd.

Roy. K.B. (1977). *Socio-political Views of Vivekananda,* Advaitha Ashrama, Calcutta, p. 30.

Saha, P. (2013, June). "Book Review: Right to Work and Rural India—Working of the Mahatma Gandhi National Rural Employment Guarantee Scheme". *Social Change, 43*(2): 326-30. https://doi.org/10.1177/0049085713493049

Sil, N.P. (1993). "Vivekānanda's Rāmakṛṣṇa: An Untold Story of Mythmaking and Propaganda". *Numen, 40*(1): 38-62. https://doi.org/10.2307/3270397

Uzuegbu, C., Iyiani, C., Obasi-Igwe, I., Anazonwu, N. & Ajibo, H. (2017). "Values, Ethics and Principles of Social Work". In Okoye, U., Chukwu, N. & Agwu, P. (Eds.). *Social Work in Nigeria: Book of Readings,* pp. 31-43. Nsukka: University of Nigeria Press Ltd.

Virajananda, Swami, ed. (2006) (1910). *The Life of the Swami Vivekananda by his Eastern and Western Disciples,* II Vols. (Sixth edn.), Kolkata: Advaita Ashrama.

Zastrow (2010). *Introduction to Social Work and Social Welfare* (3rd edn.). Brooks/Cole. http:// at www.cengage.com

16

Contribution of Mahatma Gandhi to Indigenous Social Work Practice

Pushpanjali Kumari

Introduction

Mahatma Gandhi is popularly known as "Bapu" and "The Father of Nation". The Great soul, freedom fighter, philosopher, and leader with a charismatic personality led India's freedom movement by using *Satya* and *Ahimsa* as a weapon. Mahatma Gandhi believed in social service and did charity work by adopting the way and the pattern of Social Work that is now accepted as Gandhian Social Work. Gandhiji always encouraged people to be involved in Social Work because it improves the delivery of social services and enhances the social functioning of individuals, groups, and families by providing recreational services to the community welfare systems with the needed resources. Social Work helps the individual bring about a change in the environment in favour of his growth and development of good interpersonal relationships. The various types of Social Work emphasise the multifaceted and intricate interactions between people and their surroundings. The goal is to empower individuals to achieve their greatest potential, enhance their quality of life, and prevent dysfunction. Professional Social Work focuses primarily on problem-solving and change-making and follows the ideology of Mahatma Gandhi (Mutluri, 2022).The contribution of Gandhiji to the development of indigenous Social Work is deeply rooted in the values of welfare and services. His concept of social welfare focused on the emergence of individuals and society through individual and social discipline, aiming to build a society based on moral concepts of happiness that cover all aspects. His approach to Social Work emphasised the importance of individual and collective efforts toward social reform and creating a non-violent political, economic, and social order.

Gandhi's humanism and constant efforts to abolish injustice against all individuals and groups, including women, *Harijans*, and landless farmers, set him apart as a pioneer of social welfare through social transformation. His political campaigns were also examples of Social Work, with his early efforts mainly focusing on poverty and inequality. Gandhi's contributions to social welfare initiatives influenced community empowerment, particularly in post-independence India. He applied social work techniques such as casework and group work, and his approach was like that of a professional social worker, providing the initial foundation for the establishment of the Social Work Profession in India (Bennur & Khairnar, 2013). Gandhiji dedicated his entire life to nation-building, and under his leadership, the Indian freedom movement gave a new impetus. He believed in the philosophy of upliftment of the poorest of the poor, vulnerable people, oppressed, and marginalised sections of society. He used to visit villages and meet the people to feel the pulse of the society. Various constructive efforts were made to improve their condition. Mahatma Gandhi's entire life was dedicated to social reform, and he led several movements to root out the evils prevalent in society; his contribution was appreciated not only in Indian society but worldwide.

Gandhi's philosophy as a guide for service to others and the quest for social justice complements social work practice theory, a method based on integrating social service, social action, and individual and community interventions. Gandhi accomplished this synthesis by simplifying his ethical theory into two key foci: service to others and social justice. Gandhian principles are founded on philosophical concepts prioritising corporation over competition, interdependence over individualism, compassion for others over self-sufficiency, and social justice in our achievements. The foundation of Gandhian ethics is service to others, love, respect, and care for all (Walz & Ritchie, 2000).

Gandhian Model of Human Society

The Gandhian Model of Human Society, also known as Gandhian Social Order or Sarvodaya Society, is a conceptual framework proposed by Mahatma Gandhi to create an ideal society based on his philosophical principles. Gandhi envisioned a society that prioritises the well-being and dignity of every individual while promoting social justice, equality, and sustainable development. The Gandhian Model of Human Society is characterised by several key principles and features, as discussed by Billore, (2010):

Sarvodaya (Welfare of All): The core of the Gandhian Model is the principle of *Sarvodaya*, which emphasises the welfare and upliftment of all members of society. Gandhi believed in creating a society where the needs of the most vulnerable are addressed so that everyone has an equal opportunity to flourish and reach their full potential.

Ahimsa (Non-violence): Non-violence, or *ahimsa*, is a central tenet of the Gandhian Model. Gandhi advocated for resolving conflicts peacefully and rejecting all forms of violence, whether physical, verbal, or psychological. *Ahimsa* fosters compassion, empathy, and understanding among individuals and communities.

Swadeshi (Self-Sufficiency): The Gandhian Model promotes the idea of *swadeshi*, or self-sufficiency, encouraging communities to produce and consume locally to reduce dependence on external resources and promote economic independence. Gandhi believed in empowering local economies and preserving traditional crafts and industries.

Swaraj (Self-Governance): Swaraj, or self-governance, is another fundamental principle of the Gandhian Model. Gandhi advocated for decentralised governance structures that empower local communities to decide their affairs. *Swaraj* promotes participatory democracy, grassroots leadership, and accountability.

Simplicity and Sustainability: Gandhi emphasised the importance of living a simple, sustainable lifestyle that respects the environment and conserves natural resources. The Gandhian Model encourages frugality, minimalism, and a harmonious relationship with nature to ensure the well-being of future generations.

Equality and Social Justice: The Gandhian Model envisions a society free from discrimination, inequality, and exploitation. Gandhi fought against casteism, untouchability, and other forms of social injustice, advocating for equal rights and dignified life for all individuals regardless of their background or identity.

Spiritual and Moral Values: Gandhi believed in the importance of spiritual and moral values in shaping individuals and society. The Gandhian Model emphasises honesty, integrity, compassion, and self-discipline, promoting a culture of ethical behaviour and personal responsibility.

Overall, the Gandhian Model of Human Society presents a vision of a harmonious, inclusive, and sustainable society where the needs of the society can be met through the just and equitable mechanism of resources.

The concept of *Gram Swaraj* and Its Relevance in Contemporary India

Gram Swaraj, which translates to "Village Self-Governance" or "Rural Self-Rule", is a concept proposed by Mahatma Gandhi as part of his vision for India's socio-political and economic development. Continues to inspire efforts towards building more resilient, equitable, and self-reliant rural communities in contemporary India, aligning with the broader goals of sustainable development and inclusive governance. Gandhiji believed that independence must begin at the grassroots level; thus, every village would be democratic and have full power, self-sustained, capable, autonomous, and independent. These are the areas of interventions where skilled and trained social workers are putting special efforts (Bennur & Khairnar, 2013). Gandhi believed in empowering rural communities to govern themselves and address their needs, creating a more equitable and self-sufficient society. The concept of *Gram Swaraj* encompasses several vital principles and practices as described by Pandey, (2008)—

Decentralisation: *Gram Swaraj* advocates decentralising political power and decision-making processes, transferring authority from centralised government institutions to local village councils or *panchayats*. This decentralisation aims to ensure that governance is more responsive to the needs and priorities of rural communities.

Self-Sufficiency: *Gram Swaraj* promotes economic self-sufficiency at the village level, encouraging communities to produce food, goods, and services. Gandhi believed that local self-reliance would reduce dependence on external resources and create sustainable livelihoods for the rural population. It is envisioned that self-sufficient villages are economically independent, socially cohesive, and politically empowered (Zapate, 2017).

Empowerment: *Gram Swaraj* seeks to empower villagers by giving them greater control over their affairs, including land ownership, natural resource management, and community development initiatives. This empowerment fosters a sense of ownership, agency, and collective responsibility among community members.

Social Justice: *Gram Swaraj* emphasises the principles of social justice and equality, advocating for the upliftment of marginalised and disadvantaged groups within rural communities. Gandhi believed that village self-governance could help address caste-based discrimination, gender inequality, and other forms of social injustice.

Education and Health Care: *Gram Swaraj* prioritises providing primary education, healthcare, and social services to rural populations, ensuring that every individual has access to essential resources for their well-being and development.

Cultural Revival: *Gram Swaraj* recognises the importance of preserving and promoting traditional knowledge, skills, and cultural practices within rural communities. Gandhi believed cultural revival would strengthen social cohesion and identity while fostering pride in indigenous traditions.

In contemporary India, the concept of *Gram Swaraj* remains relevant for several reasons:

- With the decentralisation of power through the *Panchayati Raj* system, *Gram Swaraj* principles are being implemented at the grassroots level, enabling villagers to participate in decision-making processes and take charge of their development. This provides the opportunity to empower local governance.
- In a country where a significant portion of the population resides in rural areas, *Gram Swaraj* offers a framework for addressing the unique challenges rural communities face, including poverty, unemployment, migration, and lack of basic infrastructure. It approaches the concept of rural interventions to promote rural development.
- *Gram Swaraj* promotes sustainable practices such as organic farming, water conservation, and renewable energy adoption, aligning with contemporary priorities for environmental conservation and climate resilience.
- By prioritising the needs of marginalised groups, *Gram Swaraj* contributes to efforts to reduce social inequalities and promote inclusive growth in rural India.
- *Gram Swaraj* fosters community-driven development initiatives that empower villagers to identify their priorities, mobilise resources, and implement solutions tailored to their context.

Contribution of Mahatma Gandhi to the Different Fields of Social Work

The contribution of Mahatma Gandhi to the various fields of Social Work has left a lasting impact on society, inspiring generations to work towards justice, equality, and peace. Gandhiji opted for the humanitarian and philanthropic approach to reduce social, economic, and political inequality and discrimination.

Here are some key areas where Gandhi's influence and contributions were significant:

Mahatma Gandhi and Women's Empowerment: Mahatma Gandhi played a pivotal role in advancing women's empowerment in India through his advocacy for gender equality, social reform, and women's rights. He emphasised the importance of women's education for leadership and societal contribution and encouraged them to participate in the freedom struggle. By providing leadership opportunities to women in the freedom struggle, Gandhiji aims to create a society where they can utilise their full potential and contribute equally to the nation-building program through equal participation in every aspect of life (Bhanja, 2020).

Mahatma Gandhi and the Farmer's Movement: Mahatma Gandhi played a significant role in various farmer's movements in India during the independence struggle. His philosophy of non-violent resistance and commitment to social justice made him a prominent leader in advocating for the rights of farmers and agricultural workers.

Champaran Satyagraha (1917): Gandhiji led the Champaran Satyagraha to support indigo farmers of Bihar exploited by the British government. It was the first movement in India in which he fought to secure justice for the agricultural community and was recognised as "barrister cum Satyagrahi" (B. Kumar, 2018).

Kheda Satyagraha (1918): In the Kheda district of Gujarat, the British authorities imposed taxes on farmers. Gandhiji stood with the farmers, advocating for tax relief and demonstrating solidarity with the agricultural community.

Bardoli Satyagraha (1928): The British government imposed a 30 per cent increase in tax on the peasants of Bardoli that exacerbated the already dire conditions of the poor farmers of the region. Gandhiji mobilised the community and successfully pressured the authorities to withdraw the oppressive tax hike. His philosophy of non-violence inspired unity and peaceful resistance among the Bardoli (R. Kumar, 2020).

Mahatma Gandhi and Education System: Mahatma Gandhi's educational philosophy emphasises holistic development, moral ideals, and social responsibility. His educational ideas, known as 'Basic Education' or *Nai Talim*, set a benchmark for the education system that continues to resonate in modern educational reforms. *Nai Talim* is based on these educational rules: who to teach, what to teach, and how to teach. Gandhiji denied the "Filtration Theory of Education" and strongly supported the "Jacksonian principle of education", which is guided by equity and universal education. It aims to bridge the gap between society and educational institutions through social reconstruction and promote communal harmony (Lawrence Sahayam, 1950). It encouraged the institution to make such arrangements where students can indulge in learning by doing, experience-based learning, and learning enhances learners' skills to become self-sufficient, independent, and assertive assets of society. Gandhiji's educational system is based on the idea that handicrafts should be taught to students for productive Work and psychological development. Education emphasises manual labour, production, and self-sufficiency in the Gandhian scheme of things. It lets students pick a job readily after completing their education, preventing them from becoming societal parasites (Bala, 2005). A reflection of Gandhiji's ideas can be directly seen in the present New Education Policy, which is more relevant and valuable in this era of revolution in the Indian education system.

Mahatma Gandhi's Efforts to Abolish Caste Discrimination

Gandhiji is a true reformer; his campaign to abolish the caste system and untouchability was multidimensional, to address the deeply-rooted social norms that sustained this discriminatory practice in Hindu society. He believed that the poor, vulnerable, and oppressed class must raise their voice against untouchability and discrimination to get their liberation (Singh, 2022).He challenged those social evils that created barriers in Indian society and established various organisations, societies, and trusts to protect the rights of an oppressed and vulnerable class. All India Anti-Untouchability League, Harijan Sewak Sangh, Harijan Ashram, Harijan Bandhu, etc., these are some examples of the organisations founded by Mahatma Gandhi played a crucial role in the campaign against untouchability and his efforts to uplift the marginalised *Harijan* Community. They served as platforms for advocacy, service delivery, education, and empowerment, contributing to the social transformation and fight against discriminatory practices in Indian Society (Ray, 1995).

Gandhiji strongly opposed untouchability, considering it the worst aspect of the caste system. He actively engaged in actions like sharing food with different castes and promoting marriages to another caste within his family. He has a strong faith that after abolishing the caste system, the entire Nation will be one family, which will enhance the growth of our country. Through public advocacy, including writing articles and speeches, he challenged societal norms and promoted equality. His personal life exemplified his commitment to inclusivity by facilitating inter-caste marriages for his sons and adopted daughter. Gandhiji made the eradication of untouchability a central aspect of Indian politics, aligning it to achieve self-rule and emphasising the importance of social reform for the Nation's progress (Biswas, 2018).

Conclusion

The contribution of Mahatma Gandhi to indigenous social work practice is deeply rooted in his philosophy of non-violence, truth, *Sarvodaya*, and trusteeship, which translates to the welfare and well-being of society as a whole. Social workers opted for the approach to address social issues and promote community well-being, which is guided by the principles, ethics, and values of Mahatma Gandhi. The approach emphasises community empowerment, self-reliance, and service to humanity as fundamental pillars of social work practice. Social workers engage in non-violent social action, community organisation, constructive programs, collective bargaining, education and awareness, social welfare services, volunteering, advocacy, policy-making, and self-transformation. These methods and techniques are grounded in the principles of *ahimsa, Sarvodaya, swaraj*, and *satyagraha*, aiming to abolish all types of discrimination and differences existing in the society and establish inclusive, equitable, and sustainable societies where the welfare of all individuals is prioritised. Therefore, by embracing Gandhian principles and methods, social workers can play a vital role in advancing social justice, promoting peace, and building resilient communities based on mutual respect and cooperation.

References

Bala, S. (2005). "Gandhian Conception of Education—Its Relevance in Present Times". *The Indian Journal of Political Science, 66*(3): 531-48. Indian Political Science Association. http://www.jstor.com/stable/41856147

Bennur, Y., Khairnar, D., Gandhi, M. & Kumar, K. (2013). "Mahatma Gandhi and Professional Social Work". *Indian Journal of Research, 3*(5), Department of Applied Sciences, ICL Institute of Engineering and Technology, Sountli, Distt. Ambala (Haryana).

Bhanja, S. (2020). "Mahatma Gandhi and Women Empowerment". *International Journal of Research and Analytical Reviews, 7*(1): 463-65. https://www.ijrar.org

Billore, S.R. (2010). "Gandhian Social Work Methods and Technique". *Origin and Development of Social Work in India*, 306-27. Indira Gandhi National Open University.

Biswas, S. (2018). "Gandhi's Approach to Caste and Untouchability". *Social Scientist, 46*(9): 71-90. https://www.jstor.org/stable/10.2307/26611325

Kumar, B. (2018). "Gandhi and Champaran Satyagraha: A conscious Idea of Justice". In Research Guru: Online *Journal of Multidisciplinary Subjects* (Peer Reviewed), *Research Guru,12(2), ISSN:2349-266X,*151.

Kumar, R.R. (2020). "Satyagrah: A Gandhian Context". *IME Journal, 14*(1): 116-122. https://doi.org/10.5958/2582-1245.2020.00016.0

Harris, S.S., Lawrence (1950). "Gandhiji's Contribution to Education". *The Phi Delta Kappan, 32-32*(2), 42-44. https://www.jstor.org/stable/20332000

Mutluri, A. (2020). "Relevance of Mahatma Gandhi's Philosophy to Social Work Profession: A Review". *Jharkhand Journal of Development and Management Studies, 20*(4). https://www.researchgate.net/publication/368243293

Pandey, A. (2008). "Gandhian Perspective on Rural Development". *The Indian Journal of Political Science, 69*(1): 141-48. https://www.jstor.org/stable/41856398

Ray, B. (1995). "Gandhi against Untouchability". *World Affairs: The Journal of International, 4*(2): 28-41. Kapur Surya Foundation. https://www.jstor.org/stable/45064288

Walz, T. & Ritchie, H. (2000). "Gandhian Principles in Social Work Practice: Ethics Revisited". *Social Work, 45*(3): 213-22. Oxford University Press. https://www.jstor.org/stable/23718604

Zapate, N. (2017). Spinning for Swaraj: Gandhi's Idea of Economic Self-sufficiency and Self-government (1920 to 1927)". *Proceedings of the Indian History Congress, 78-78*, 812-819. https://www.jstor.org/stable/10.2307/26906155

Singh, P.K. (2022). "Relevance of Gandhian Philosophy in Social Work Practice. *Central Asian Journal of Social Sciences and History*, pp. 76-77. [Journal-article]. https://www.cajssh.centralasianstudies.org

Index